THE RISE AND SPLENDOUR OF THE *Chinese Empire*

BY RENÉ GROUSSET

This edition published by Barnes & Noble, Inc.

1992 Barnes & Noble Books

ISBN 1-56619-063-0

Printed and bound in the United States of America

M 9 8 7 6 5 4 3 2 1

CONTENTS

CHAPTER I

CHINESE EARTH

ASIATIC civilization is the product of "Mesopotamias", of great alluvial plains where the natural fertility of the soil stimulated man's agricultural vocation. Such was the case of Babylon in western Asia; such is the case of the "Central Plain" of China in eastern Asia.

This great plain, from Peking in the north as far as the Huai River in the south, from the approaches of Loyang in the west to the mountain spur of Shantung in the east, covers more than one hundred and twenty-five thousand square miles, an area greater than England and Ireland. In the same way that Egypt, according to Herodotus, is a "gift of the Nile", the Central Plain is a gift of the Yellow River and its tributaries. "At a relatively recent period—using that adjective in the sense which geologists give to it—this plain was an arm of the sea, the cliffs of Shansi were lashed by its waves and the present-day peninsula of Shantung was an island." Since time immemorial the Yellow River has carried away immense accretions of mud from the plateaux of yellow earth farther west and deposited them in this area, thus creating a marvellously fertile alluvial soil. As a result of this accumulation of muddy sediment, the sea has been checked and the coastline has receded ever farther eastward; a process which is still continuing today. Thus it has come about that year after year the mud has raised the bed of the Yellow River and the riverside dwellers have been obliged to build up their embankments proportionately, with the result that the river has ended by flowing in a great gutter above the level of the plain; a paradoxical situation and one fraught with extreme danger.

Towards the west and beyond the Central Plain stretch the

terraces of yellow earth, covering an area of more than two hundred and sixty thousand square kilometres, from which the nutritive stream descends. All this hilly country is in effect covered by an immense blanket of yellowish earth analogous to the Alsatian loess, a fine dust of clay, sand, and limestone deposited by the wind in past millennia, formed into a great mass and cut in terraces by erosion. A land which (when there is no lack of rain) is on the whole as fertile as the Central Plain and equally destined for agriculture. It is the kingdom of millet and wheat.[1] Finally there are immense areas, from Peking to Kaifeng and from Kaifeng to the approaches of Nanking, where the yellow earth of the terraces of the northwest and the alluvial mud of the Central Plain fuse imperceptibly and constitute the most fertile part of the whole. In this area the cultivation of millet, suited to the terraces of loess, is combined with that of rice,[2] more properly suited to the basins of the Huai River and the Long River.[3]

Chinese civilization arose in this area, hand in hand with the development of agriculture, or more specifically with the cultivation of millet and later of rice. The unknown centuries before history were employed in burning and clearing the undergrowth, which covered the plateaux of loess in the northwest, and in draining the marshes which must have covered the larger part of the Central Plain in the northeast. The ancient songs of the *Shih-ching* celebrate this work: "Ah! They are clearing the land! Their ploughs are opening up the earth. Thousands of couples are digging up roots, some in the lowlands, others on the high ground." And again: "Why have they torn up the thorny brushwood? So that we may plant our millet." Among the divine heroes glorified for the direction of this

[1] Nowadays nearly all of North China grows either millet or wheat. Shansi is about 43 per cent millet, 16 per cent kaoliang, and 14 per cent wheat; Honan, Shensi and Kansu from 45 to 60 per cent wheat.

[2] Rice is foreign to North China, but must have been grown in the south at a very early date; in the eighth century B.C. it is listed as one of the Five Grains.

[3] Usually known to foreigners as the Yangtze; but only the reaches near Chinkiang are called Yang-tzu-chiang by the Chinese, while *Ch'ang-chiang* (Long River) is the common name for the whole course of the river.

collective labour were Shen Nung, who taught men to burn the brushwood and use the hoe, and Hou Chi, "Prince Millet". A labour of no less importance was ascribed to Yü the Great, the founder of the legendary dynasty of Hsia. In his work of draining and ditching, he reclaimed the land from the water, "led the rivers back to the sea", and increased the number of ditches and canals.

It was the agricultural and sedentary life led by the ancestors of the Chinese in the loess lands and the Central Plain which differentiated them from those tribes—presumably of the same racial stock—who continued to lead the lives of nomad hunters, either on the steppes of Shensi and northern Shansi or among the marshy forests of the Huai River and Long River valleys. There is no reason to suppose a difference of race, still less to imagine the immigration of a race of proto-Chinese, said to have come from Central Asia. Moreover these "barbarian" tribes, who encircled the narrow domain of primitive China, were destined in course of time themselves to adopt a Chinese way of life and thought. From the end of the archaic period onwards they gradually abandoned their nomadic life (spontaneously in the case of the tribes of the lower Long River), and took to agriculture. In the same way, in Tonking, if the Annamites are unlike their kinsmen the Muong, it is because they became cultivators of the paddy fields in the flat plains of the littoral, whereas in the inland forests the Muong made no attempt to learn anything about agriculture.

The life of peasant society in archaic China cannot have differed greatly from what it is today in the same regions. In the Great Plain they lived in mud huts (brick was to be used later) which generally failed to resist the monsoon rains and destruction by rodents, while on the plateaux of loess they inhabited caves hollowed out from the side of cliffs in such a way that the fields overhung the farmhouse and the air vents from the caves sometimes opened strangely into the midst of cultivated fields. The breeding of silkworms would also appear to have a very ancient origin. If we can believe the economic map suggested by the *Tribute of Yü* (about the seventh century B.C.),

Shantung and the neighbouring districts may well have been the "land of the mulberry". Apart from this, it is traditionally held that the second of the mythical "three kings", the legendary Huang-ti, himself taught the Chinese to breed silkworms and replace with textiles their "barbarian" garments, made of straw or from the pelts of wild beasts. Finally, it would seem that from time immemorial the Chinese peasant, having once reclaimed the soil from brushwood and marshland, in order to ensure his conquest adopted a system, still in force among his present-day descendants, of intensive cultivation. It has been written that "Chinese agriculture is no more than gardening on a larger scale". It may be added that, having failed to find real woodlands at his cradle, either on the plateaux of the loess or in the alluvial soil of the Central Plain, the Chinese was to acquire an antipathy to the forest no matter where he found it. Central and southern China, which he was to colonize in the course of time, was originally a wooded region. After they had become masters of the country, the Chinese systematically felled the trees and overcame their immediate need for fuel without troubling to make any further use of the hills they had thus laid bare. For, having been bred on the terraces of the northwest or in the immense low-lying stretches of the northeast, they were reluctant to establish themselves on the heights. The yellow earth of the plains was thus instrumental in fashioning the Chinese for all time.

There is no life more laborious than that of the Chinese peasant. In spite of his obstinate and tireless patience, and notwithstanding the natural fertility of the plateaux of the loess and the Central Plain, he is constantly at the mercy of the elements. The lands of the loess are threatened by appalling famines in time of drought, while on the Central Plain, although there is less danger of drought owing to the monsoon rains, there is the danger of floods and the terrible divagations of the Yellow River. The superstitious dread in which the Chinese held the god of waters, "The Lord of the Rivers" as they called him, bears witness to the terror felt by the riverside dwellers of primitive times for this untamed neighbour. In order to propitiate him they used to offer periodic sacrifices of youths and maidens. In these great tracts of low-lying ground, defenceless against flood or drought because of the lack of forestation, the peasant was more narrowly dependent on the soil than in any other part of the world. The order of his daily life was controlled by the rhythm of the seasons.

More than in any other agricultural country, rural life was broken up into two clearly divided phases; work in the fields from spring to autumn, followed by the indoor winter season. At the spring equinox the "interdict", which had been laid on the fields during the winter months, was lifted and the soil was "desanctified" by a ceremony of prime importance, the first tilling of the sacred field, which was solemnly carried out by the king in person. The spring equinox augured not only the fertility of the soil, but also that of the race. On the "day of the swallows' return", marriages, which were forbidden in winter, began to be celebrated. In the country, "at the first crash of thunder", young peasants and peasant girls gathered together to sing love-songs and to be united among the fields:

The Chen and the Wei
Have overflowed their banks.
The youths and the maidens
Come to the orchids.
The girls invite them . . .
Suppose we go there?
If we cross the Wei,
There stretches a fine lawn,
Then boys and girls
Play their games together,
And the girls receive
The token of a flower.

At the autumnal equinox, after the harvest festivals had been celebrated, the closed winter season began for the villagers, during which the women devoted their time to weaving.

It can be seen that the pattern of peasant life followed closely on the cycle of the seasons. From this conformity may well have been derived the first Chinese conceptions of the universe, and especially the first "classification" of objects into two general categories, a classification which up to modern times was to dominate all Chinese systems of philosophy without exception. Peasant life in early times was rigorously divided into the period of the closed winter season, when female work was pre-eminent (it was the season of the weavers), and the period of agricultural labour, principally carried out by men. Following an analogous distribution, everything was divided into two principles or modalities: *yin*, which corresponded to shadow, cold, contraction, moisture, and the female sex, and *yang*, which corresponded to heat, expansion and the male sex. These two principles, like the seasonal phases on which they appear to be modelled, are in opposition, and at the same time are modified, called forth and transformed the one in the other. Their interdependence, or the order which presides over their alternation and mutation, is the order of the universe and of society, or as the Chinese say, it is *tao*, the central notion which came to be the keystone of all subsequent philosophic doctrines.[1]

Primitive Chinese religion had as its primary objective to assure the concordance of the seasonal cycles with the cycle of agricultural life, or, as was to be said later, between Heaven and Mankind. The celestial order was regulated by August Heaven (*Huang-t'ien*), also known as the Sovereign On High (*Shang-ti*), who dwelt in the Great Bear.[2] In the same way, human order was assured by a king, invested for this purpose with the "Mandate of Heaven" (*T'ien-ming*), which made him "the Son of Heaven" (*T'ien-tzu*). It was the king's duty to fix the calendar for the regulation of agricultural work and to inaugurate the seasons with the necessary sacrifices and ritual acts in harmony with the Sovereign On High. His first duty, in his role of high priest, was to inaugurate the new year and invoke the spring by sacrificing a red bull as a burnt-offering to the Sove-

[1] *Tao* is a term whose sense varies greatly in different schools of philosophy. Originally it meant "road" or "way". In *Yin-yang* speculation it is either the order controlling the alternation of *yin* and *yang*, or their synthesis.

[2] *Shang-ti* is also the Protestant word for God.

reign On High. This was followed by the tilling of the sacred field, which was a signal for the beginning of agricultural work. With the second month of summer he offered a further sacrifice accompanied by prayers for rain, which if unsuccessful were followed by the execution of all the wizards and witches, who were burnt alive because their incantations had proved fruitless. Finally, at the approach of winter he celebrated the abandonment of the fields and the return to winter dwellings with a sacrifice (like the Roman *Suovetaurilia*) in which the victim was a black bull. This sacrifice, offered to the "sun-god", was followed by another, offered to the Ancestors. The cycle was closed by the harvest festival, the most important of all, in which the whole population joined in the general feasting and carousal. At each season the king was dressed in garments appropriate to the "orientation" of the season; black in winter, green in springtime, red in summer and white in autumn: these being the priestly robes with which he officiated in his pontifical career. In his various duties he was aided by a whole "clergy" of diviners and sorcerers—whose role in the elaboration of early Chinese philosophy will be examined later.

Apart from this "seasonal cycle" there was the "ancestral cycle", nowadays common to the whole Chinese population, but in early times restricted to the noble class. Indeed it was only the nobles who had any reason to be preoccupied with their ancestors, as that class alone possessed a soul capable of survival. They possessed in fact two souls, one a mere animal exhalation, destined to become a sort of ghost which hovered round the corpse; the other the spiritual soul, which after death ascended to heaven in the form of a genie, but was only able to exist there when its substance was nourished by the funeral offerings of its descendants. This "ancestor worship" was essentially concerned with the daily or seasonal offerings which enabled the corpse, represented by its funeral "tablet", to take part in the life of the family. In its origin, the cult of the "Earth God", represented in primitive times by a tree or rough stone, was likewise connected with this seignorial religion. This god, the deity of the earliest territorial groupings, was fierce and cruel: "He loved blood," notes Henri Maspero, "and the sacrifices that were offered to him began with the anointing of his stone tablet with the fresh blood of the victim. This was generally a bull, but human victims were not unpleasing to him."

In these earliest times we find a peasant society, living at the junction of the Central Plain and the deposits of yellow earth, and engaged in clearing the undergrowth in this primitive Chinese domain, a society with a class of nobles and a monarchy. The presence of these war leaders proves that the Chinese farmer was forced to live in a state of constant alertness against the tribes of semi-nomad hunters who surrounded him.

The riches accumulated by the toil of this peasant society soon produced a state of luxury at the top of the social scale. Although we know practically nothing of the political history of the first royal dynasty, the Hsia, archaeology has recently given us certain indications as to the utensils which they used in this distant epoch, and during the last seven years it has provided us with a store of unexpected discoveries about the second dynasty, the Shang (1558–1050 B.C.?).

The earliest discoveries, dating from the Hsia period, have brought to light a roughly decorated pottery, ornamented in the so-called "comb" patterns. It was a style in general use in European Russia and well known in Siberia between the years 2000 and 1500 B.C., and its discovery may indicate that there were already some relations between the two continents.[1] This was followed by the excavation of painted vases, discovered in recent years in the villages of Yang-shao and Ch'in-wang-chai in the province of Honan, brick-red earthenware vases painted with a spirited and sensitive decoration of unexpected groups of bands, triangles, spots, crossed lines and eyes fringed with lashes. This Yang-shao pottery made its appearance

[1] One should note especially the incised and painted ceramics, with parallel lines and simple chequer work, recently discovered at Hou-kang, near An-yang in the extreme north of Honan. Also the ceramics of near-by Hou-chia-chuang, decorated with an impression of fibres and basketwork. The two groups may date from the beginning of the Hsia dynasty. (G. D. Wu, *Prehistoric Pottery in China*, 1938.)

about 1700 B.C., a date which corresponds to the second phase of the Hsia dynasty.

The Pan-shan pottery, thus named after a site in the province of Kansu which has been excavated since 1921, dates from between 1500 and 1400, or according to some opinion between 1400 and 1300 B.C., and is thus contemporary with the first period of the Shang dynasty. These vessels were real works of art with a magnificent ornamentation of red and black spirals of a decorative quality worthy of the Aegean. Moreover this resemblance is not merely stylistic, for analogous themes have been discovered in the painted ceramics of prehistoric Ukraine and Rumania, which leads one to suppose that they may have been transmitted from the Aegean Sea to northwest China by way of the Russian steppes. But without doubt this imported decoration cannot have taken lasting root in Chinese soil. At Pan-shan, in addition to the "Aegean" spirals we have evidence of a much simpler form of decoration, that of the draught-board, clearly imitated from basketwork. This form of decoration—an indigenous one—is the only form to be found (the spirals having been abandoned) from the following period (about the fourteenth century B.C.), among the ruins of Ma-ch'ang, in Kansu.[1] We see there the transference of the various interlacing patterns of basketwork into painted ceramics, while in the next period we shall see them pass into the decoration of the first bronzes.

We touch here on the mystery of the appearance of bronze in China. Bronze, according to the archaeologist Menghin, was introduced into Siberia about 1500 B.C. However, several very early bronze arrow heads discovered in China, notably at An-yang, indicate a Siberian origin. Moreover, several early bronze vases of the Shang period betray a naïve imitation of woodwork, the bronzeworker having copied his model faithfully, even to imitating the notches and knife-marks. The Chinese, suddenly encountering the

[1] In fact, on certain of the Ma-ch'ang vases one finds circular waves which are reminiscent of the Pan-shan decoration, only in this case they are used not so much for their own sake as to serve as surrounds for the characteristic decorative circles of chequer work. (See the plates in G. D. Wu's *Prehistoric Pottery in China*, 1938.)

Siberian technique of metal working, seem as it were to have taken their ancient earthenware and wooden ritual vases and converted them into bronze overnight.

Various problems face us in the discoveries made in 1934 and 1935 at An-yang, situated in the most northerly part of present-day Honan. In this ancient capital of the Shang dynasty, which flourished in the twelfth century before Christ, we find ourselves abruptly confronted with a material civilization already at its height, although so far nothing has been found to throw light on its beginnings. One of the sites of excavation, about six hectares in size, is entirely taken up by the foundations of a building of considerable size thought to be a royal palace. Tombs show traces of funeral sacrifices with human and animal victims. We know in fact that human sacrifice continued for a long time to play an important part in religious ceremonies; for example, the new year was inaugurated at court by quartering victims at the four principal gates of the city. Bones and tortoise shells used in divination, and found in the tombs of Anyang, bear the first Chinese characters which have come down to us. They indicate a writing still little removed from the pictorial. Egyptian hieroglyphics, Babylonian cuneiform script and Chinese characters have all evolved from similar drawings of objects. Nevertheless the characters discovered at An-yang are sufficiently stylized to force us to acknowledge a long period of preliminary elaboration since the really "primitive" drawings, the originals of which have so far never come to light.

The most characteristic discoveries in the excavations of An-yang are the admirable bronze vases, which since 1934 and 1935 have been found in considerable quantities. Great was the astonishment of archaeologists when they were obliged to admit that, in this far-distant period, the ritual form and decoration of various types of bronzes were already well established.[1] It would indeed be little short

[1] This fixation of the style of the various bronze vases, almost unvaried from the earliest times onwards, was evidently due to their ritual importance for sacrificial purposes.

of a miracle, like Athene coming fully armed from the brain of Zeus, if we did not already know that according to Chinese tradition An-yang was only one of the latest capitals of the Shang dynasty. The earlier capitals, doubtless contemporary with the first rough efforts of Chinese bronze work, have never been excavated. If we admit that the art of working in bronze was introduced from Siberia into China during or towards the end of the fifteenth century B.C., there remains a period of some three centuries to be explored before we can arrive at the beginnings of Chinese bronze.

Thus it is the zenith of an art, without the inevitable fumbling beginnings, that is revealed to us by the Shang bronzes discovered in recent years at An-yang. In later periods, Chinese bronze workers were never able to attain the same power of architectural construction in ritual vases or a similar equilibrium of masses. The most notable examples are the great lidded cooking-pots (known as *yü* or *lei*), but a similar forcefulness is shown in some of the more sober forms, such as the pot tripods and goblet tripods (known as *li* or *ting*, and *chüeh* respectively). Indeed this sobriety in no way destroys the elegance of form, as one can see in the vases (*ku*), great bell-shaped chalices of an astonishing slenderness. The geometric and mythological motifs which ornament most of the ritual bronzes have a corresponding decorative splendour. One is struck by the vigour of these masks of monsters, above all the *t'ao-t'ieh*, which began as realistic heads of bulls, rams, tigers or bears, and became progressively stylized into apparitions of terror. Another mythological figure found on Shang bronzes (and also on jades) is the dragon *k'uei*, "an ox-dragon which makes the noise of thunder". The heroes of Chinese legend made drums "which gave orders like a clap of thunder" from the skin of this monster. "Symbols of cosmic force," says Georges Salle, "the fabulous animals invested the object which they decorated with a secret and formidable power."

Among the ruins of An-yang have been found vigorous marble sculptures in the round, or rather incised blocks of marble, representing mythological monsters. (This "trend towards sculpture in the round" seems to have stopped after the Shang dynasty and does not reappear until much later, in the period of the Warring States.)

Finally, in addition to the bronzes the civilization of An-yang produced some remarkable jades, also of a ritual significance. Jade, the symbol of purity, according to ancient Chinese beliefs possessed an intrinsic "virtue". We learn from the Chinese classics that it was permissible for the royal headdress to be adorned with jade ornaments, while the pre-eminent symbol of kingly power consisted in a large jade tablet, the *kuei*, fastened to the royal girdle. Excavations of the Shang period have brought to light great knives, axes, and hatchet-daggers (*ke*) of jade (some of them of a brown or black tint, seemingly chosen in imitation of the colour of bronze); also two very characteristic types of jade ritual objects, the *pi*, a disc with a pierced centre, representing the sky, and the *tsung*, a cylinder fitted into a cube, which represented the earth. These two forms of jade may possibly have figured, as did the bronzes, in the seasonal sacrifices which the king offered to heaven to assure the fertility of the soil.

The wealth of this material civilization bears out what the ancient Chinese annals say of the kings of the Shang dynasty. The last of them, Chou Hsin, has left behind him the reputation of a Chinese Nero, the product of a refined, sumptuous and corrupt court and an example of an already decadent civilization. "His knowledge permitted him to gainsay correction, his eloquence enabled him to dissemble his misdeeds. He collected ever-increasing numbers of horses, dogs, and rare objects, he extended without limit the parks and terraces of his capital. He organized great entertainments and held orgies which lasted throughout the night." However, behind this Babylonian façade the expansion of the Chinese race continued.

CHAPTER II

THE EXPANSION OF A RACE OF PIONEERS

PARADOXICAL as it may seem, if one is to compare the history of China with that of any other great human society it is to Canada or the United States that one should look. In both China and America the fundamental and essential concern, far beyond the vicissitudes of politics, was the conquest of immense stretches of virgin territory by a labouring people who found only semi-nomadic populations in their path. The hardest part of this struggle had to be directed against Nature herself, clearing the soil, cutting down the primitive forests, taming the rivers, and everywhere creating arable land. Whereas the French-Canadians and the Anglo-Saxons needed only three centuries to put the North American continent under the plough, the agricultural conquest of China took nearly four thousand years. Starting within the confine of the loess lands and the Central Plain about the second millennium before Christ, it is not entirely finished today, since in the mountains of the southwest the Lolo and Miao-tzu "aborigines" continue to hold out against the encroachments of the Chinese farmer.

It was doubtless in the middle of the Shang dynasty (fourteenth century B.C.) that Chinese colonists started swarming in compact groups, beyond the limits of the Central Plain, to create new areas of clearing among the "barbarian" peoples whom they subdued, assimilated or won over. This process cannot have differed greatly from that which in the nineteenth century marked the encroachment of Chinese ploughlands upon the grasslands of Mongolia, or their twentieth-century inroads into the forests of Manchuria. This first Chinese expansion was directed in the south towards the basin of the Long River, then almost entirely covered in forests, in the north towards the yellow-earth terraces of Shansi, and in the north-west towards the enclosed valley of the Wei in Shensi, a land likewise carved out of the yellow earth. At the approaches of the Long River the Chinese farmers came into contact with tribes still half-savage (although doubtless of the same race as themselves), who lived by hunting and fishing, and who were gradually led by the Chinese example to adopt an agricultural way of life.

The same thing happened in the northwest. In this area a clan of hardy pioneers, the Chou, who symbolically placed themselves under the protection of an agricultural demigod, "Prince Millet", became established and undertook the clearing and sowing of the rich alluvial plain. It was a country cut out from the loess and covered with its fine yellowish-grey loam, where the town of Sian or Ch'ang-an, the capital of Shensi, was later to be built; a land so rich in corn and millet that it might be compared with Canada. The ancient annals speak with a restrained enthusiasm of the first barons of the Chou family to be established there, who before all else "set to to till and sow". They were to produce a line of soldier-farmers capable of carrying on the perpetual struggle against the barbarian tribes amongst whom they were established. The settlers of this Chinese Wild West led the rough existence of all colonists placed in a similar position. Their obstinate determination to create arable land, to the detriment of the clans of semi-nomad hunters who ranged the neighbouring terrace lands, cost them heavily. The old annals show them for a time obliged to retreat before the onslaught of savages, and then once more descending the plateaux of loess towards the valley of the Wei, "the warriors helping the aged and supporting the weak".

In their rugged task as defenders of the marches and pioneers of the highlands, the Chou barons became inured to the hardships of war. In the middle of the eleventh century B.C. one of them, known to history as King Wu ("mighty"), profited from the unpopularity of Chou Hsin, the last of the Shang kings, who was hated for his cruelty and debauchery. Wu led a revolt and decimated the royal army. Chou Hsin, fleeing back to his palace, killed himself in a dramatic manner: "He climbed on to the Terrace of the Stag. He arrayed himself in his pearls and jade and hurled himself into the flames." Wu made a triumphal entry into the capital. "He seized the great white standard. The nobles came to pay homage to him. He entered the place where lay the body of Chou-Hsin and got down from his chariot; he struck the corpse with his dagger, then with the great yellow axe he struck off the head; and this head he hung on the great white standard."

It was the victory of the men of the marches, of the rough pioneers of the high valleys of the west, over the luxurious court and the rich cultivators of the Central Plain. Thus raised to the throne, the Chou had the wisdom to maintain their residence for nearly three centuries in the high valley of the Wei, to which position they owed their strength, and whence they could dominate the Central Plain. The art of this epoch (the eleventh and tenth centuries B.C.), quite lately identified beyond doubt by the Swedish archaeologist Karlgren, is characterized by bronzes of a rougher style than the preceding era, with a rhythm of lines (or "dragon" motifs) of a severe and sometimes rather heavy geometrical pattern.[1] If we can rely on these indications, the material civilization of the first Chou rulers seems, as might well be expected, to mark a certain regression from the luxury and the dazzling artistic creations of the Shang dynasty.

A disaster put an end to the power of the Chou. In 771 their capital was surprised and pillaged by the Barbarians of the West. The dynasty, abandoning their residence in the marches, fell back on the region of Loyang, on the threshold of the Central Plain, and the centre of the China of those times. It found far greater security there, but rapidly lost its warrior character; its princes degenerated into royal figureheads, while the real power passed into the hands of the feudal nobility.

[1] Bronzes of many forms appeared at this period, such as the *chung* or Chinese bell, and the *yi*, a sort of "sauce-boat".

CHAPTER III

FEUDALISM AND CHIVALRY

ANCIENT China from the eighth to the third century B.C. could provide western students of the middle ages with material for a comparative study of feudal systems. In Chinese society of that time, the breakdown of royal power involved somewhat similar institutions to those of tenth-century France. The partition of the seignories was carried to similar lengths; and then, as in France, a certain number of great baronies brought about a territorial regrouping.

We will not attempt to enumerate all the feudal Chinese states, but it should be noticed that in most cases their formation was the result of geographical factors. The Chinese provinces of today often as large as several European states, correspond, as do the latter, to permanent units which are always reappearing throughout the vicissitudes of history. These great regional units were already apparent in the principalities of ancient China. In the northwest, for example, the present-day province of Shensi in the valley of the Wei—a valley hollowed out from the loess and dominating the plain of Honan—has been fixed since the dawn of the historic period. We have seen how the Chou princes departed from these western marches to win the throne. The role of marcher princes, which they consequently abandoned, was assumed by their vassals the Counts of Ch'in, who founded in Shensi a barony destined to have a spectacular career. On the yellow-earth terraces of Shansi another principality was founded, which owing to its advantageous geographical situation above the Great Plain succeeded in establishing a hegemony and keeping it over a considerable period. A third dominant principality was created to the east in Shantung, a province of individual character extending from the massif of sacred T'ai-shan to China's "Brittany", the rocky Shantung Peninsula. On the middle Long River in Hupei (a shallow basin intersected with lakes and at that date covered in forest), barbarian tribes attracted by the example of Chinese civilization spontaneously adopted a Chinese way of life and thought and founded a fourth great state. So far we have only mentioned the most powerful baronies. If we were to enumerate all the others, born by chance in the feudal parcelling-out of the more modest regional sub-divisions, we should have some sixty fiefs.

Likewise we shall not enter into details of the struggles between the various principalities. They were as tedious as the feudal quarrels in eleventh-century France, and only interesting from the point of view of historical geography. What is important here is the social structure itself and the social life of those times, the equivalent of our feudal society.

This was the period of Chinese chivalry. War in those times was a chivalrous warfare, waged with that pre-eminently noble arm, the chariot. These war chariots are familiar to us, not only from the ancient annals, but from the bas-reliefs of the Han period. The chariot was harnessed to four horses, two at the shaft and two others drawing it by leather straps from the "wings". They were short, thick-set, muscular steeds, well-fed and full of fire. Their bits were ornamented with little bells. The chariot consisted of a short narrow frame, open at the rear and mounted on two wheels. The Chinese war chariot, like the Assyrian, carried three men: the driver in the centre, a lancer on the right, an archer on the left. All three wore breast plates, armlets, and kneepieces of varnished ox-hide. The lance was armed with a small hook for harpooning the enemy, and the bows were tipped with ivory. The three companions had shields painted in brilliant colours; the varnish of their armour glittered in the sunshine; while at the vanguard, rearguard, and flanks, floated standards depicting the symbolic animals of the four cardinal directions—the Red Bird of the south, the Black Tortoise of the north, the White Tiger of the west and the Green Dragon of the east.

When the army of one seigniory invaded a neighbouring principality, the seigneur of the latter, from defiance and bravado, would send a convoy of provisions to the invading army. Sometimes this defiance took a more sanguinary turn; the barons would send messengers to their enemy, braves who would cut their throats in his presence. Sometimes a war chariot would come at full speed to hurl insults at the gate of an opposing city. Then followed a mêlée of chariots in the Assyrian manner. "The thousand chariots charge, pennon against pennon, honour against honour." As in the Homeric period, when the warriors of the two armies recognized each other, they would exchange "haughty compliments" from the height of their chariots. Sometimes before the battle they would drink together, or even exchange weapons. Warfare between such adversaries had to be carried on in conformity with a strict code of courtesy. The vanquished were spared if they had given proof of their bravery, or if they knew how to address their victor with true chivalry. As later among the samurai of Japan, "fame was gained by acts of generosity". There was already an equivalent of Japanese *Bushido*, the code of chivalrous honour, with its paladins who before drawing their bows exposed themselves impassively to the arrows of their enemies, and with squires who deliberately courted death so as to bring honour to the blazon of their master. More than one passage of the early chronicle *Tso-chuan* illustrates these epic virtues. The chief charioteer of the prince of Chin, although pierced with arrows, continues unceasingly to beat the drum, "for he who is armed in breastplate must go on resolutely, even to death"; "the left wheel of my chariot is dyed purple in my blood. My Lord, did I dare to say that I was hurt?"

In peacetime the gentleman was imbued with this same ideal. His belts ornamented with jade trinkets which made "a harmonious tinkling sound", he would come to the court of his seigneur to take part in tournaments of the noble sport of archery which was accompanied by musical airs and interspersed with elegant salutations, the whole regulated like a ballet.

This chivalrous ideal of loyalty towards one's seigneur and fair dealing towards one's enemy, this regard for military integrity, this code of noble courtesy expressed in peacetime in "the religion of etiquette", were to leave a deep impression on the Chinese spirit. From them came a part of the teachings of Confucius.

CHAPTER IV

THE SAGES OF FORMER TIMES

CHINESE philosophy, like Greek and Indian philosophy, represents an original aspect in the history of human thought.

Philosophical speculation in China may well have grown out of very ancient naturalistic conceptions of the alternating seasons. Observation of this seasonal rhythm must have moulded Chinese thought in archaic times in its classification of objects into two general categories, *yin* and *yang*, which represented darkness and light, moisture and heat and, by analogy, earth and sky, contraction and expansion, feminine and masculine. The opposition and alternation of these two principles, and also their interdependence, or rather their mutation, explained the course of things and the whole life of the universe. Upon these two opposing principles a third was then superimposed—*tao*, which might be described as the principle of their inseparability, interdependence, and endless procession.

These naturalistic conceptions, which are inherent in the earliest classifications of a primitive mentality, were followed by more complicated notions drawn from the schools of divination.[1] Diviners, who played a considerable part in early Chinese society, imagined for the convenience of their performance an abstract world, above the perceptible world and governing it, rather like the Platonic theory of Ideas. Chinese divination, however, was concerned with geometric abstractions, with the knowledge of the different combinations which form a whole system of broken and continuous

[1] Early China knew two forms of divination: by tortoise shell (interpretation of cracks appearing on a shell in contact with fire), and by shuffling yarrow stalks. It was the various possible arrangements of yarrow stalks that brought about the theory of hexagrams which we will discuss later.

lines arranged in "trigrams" and "hexagrams" and symbolizing the various combinations of *yin* and *yang*, that is to say the divers aspects of the universe and the various contingencies of the future. Add to this the purely Chinese ideas about the qualitative value of numbers,[1] and we can appreciate the special conceptions which served as a point of departure for the subsequent evolution of Far Eastern philosophy.

It was into this intellectual setting that Confucius—in Chinese K'ung Fu-tzu, "K'ung the Master"—was born (traditional date 551 B.C.). The son of a noble but impoverished family in the principality of Lu (in the present province of Shantung), he left home for a time to visit neighbouring courts and then returned to found a school of wisdom. By reason of the moral character of his teaching he has been compared with Socrates. They have another point in common, that neither left any written work behind him. We are obliged to reconstruct the likeness of Socrates from portraits—sometimes divergent—left us by Plato and Xenophon. In the case of Confucius, the task is possibly even more delicate. His aphorisms and those of his conversations that we possess have reached us only by way of an emended edition of some five hundred years after his death. Yet from this text emerges the outline of an engaging personality, with delightful revelations of sensibility and a spontaneous repartee which could never have been fabricated by conventional eulogists.

In so far as we are able to follow the course of his thought, it would seem that Confucius in no way sought after innovations. After the fashion of the old schools of the scribes with which he was connected, his teaching appears as a commentary on the tradition of the ancients. One finds in him again the respect proper to Heaven, that is to the cosmic order, the classic ideas of *yin* and *yang*, and the

[1] The number 1 = water = the north = black.
2 = fire = the south = red.
3 = wood = the east = green.
4 = metal = the west = white.
5 = earth = the centre = yellow.
The symbolic animal of the north is the black tortoise, that of the south the red bird, that of the east the green dragon, and that of the west the white tiger.

higher conception of *tao* which, while used in a different sense in the works of his Taoist rivals, in Confucius generally means the right (*i.e.* the ancient) way of government.

Like all the sages of his school, Confucius preaches filial piety and piety towards the *manes*, that is, the cult of ancestors. Despite this traditionalism, certain anecdotes show us that he did not consider himself absolutely bound by ritual formulae; what he appears to have prized above all was purity of intention and sincerity of heart.[1] His doctrine appears to be essentially one of action, his teaching an active morality. "It is as a director of conscience that he appears to have won his prestige."

Confucianism may be summed up in the notion of *jen*, a notion which implies at the same time a feeling of humanity towards others and a feeling of human dignity in oneself; in brief, a respect for oneself and others with all the subsidiary virtues that this ideal involves: magnanimity, good faith, and charity. In external relations *jen* is expressed in a constant self-control, a respect for ritual, and a formal politeness which, as has been said, is but an external manifestation of the politeness of the heart. One finds here the kind of courtesy which, under the dominion of the ideal of chivalry, inspired in the noble classes of Europe the etiquette of feudal times.

Like the teaching of Socrates, Confucianism tends first of all to teach man to know himself in order to cultivate self-perfection. Just as Socrates renounced the researches of the Ionian philosophers into cosmic origins, Confucius—without being in any way agnostic—refused to probe into the mysteries of destiny, to discourse on spirits or "speak of prodigies". "Recognize", he said, "that you know what you know, and that you are ignorant of what you do not know." And again, "If you do not know about the living, how can you know about the dead?" His teaching recognizes no difference between individual morality and civic and social morality. Its aim lies in the good government of the people, assured, as in all Chinese philo-

[1] But Confucius was famous as an upholder of ritual, which he regarded as essential for the expression of, and the incitement to, moral virtue.

sophic systems, by a harmony of the virtue of the prince and the order of Heaven. "It is the moral power of the sovereign, the supernatural influence which he draws from the mandate of Heaven, which makes for the good or evil conduct of his people." Because of the stress laid on these maxims, Confucius was later to qualify as the archetypal sage and the pre-eminent authority in the school of the literati.

If we had to condense the spirit of Confucianism into a single formula, we would say that it is a civic order in communion, or rather in collaboration, with the cosmic order.

The successor of Confucius who was to show the greatest originality was Mo Tzu (who lived during the late fifth century B.C. and the first years of the fourth century). By a bold flight, this distinguished thinker came singularly near to theism. In place of the impersonal Heaven of his predecessors, he invoked the Lord On High, a personal god, omnipotent, omniscient, and essentially moral: "The main reason for good behaviour should be fear of the Lord On High, of Him, who sees all that passes in the woods, in the valleys, and in the hidden retreats where no human eye can penetrate. He it is that one should strive to please. He loves good and hates evil, loves justice and hates iniquity. All power on earth is subordinate to Him and must be exercised according to His views. He desires that the prince be good to his people and that all men love one another, for He, the Lord On High, loves all men."

From this theism Mo Tzu extracted a morality of a very high order. With him the altruism of Confucius became universal love, carried to the length of self-sacrifice: "To kill a man in order to save the world is not acting for the good of the world. To sacrifice oneself for the good of humanity, that is acting rightly!" In the same way Mo Tzu strongly condemned the feudal wars. The following maxim summed up his thought: "Knowledge consists in the adoration of Heaven and the love of mankind."

The Taoist school was of a very different nature. Its origins go back to the speculations of the prehistoric diviners on the ideas of *yin*, *yang*, and *tao*, which we have already discussed. They are also connected with the practice of autosuggestion by the ancient wizards and witches, whose frenzied dances resulted in states of trance capable of capturing the attention and retaining the presence of the gods. It is however a long way from these savage practices, still full of primitive magic, to the lofty thought of the "fathers of Taoism", and orthodox tradition prefers to ignore its dubious ancestry. According to tradition, philosophical Taoism was founded by a sage called Lao Tzu, of whom we know nothing positive, but who according to the legend must have lived towards the end of the fifth century B.C. We know no more of the second Taoist sage, Lieh Tzu. The third, Chuang Tzu, on the contrary, is clearly shown as having lived in the second half of the fourth century; he must have died about the year 320 B.C.

Taoism has retained from the ancient practices of magic which gave it birth some curious exercises in breath control, or rather a real system of "respiratory gymnastics", designed to transport the initiate into a state of ecstasy and levitation. The methods are not peculiar to ancient China, for one finds them among the yogis of India. These methods of autosuggestion were ennobled by the practice of a mysticism which was intended, as was Indian yoga, to "render the soul empty of all save its pure essence". The Taoist saint thus attained a kind of permanent ecstatic condition, "a state of magical grace which was also the truly natural state".

Taoist texts reveal to us the various stages of this mystic way. "After listening to your instructions", declares one of the sage's disciples in the book *Chuang Tzu*, "I first learned to consider my self as an external object, then I no longer knew if I were dead or living." And similarly in another passage: "After having seen the One (*tao*), he (the disciple) is able to attain a state where there is neither past nor present, and then a further state where he is neither dead nor living." The book *Lieh Tzu* analyses with greater precision these contemplative states which could be sustained even amid the vortex of affairs, since they were in communion with it: "My heart was concentrated, my body was dispersed. All my feelings were alike. I had no longer any sensation from what my body was leaning against nor from what my feet were standing on. I drifted from east to west at the will of the wind, like the leaf of a tree or a withered twig, until at the end I was uncertain whether it were the wind that was bearing me or I who carried the wind."

This intellectual asceticism endowed the Taoist with extraordinary powers. Granet writes that "having attained a state where he was no longer anything but a pure force, imponderable, invulnerable, and entirely autonomous, the saint passed through the elements with complete freedom".

In this transcendence, teaches Chuang Tzu, the sage is above all earthly contingencies: "Were the thunder to bring down the mountains or the hurricane to spill the ocean, he would not care. He is borne up by the air and the clouds, he rides on the sun and moon and frolics beyond the limits of space!" Like a pure spirit he passes through all matter, for to him all matter is as if porous. The book *Chuang Tzu* opens with the Platonic myth of the great celestial bird rising in search of *tao*. "The great bird rises on the wind to a height of a thousand miles. What does it see from on high there in the blue? Is it droves of wild horses galloping? Is it primeval matter whirling in atomic dust? Is it the exhalations that give birth to all things? Is it the blue of the sky itself, or is it only the colour of infinite distance?" In this planetary flight on the wings of the great mythical bird, in this wild aspiration to reach in one swoop the nameless force which moves the world, Chuang Tzu feels himself master of the universe.

In order thus to unite himself with nature and associate himself with the cosmic forces, the Taoist must first suppress his logical reasoning and "vomit his intelligence". "Let your eyes have no longer anything to see," teaches Chuang Tzu, "your ears nothing to hear and your heart nothing to know." Society and civilization are mere conventions. Like a disciple of Jean-Jacques Rousseau, he must return to a stage of nature and live in a kind of intimacy with the wild and free animals. To rediscover in himself the natural man, he has only to cast off the veneer of civilization.[1] There in himself is to be found the secret of longevity sought by all schools. In order to prolong our lives indefinitely, we need only preserve in peace our vital forces, without artificial interference. In its daily application Taoist wisdom consists essentially in the avoidance of all useless agitation. Lao Tzu [2] said:

> Without crossing his threshold
> He knows the whole world;
> Without looking from his window
> He perceives the ways (*tao*) of Heaven.

By deepening the ancient notion of *tao*, Taoism gave to Chinese thought a metaphysic of remarkable power, even though it avoids any attempt at precise definition. *Tao* is the cosmic substance before all determination.

"Before time and in all time", said Lao Tzu, "there was an existence existing by itself, eternal, infinite, complete, omnipresent. It is impossible to name it, for human language is confined to objects of the senses, and this primordial existence is essentially non-sensible. Outside this existence, before the beginning, was nothing. We call it the Formless or Mystery or *Tao*."

"It permeates all things," confirms Chuang Tzu; "it is in this ant; lower still, in this tile; yet lower, in this dung." A unique substance of which *yin* and *yang* are only the modes, a cosmic continuum

[1] Oscar Wilde wrote in *The Speaker* a delightful essay on a book about this Chinese sage and mystic, in which he said: "Chuang Tzŭ, whose name must carefully be pronounced as it is *not* written, is a very dangerous writer, and the publication of his book in English, two thousand years after his death, is obviously premature, and may cause a great deal of pain to many thoroughly respectable and industrious persons. It may be true that the ideal of self-culture and self-development which is the aim of his scheme of life, and the basis of his scheme of philosophy, is an ideal somewhat needed by an age like ours, in which most people are so anxious to educate their neighbours that they have actually no time left in which to educate themselves. But would it be wise to say so? It seems to me that if we once admitted the force of any one of Chuang Tzŭ's destructive criticisms we should have to put some check on our national habit of self-glorification; and the only thing that ever consoles man for the stupid things he does is the praise he always gives himself for doing them" (*Oscar Wilde*, by Hesketh Pearson, published by Methuen & Co, Ltd.).

[2] *i.e.* the book *Tao-te-ching*, claimed to be the teaching of "Lao Tzu".

which allows of their eternal reversibility, it remains completely unknowable and inexpressible. "The *tao* which can be named is not the true *tao*." [1] One can only define it negatively. This is expressed in the often quoted lines of Lao Tzu:

> The greatest square has no corners,
> The greatest pot is slowest made,
> The greatest melody makes the smallest sound,
> The greatest image has no shape.

Nevertheless it would be a mistake to regard this monism as a static monism. It is a genuine dynamism. As Maspero and Granet have observed, *tao* is conceived less as a being than as a force. It is all upsurge and vital impulse. It is the "innate power which moves worlds", or rather the "permanent principle of universal innate powers", the cosmic force identical with the vital force.

By a curious inversion, this absolute monism ends by being a radical relativism. If the "ten thousand things" are but one, they become interchangeable and inter-reversible. The sage himself, having cast off his name, his personality and his individuality, becomes identified with the rest of the universe. "How", says Chuang Tzu, "can we know if the self is what we call the self? Once I, Chuang Chou, dreamed that I was a butterfly, a fluttering butterfly, and I felt happy. I did not know that I was Chuang Chou. Suddenly I awoke and was myself, the real Chuang Chou. Then I no longer knew if I were Chuang Chou dreaming that he was a butterfly or a butterfly dreaming that he was Chuang Chou." Or take again the Shakespearian scene where Lieh Tzu, holding a skull picked up at the roadside, murmurs like a Chinese Hamlet, "This skull and I, we know that there is nothing really living, nothing really dead." Like Renan with his "Sirius View", so Chuang Tzu, in order to establish his universal relativism, invites us to view things from a similar observatory: "If you ascend in the chariot of the sun . . ." then from

[1] Hence the uselessness in these matters of logical reasoning; "those who would obtain *tao* by study", says Chuang-Tzu, "seek what study cannot give. Those who would obtain it by reason, seek what reason cannot give."

such a height "the self and the others", or as we would say the subject and the object, become identical: "A centenarian is not old, a stillborn child not young; a mite is equal to a mountain, a blade of grass to the universe."

This relativism, or rather this universal reversibility, produces an attitude of detachment, of quietude and of serene acceptance of all the vicissitudes of human life. "O world! all that you bring is of benefit to me," wrote Marcus Aurelius. Chuang Tzu in the same way says: "When we have understood that the sky and the world are a vast crucible and the Creator a great smelter, where could we go that would not be for our good." "O my master, O my master," he cries, addressing himself to *tao*, "you annihilate all things without being cruel, you give charity to ten thousand generations without being kind." The final lesson of Taoism is this lesson of indifference.

A singular philosophy is that of Yang Chu, who lived in the middle of the fourth century B.C. We have now reached the terrible epoch of the Warring States, a period of endemic warfare with appalling slaughter and massacres of whole civilian populations, and the vision that Yang Chu has left us of these centuries of the sword is desperate and cynical. His teaching is a pessimistic fatalism, whose bitterness has a personal note reminiscent of Lucretius. "A hundred years is the extreme limit of human life. A helpless infancy and a drivelling dotage take up half. Sickness and suffering, loss and trouble, fear and anxiety, occupy the rest. What is the life of man, where is the pleasure? Dead, he is stinking corruption, but how much worse eternal life!"

If the thinkers were deeply disappointed by the spectacle of the real world, there was one school which accepted it resolutely; that of the Legalists. In this century of the sword, they attempted to set up a doctrine of statecraft independent of morality. Taking man for what he was, with all his vices, the Legalists constructed a theory of good government on essentially empirical foundations. The laws, even under personally mediocre princes, should assure the health of the state, and indeed the well-being of the people, through the alternate employment of "the two handles", the awareness of punishments and rewards. Politics are a technique; the criterion of the value of laws is not their theoretical moral quality, but their practical effectiveness. In this respect the main thing is that the laws should be backed by force: "It is by their claws and their fangs that tigers can triumph over dogs."

Mencius (Meng Tzu), who lived approximately from 372 to 288 B.C., was a moralist of the Confucian school. He taught a doctrine of the golden mean, equidistant from the egoistic individualism of Yang Chu and the complete self-sacrifice preached by Mo Tzu, and protested no less against the harshness of the Legalists. In short, he returned to Confucian humanitarianism, balancing it with a more realistic theory of justice.

Particular stress was laid on education: "Excellence of heart is achieved by cultivating a germ of kindness, like a seed of barley which profits from a rich soil and a good year." This doctrine of moderation was not to reap its full success until later, under the settled government of the Han dynasty. For the time being, the epoch of the Warring States was at its most terrible stage, and all the realism of the Legalists was hardly sufficient for the lessons which tyrants and adventurers demanded of them.

CHAPTER V

BY FIRE AND SWORD

OUT of feudal chaos there finally emerged several great principalities, which absorbed the secondary seigniories and soon engaged each other in struggles to the death. All were rivals in the competition to determine which of them was to profit by bringing about the unification of Chinese territory. From the year 335 B.C. onwards, the most important territorial princes, without troubling themselves about the royal figureheads of the Chou dynasty, began themselves to assume the royal title (as in the Greek world Alexander's generals the Diadochi were to do the same thing after his death in 305 B.C.). The period of the Warring States was now at its height.

With the advent of the Warring States, the earlier chivalrous warfare gave place to wars of adventurers devoid of pity or loyalty, and this in turn developed into mass warfare, where the entire population of one state would be hurled against its neighbours. That pre-eminently noble arm of warfare, the chariot, the arm of fine tournaments in the style of the Iliad, began to give place to the cavalry proper, the arm of surprise attacks and sudden raids. This revolution in military technique was introduced in 307 B.C. by a king in the state of Chao, in the north of the present-day province of Shansi. Having to contend with the Huns of Mongolia, he realized that these nomads owed their superiority to their mounted archers, whose mobility and rapid evolutions always took the slow-moving Chinese charioteers by surprise. Adopting their tactics, he formed companies of mounted archers. His neighbour and rival, the king of Ch'in (in modern Shensi), went still further; he equipped himself not only with cavalry, but with companies of lightly equipped foot-soldiers as a standing "national" army to replace the unwieldy feudal levies. At this time, too, siegecraft made its appearance with the invention of siege machines, movable towers, and catapults which constituted a veritable artillery. The courtesies of feudal warfare were a thing of the past. The struggles between the Warring States were implacable. Instead of nobly holding their prisoners to ransom, from now on conquerors put them to death in mass executions. The soldiers of the kingdom of Ch'in, the most bellicose of the Warring States, received their pay only on the presentation of the severed heads of their enemies. In towns taken by assault, or even in those that capitulated, the whole population, women, old men, and children, were often put to the sword. Reverting once more to the cannibal practices of primitive humanity, the chiefs, in order to "increase their prestige", did not hesitate to throw their conquered enemies into boiling cauldrons and drink this horrible human soup, and even forced the kinsmen of their victims to drink it.

Among the Warring States, the principality of Ch'in enjoyed a great advantage because of its geographical situation. From the high valley of the Wei it dominated the rich plains of Honan, the chief prize in all this rivalry. The Han historian Ssu-ma Ch'ien, the Herodotus of China (died about 80 B.C.), drew attention to this in striking terms: "The country of Ch'in was a state whose position alone predestined its victory. Rendered difficult of access by the girdle formed around it by the Yellow River and the mountains, it was suspended a thousand li above the rest of the empire.[1] With twenty thousand men it could hold back a million spearmen. The position of its territory was so advantageous, that when it poured out its soldiers on the seigniories, "it was like a man emptying a jug of water from the top of a high house." Added to these geographical advantages was the military character of its people, a race of pioneers and soldier-farmers in these outer marches of the Chinese Wild West, plus—to turn these natural gifts to account—a tough and realistic

[1] One li is usually about one-third of a mile. "One thousand" or "ten thousand" often simply mean "many" or "myriad".

local dynasty that early recognized the secret weakness of the rival dynasties, namely the crumbling of the princely domains into sub-fiefs and estates for the benefit of the royal entourage. So as to avoid this weakening process, the kings of Ch'in learned how to reward their subjects without breaking up the royal domain. Lastly, they surrounded themselves with a school of Legalists—we have already referred to this school of philosophers—who in order to establish royal authority and justify conquest built up a comprehensive theory of the absolutism of king and state.

Also significant are the harsh regent-ministers, who during minorities assured the continuity of royal policy, often more vigorously than the kings themselves. One of these regents was the remarkable Wei Yang, of whom the annalist, under the year 359, says briefly that "he encouraged tilling and sowing. In the army he increased rewards as well as punishments. At first the people suffered by his policy, but the state benefited from it." This Chinese Richelieu was ill-paid for his services. A new king, whom as heir to the throne he had once reprimanded, had him "torn limb from limb between chariots". So severe a punishment for a personage of such high rank bears witness to the rigour of the Ch'in laws, which were equally merciless to all degrees of the social hierarchy. "Those who offered criticism were put to death with all their kin; the bodies of those who held meetings in secret were exposed in the market place." A strict discipline was imposed on the entire population.

Even under such leaders, the conquest of contemporary China—the basin of the Yellow River and the valley of the Long River-took a century and a half to complete.[1] Only the annals of the kings of Assyria, the Sennacheribs and the Assurbanipals, can display such a wealth of atrocities. In 331 Ch'in captured the army of Wei and decapitated 80,000 men; in 318 they broke up the coalition of Wei, Han, and Chao, which had aided the Huns, and cut off 82,000 heads;

[1] For the historical geography and the wars cf these feudal states, see Grousset, *L'Asie Orientale*. Here we may recall that while Ch'in corresponded to the modern province of Shensi, Chao and Wei corresponded roughly to Shansi, Ch'i to Shantung, Han to north-central Honan, and Ch'u to Hupei.

in 312 they beat Ch'u and 80,000 heads fell. In 307 they contented themselves with the score of 60,000 heads, but with the accession of King Chao Hsiang (he reigned over Ch'in from 306 to 251 B.C.), the scale of the massacres increased. In 293 he defeated Han and Wei and won himself, for a start, a trophy of 240,000 heads. In the campaign of 275 against Wei only 40,000 heads fell, but in a new expedition against the same adversary, a further 150,000. In 260, in a major success against Chao, "although he had promised to spare the lives of the conquered, more than 400,000 were decapitated". The other kingdoms of China were filled with a growing terror. Scarcely a decade passed in which Ch'in, "the wild beast of Ch'in", failed to devour one of them. It was at this point that there ascended the throne of Ch'in a prince who was successfully to conclude the work of his predecessors. This was the unifier of the lands of China, the future Ch'in Shih-huang-ti.

CHAPTER VI

A CHINESE CAESAR

IN the year 246 B.C., the future founder of Chinese autocracy, then known simply as King Cheng, ascended the throne of Ch'in. He was only thirteen years old. His youth allowed a certain respite to the other Chinese kingdoms, but it was a short reprieve. "He was", relates one of his counsellors, "a man with a prominent nose, large eyes, the chest of a bird of prey, the voice of a jackal, and the heart of a tiger or wolf." He was twenty-five years old when one of his generals, the conqueror of the rival kingdom of Chao (in present-day Shansi), offered him the colossal trophy of 100,000 heads. The other princes considered themselves doomed and felt that only the assassination of the young king could save them. One of them organized the murder, but the king escaped and it was the assassin who was cut to pieces. From then onwards his conquests succeeded one another at a lightning pace. Between the years 230 and 221 B.C. all the other Chinese kingdoms (corresponding to the present-day provinces of Shansi, Honan, Hopei, Shantung, Hupei, and Anhui) were annexed, one after another. In the year 221 the entire Chinese territory of those times was united under the king of Ch'in, who then assumed the title of supreme ruler or emperor (*huang-ti*) and it is by the name of "first emperor of the Ch'in dynasty", in Chinese, Ch'in Shih-huang-ti, that he is known to history.

The Chinese Empire was founded with the realization of Chinese unity. Under various dynasties, it was to endure for a period of two thousand one hundred and thirty-three years (from 221 B.C. to A.D. 1912).

The territorial unification of China by Shih-huang-ti was followed by a work of political, social, and even intellectual unification which was not the least remarkable part of his achievement. A personality without equal, this Chinese Caesar was not only a conqueror, but an administrator of genius. He extended to the entire empire the military and civil centralization created by his forebears in Ch'in. By mass exchanges of populations he succeeded in breaking down the most stubborn regionalism. His authoritarian caesarism ended a feudal system which seemed inherent in Chinese society. Far from creating a new feudal class in their favour, as his generals had hoped, he divided the empire into thirty-six commanderies, each directly administered by a civil governor, a military governor, and a superintendent. His minister Li Ssu standardized the written characters throughout the empire; a reform of far-reaching importance for the future, because difference of dialect was often to make the standard written language the only means of communication intelligible anywhere from Peking to Canton. Furthermore, "he standardized laws and regulations, weights and measures; carriage axles had to be of a uniform length".[1] This last measure had reference to the creation of a system of imperial roads of a uniform width of "fifty paces", planted with trees and built up on embankments to guard against the danger from floods.

At the instigation of his minister Li Ssu, this Chinese Caesar in 213 B.C. ordered the destruction of the classics, more particularly the books of the Confucian school; a measure which has earned him the hatred of the literati throughout the ages. At this period the literati, traditionally attached to the cult of a feudal past, were conscious or unconscious partisans of the regime which Shih-huang-ti abolished. In order to put an end to this covert opposition, the emperor "proscribed the books"; a radical measure which cannot have been as general as was said, for despite everything the classics have survived. In any case, it is the achievement of Shih-huang-ti that counts, an achievement equal to that of Caesar or Alexander the Great, but which was to endure much longer than theirs. In the most divided

[1] Because it was difficult to drive a cart if it did not fit into the wheel-ruts.

and most feudal of countries, his caesarism was able in some twenty years to create a centralization strong enough to last for twenty-one centuries. In short, he was one of the mightiest geniuses to whose lot the reshaping of humanity has fallen.

The inscriptions which this Chinese Caesar had engraved throughout his empire prove that he was not unconscious of the historic grandeur of his achievement. The inscription at T'ai-shan reads impressively: "For the first time he has united the world." "The inner ramparts have been cast down and destroyed," said the inscription at Chieh-shih. "He has regulated and made equal the laws, measures and standards for all men", said the stele at Lang-ya, "he has brought order to the eastern land, he has quelled the battles"—the formula of *Pax Sinica* for the Far East, equivalent to the *Pax Romana* of the Mediterranean world. Further on, to the same effect, one reads: "The black-haired people (that is the Chinese) enjoy calm and repose, arms are no longer necessary and each is tranquil in his dwelling. The Sovereign Emperor has pacified in turn the four ends of the earth"; a formula which evokes the picture of an *Orbis Sinicus* self-sufficient and analogous to the *Orbis Romanus*.

The rock inscriptions of Shih-huang-ti commemorate his journeys. Having finally brought unity to China, he set out on a grand tour of the principal regions; he ascended the sacred mountain of T'ai-shan in order to converse with the celestial spirits, and gazed at the ocean from the terrace of Lang-ya, trying to enter into communication with the genii of the sea, the inhabitants of the mysterious islands of the rising sun.

One of the preoccupations of Shih-huang-ti was to make China safe from the incursions of the Turco-Mongolian nomads; these barbarians, then known as the Huns (Hsiung-nu), ranged the Mongolian frontiers of the empire. In an attempt to hold them back the ancient princes had built stretches of wall at various points on the northern marches. In 215 B.C. the emperor joined up these ancient rudimentary fortifications into a continuous line of defence. This was the Great Wall. It ran from the pass of Shan-hai-kuan on the Gulf of Po-hai, as far as the sources of the Wei in Kansu, in the marches of the northwest.

Chinese territory, up to this period, had consisted only of the basin of the Yellow River and the valley of the Long River. Southern China and more particularly the Cantonese region remained foreign and barbarous. In 214 B.C. Shih-huang-ti sent an expeditionary force which occupied Canton and set about "Sinicizing" the country it had conquered. To this end the emperor ordered the rounding-up of vagrants, and sent them off to populate the new territories from the Long River estuary to Canton. The history of European colonization could furnish many similar examples of the application of this system of populating lands by the importation of convicts.

Shih-huang-ti died in 210 B.C. He was buried in accordance with his wishes, and at a spot near the present-day village of Hsin-feng in Shensi. His tomb is an immense tumulus, of a height of 48 metres from its base and some 60 metres from the surrounding land—a veritable mountain constructed by human hands. Inside the tomb were immured a number of his wives, as well as the workmen who carried his treasures there.

That part of the epoch of the Warring States which saw the rise of the kingdom of Ch'in (from the second half of the sixth century B.C. onwards) and the brief imperial apotheosis of this royal house under Shih-huang-ti (221–210 B.C.), witnessed the development of a new and distinct style in the art of bronzes. This style, formerly called "Ch'in technique" and now known as the "technique of the Warring States", is characterized by a "liberation from relief" in the representations of animals on the sides of vessels, as can be seen in the celebrated Li-yu vases now in the Louvre. It is distinguished above all by a new form of decoration, with interlacing and overlapping lines, loops, hooks, braids, spirals, and undulations, giving an impression of pullulation, or of a dance in perpetual motion. Lizard-like dragons, already to be found against the slower movement of the decorations of Chou bronzes, are swept into this quivering rhythm and leap up in a wild saraband. A similar animation is found in the hunting scenes which decorate the later bronzes in the period of transition to the art of the Han dynasty. It is worth noting that this style, while it is a logical development from the art of the Chou period, may at the same time have been influenced by a neighbouring art which was making its first appearance on the northern frontiers of China: the art of the steppes.

At the period which concerns us the immense zone of the steppes, which stretched from the north coast of the Black Sea in southern Russia, across southern Siberia and Mongolia as far as the Great Wall of China, was occupied by nomads of various races—Scythians of Caucasian stock in Russia, Huns of Mongolian race in Mongolia—all moving with their herds after seasonal pasture. These horsemen of the steppes, Scythians and Huns, possessed an individual style of art represented especially in ornamental bronze plaques decorated with fighting animals—wild beasts and horses, birds of prey and deer—curiously contorted and tormented in a style full of movement. We have seen that the Chinese, in an attempt to combat the Huns of Mongolia on an equal footing, created companies of mounted archers after their example. At the same time they adopted a part of their dress—the trousers of the horseman which replaced the long robe of the charioteer—and a part of their equipment, notably the bronze clasps and trimmings. Contemporary with these plaques and buckles we notice the appearance in Chinese art of stylized animal motifs whose rhythm is in close relation to the art of the steppes, although they belong to the Chinese style of the Warring States and the Ch'in period—a style whose blossoming they may well have assisted. This fact is interesting, since it enables us to discover certain contacts of Chinese art not only with the animal art of the Huns of Mongolia and the Siberian bronzes of the Minusinsk region, but also, through this intermediary, with the Scythian art of southern Russia, which latter is well known for its relationship with Greek art.

Whatever may be the significance of these archaeological comparisons, which are still in their infancy, China at the period we have reached was well on the way to entering into the current of world history. The unified empire created by Shih-huang-ti was destined, under the following dynasty, to come into contact with the Indian world, Persia, and the Roman Empire.

CHAPTER VII

A PERIOD OF TRANSITION

THE absolute monarchy created by Ch'in in Shih-huang-ti was only amenable to the leadership of a strong man. The son and successor of this Chinese Caesar was an incompetent youth. At the end of three years of disorders he was forced to commit suicide amid a general revolt. The country relapsed into the most appalling anarchy and the chiefs of the army seized the various provinces.

Chinese historians delight in contrasting the characters of the two principal captains in the ensuing struggle for power. Hsiang Yü, a coarse giant with the manners of an old soldier, and Liu Pang, a typical Chinese politician, wily and shrewdly generous, who was equally an upstart adventurer. The historians have left us a highly coloured portrait of him: "He was a man with a prominent nose, the forehead of a dragon and a handsome beard. His left thigh was marked with seventy-two black spots"—the latter an evident sign of his future greatness. "Although very poor, he loved wine and women." We are told that he used to drink at the house of an old shopkeeper, the woman Wang; where, either through generosity or boastfulness, he always offered to pay for his wine above the standard price, though in point of fact he always bought on credit. It is true that one day, when he had fallen asleep in a drunken stupor, the old woman thought that she saw a dragon hovering above his head; a further omen of the great destiny that lay before him. After this she was more willing than ever to allow him his wine on credit.

Early forsaking his peasant life, he took service as a police officer in a rural district. At this point in his career his biographer regales us with some jovial anecdotes about him. On one occasion, when asked by the prefect of the district to hand over a thousand cash as a "gift", he got out of it by sheer effrontery, and without paying a farthing. The collapse of the Ch'in empire offered an ideal opportunity to an adventurer seeking to make his fortune. Liu Pang started his career by forming a band of men in a rather original fashion. One day, when charged with escorting a column of prisoners, he thought it better to remove their chains and put himself at their head as captain of the band. "He anointed his drum with blood, took red for the colour of his standards", and carved out a fief in his native province of Kiangsu. In the year 207 B.C. he marched against the imperial province of Shensi, and won over the people by his humanity. His rival Hsiang Yü, who occupied Shensi in his wake, laid waste the country. Hsiang Yü having captured Liu Pang's father, threatened his rival that, if he failed to surrender, he would boil the old man alive. Liu Pang was not so easily intimidated. He replied to this horrible threat in the most amiable tone: "Hsiang Yü and I were formerly brothers in arms, my father is thus his father too. If he absolutely insists on boiling *our* father, let him not forget to save me a cup of the soup!" Disconcerted by such sang-froid, Hsiang Yü at once released his prisoner.

Soon Liu Pang's cunning had driven his rival to final disaster. In a furious battle, which was joined on the banks of the Huai River (203 B.C.), Hsiang Yü performed prodigies of valour, crossing and recrossing the enemy lines with his cavalry and killing one of Liu Pang's lieutenants with his own hands, until in the end, pierced with ten wounds, he found himself surrounded by overwhelming forces. Among his pursuers he recognized one of his former companions in arms and cried out to him: "I know there is a price on my head. Take it!" With which he killed himself by cutting his throat.

Liu Pang had no other rival. The soldier of fortune had become emperor! By an unforeseen turn of fortune it came about that this peasant's son was to profit from the labours of thirty-seven generations of the princes of Ch'in, and it was in the end for his benefit that Ch'in Shih-huang-ti had created the Chinese autocracy. In less than five years this lucky adventurer had become the unexpected heir to a long line of proud feudatories, and the beneficiary of a man of genius who had created a centralized empire and united China. None the less, the outset of his reign was modest and even difficult. He was forced to reward the other *condottieri*, who had helped him to the throne, with large fiefs and local princedoms—apparently restoring in their favour the old feudal system abolished by Ch'in Shih-huang-ti. Yet what he gave with one hand he took away with the other; he took advantage of the least pretext to transfer the local princes that he had been obliged to create, as if they were mere prefects. Alternately, he drove them to revolt and then got rid of them. In the end the new Han feudatories, tamed and deprived of all administrative power, were reduced to the state of a mere court nobility which in no way hindered the absolute power of the emperor.

Liu Pang was to be blessed with that which to the founder of a dynasty is the greatest fortune—a line of descendants who maintained the empire for four centuries. At the outset there was no authority more doubtful and precarious than his, but as time went on there was no legitimacy more sure than that which claimed descent from him; for his line, the Han dynasty, was to rule over the empire from 202 B.C. until A.D. 220 and leave so strong an imprint on the destiny of the Chinese people that to this day they are proud to be called "The sons of Han".

Meanwhile nobody could have been less intoxicated by his good fortune than this founder of a dynasty. At the zenith of his power he never forgot the simplicity of his origins: "It was while dressed in rough cloth and wielding a three-foot sword that I conquered the empire!" He was only really happy when he was among the humble people of his native province (the present Kiangsu), with whom he loved to recall the days of his youth. Yet he was forced to leave them and take up residence in his new capital of Ch'ang-an (the present Sian) in the province of Shensi, the true heart of the empire. Before taking leave of his native province, he gave a great banquet to the people. "He invited all those, young and old, whom he had known in former times and passed round the wine. He drank and danced with them. Old men, married women, and all the former friends of Liu Pang passed days in drinking and rejoicing. They laughed and made merry, telling stories about the old days." Before leaving, the emperor could not restrain his tears: "The traveller is sad when he thinks of his native land; although I must go and take up residence in the west, when I am dead my spirit will still be happy thinking of this land of yours."

As with his compatriots the villagers, so did Liu Pang take pleasure in the company of his soldiers, men whose tastes he shared. While he did not systematically persecute the Confucian literati, as his predecessor Ch'in Shih-huang-ti had done, he profoundly despised them and riddled them with sarcasm. Those who would fill his ears with classic texts from the *Book of Songs* and the *Book of Documents* brought on themselves a sharp rebuke: "I conquered the empire on horseback! What are your *Songs* and *Documents* to me?"[1] Indeed it was hardly the moment to slacken military control in the empire. In the year 200 B.C. the emperor himself had the misfortune to be surrounded by the Huns on a plateau near P'ing-ch'eng in the north of Shansi; for seven days he was cut off from the main body of the army and unable to obtain rations. He managed to escape in the end by a ruse, presenting the king of the Huns with the portrait of a Chinese beauty. Two years later he did in fact resign himself to sending one of the beautiful girls from his harem to the barbarian chief, and poets have never ceased to lament the sad fate of the poor little "Chinese partridge" surrendered in marriage to the "savage bird of the north".

Liu Pang included doctors in the general contempt which he showed for all intellectuals. Suffering from a war wound, he refused to accept their aid. The wound became septic, and he died at Ch'ang-an on June 1, 195 B.C., when only fifty-two years of age.

[1] The *Shih-ching* ("Song Classic") and *Shu-ching* ("Documents Classic") were the two books taught by Confucius. The *Shu-ching* is a collection of legends and chronicles relating to ancient history, from the appearance of the first sage-kings down to Chou times. Much of the existing text is said to be spurious.

The founder of the Han dynasty bequeathed the throne to one of his sons, a boy too young to exercise authority. The power was assumed by the boy's mother, the dowager empress Lü, a woman of ferocious energy whose advice in former times had aided Liu Pang to consolidate his successes. At one time the Lady Lü had been forced to contend for her position with a concubine who was younger than herself and who, in the latter years of the emperor's reign, had found favour in the eyes of Liu Pang. The emperor was scarcely dead before the dowager empress took an appalling revenge on her rival. She caused her hands and feet to be cut off, her ears to be burnt, and her eyes to be put out, then after a narcotic had been administered to the unhappy woman, she had her pitched into the palace pigsty, where she was fed on refuse as a "human sow". This Chinese Agrippina had a further cause for anxiety in the shape of a young prince, the child of the late emperor by a third concubine. At a banquet she prepared for him a death like that of Britannicus. But the young emperor, who had not been warned about the plot against his half brother, was the first to put out his hand to empty the poisoned cup. The empress had scarcely time to spring up from her seat and upset the fatal drink. It is unnecessary to add that the victim, after his miraculous escape from death, hastened to leave this dangerous household.

The dowager took advantage of her authority to place members of her own clan in all the key positions, but the day after her death, in a fresh palace drama, they were collectively massacred by the imperial princes (180 B.C.).

Despite these disturbances, the Han dynasty daily assumed greater authority, and one might say, "legitimacy". Its first rulers—with the exception of Liu Pang—were perhaps men of no great distinction. Yet like the first Capetian kings in the direct line, they had not only the advantage of endurance, but also of being excellent representatives of the principles on which the moral and religious systems of their times were based. The best known among them, the emperor Hsiao-wen-ti (180–157 B.C.), talked like a Confucian scholar, having constantly on the tip of his tongue "the holy wisdom of the Emperor On High", "the supernatural influence of Heaven and Earth", the cult of ancestors and the importance of agriculture, "the blessing of the gods of the earth and of the crops", and the patriarchal regime that the Confucian literati projected back into the mirage of mythical times.

These virtuous speeches are not without significance. Their very repetition shows that Imperial absolutism, the brutal Caesarism created by Ch'in Shih-huang-ti and maintained by Liu Pang, was winning the support of the literati. Their adherence sanctioned the regime from a traditionalist point of view, since it linked it, back beyond the centuries of the sword, with the saints and sages of the "golden age".

CHAPTER VIII

PAX SINICA

THE most outstanding personality produced by the Han dynasty was the emperor Wu-ti. This prince enjoyed an exceptionally long reign; he ascended the throne at the age of sixteen and ruled for fifty-three years (140–87 B.C.). Gifted with a prodigious energy and an extraordinary vitality, he took no thought of conserving his strength. One finds him, like the Assyrian kings of former times, bringing wild beasts to bay in the high grasses, reckless of his life and the great consternation he caused his attendants. A man of remarkable intelligence, full of bold and original ideas and with a taste for autocracy, he nevertheless understood the wisdom of listening to the opinions of others. Thus at the outset of his reign he surrounded himself with Confucian literati and openly solicited their advice. The men of letters, as we have seen, had long remained in aloof opposition to the autocracy, an attitude which led to Ch'in Shih-huang-ti's proscription of the "books" and provoked the sarcasms of Liu Pang. How then is one to explain the favours which Wu-ti lavished on them—Wu-ti, who seemed to combine the fiery absolutist temperament of the First Emperor with the political realism of the founder of Han? Certainly nobody was less likely to be taken in by the utopian theories of which the literati were the tireless defenders. The answer is that without knowing it they served his policy against the nobility. The scholar class, which began to assume the shape of the future mandarinate, made it possible for the emperor to gain the upper hand over the landed aristocracy, the new feudal class of imperial princes which had been allowed to develop. Relegating these noblemen to purely nominal positions of honour, he replaced them by a government of sons of the people distinguished for their knowledge, and in the same way he replaced them in the army by commanders of humble birth. Through these changes, the future mandarinate enabled Chinese autocracy to achieve its task of "levelling". In addition, Wu-ti took a radical measure aimed at reducing the importance of the feudal appanages. Under the semblance of interesting himself in the position of younger sons, he compelled the princes to bequeath their estates among all their children without distinction, and to make no special provision for elder sons. Within two or three generations this egalitarian legislation, like the *Code Napoléon*, had broken up, impoverished, and wiped out the great feudal estates.

In his foreign policy Wu-ti undertook the conquest of those parts of Asia that were known to the Chinese of his age, beginning with the conquest of Upper Asia.

From the Great Wall of China to the Siberian forests, Upper Asia was under the domination of the Huns, the ancestors of the Turks and Mongols of our Middle Ages. Their various hordes shared the Mongolian steppes; both that part of Mongolia situated to the north of the eastern Gobi called Outer Mongolia, and the grasslands which stretch along the southern fringe of the Gobi and are known as Inner Mongolia.[1] These nomad herdsmen, whose flocks constituted their sole riches, migrated with their animals in search of fresh pastures, pitching and striking their temporary encampments of felt *yurts* as they went. As they are described by Latin authors of the fifth century A.D., so they appear already in the old Chinese annals, which likewise portray them as perfect barbarians: their heads are too big, their features undefined, but their eyes like burning coals; they have massive chests, framed to withstand the icy nights and scorching days of the Gobi, and their legs are bowed from constant riding. Born horsemen and archers incomparable, to the Chinese peasant of the northern marches—the northern parts of Hopei, Shansi, and

[1] This has also been a political division since 1912, when the Chinese Republic was only able to gain control of Inner Mongolia. In 1924 the Mongolian People's Republic was formed in Outer Mongolia, and its sovereignty was recognized by China in 1946.

Shensi—these men were the most dreaded of neighbours. When drought exhausted the water holes and burned the grass of the steppes, then the Huns whose herds had perished would descend on the farmlands. They would appear unexpectedly, raiding and killing, and disappear again across the vast spaces of the desert before the Chinese garrisons had had time to muster their forces.

Before undertaking a major war against the Huns, the emperor Wu-ti planned a policy of encirclement of "world-wide" scope. At the opposite end of Central Asia, in the steppes of present-day Soviet Turkestan, lived other nomads, Scythians it would seem, whom the Huns had driven out of the Gobi at an earlier date. Wu-ti sent an emissary who found them on the borders of Sogdiana and Bactria, that is to say on the threshold of the Greek kingdoms which were successors of Alexander the Great in this area. Wu-ti proposed that the Scythians should attack the Huns from the west, while he himself would take the offensive by way of Mongolia. When this offer was declined he started operations alone. In the year 128 B.C. his general Wei Ch'ing—a former herdsman who could rival the Huns themselves as an archer and horseman—carried out a "counter-raid" across the Mongolian Gobi, penetrated as far as the Ongun River, surprised the enemy, and "cut off heads". This system of "counter-raids", which turned against the Huns their own time-honoured tactics, was complemented by the creation of military colonies. These camps of soldier-farmers were analogous to the military outposts of the Roman Empire and were likewise intended to protect the boundaries (*limes*)—as well as to increase the Chinese cultivated lands at the expense of the Hunnish grasslands. In particular, these colonies picketed the great loop of the Yellow River, so as to include within the limits of the empire that part of the Gobi which the river loop brings within the natural boundaries of China proper. This is the Ordos steppe, a land which in times of decay has always served as a point of concentration for nomad forces intent on invading the northern provinces.

Wei Ch'ing's nephew, Huo Ch'ü-ping, was a man even more

remarkable than his uncle. He was only about twenty years old when he reorganized the Chinese light cavalry after the Hunnish pattern. In the year 121 B.C., with ten thousand horsemen he drove the Huns from eastern Kansu, the departure point of the Silk Road. In 119 B.C. he and his uncle Wei Ch'ing, with fifty thousand horsemen carried out an overwhelming raid into Outer Mongolia. Wei Ch'ing, with the column of the left, penetrated as far as the lower stream of the River Ongun, took the king of the Huns by surprise and, in the middle of a storm which drove the sands of the Gobi into the eyes of the barbarians, inflicted a crushing defeat. Huo Ch'ü-ping, with the column of the right, crossed the entire length of the eastern Gobi and reached the upper Tola, towards the Khangai Mountains. There, after capturing eighty Hunnish chieftains, he made solemn sacrifices to the spirits to symbolize the capture of Outer Mongolia by Chinese arms. This young hero died shortly after his return to China (in 117 B.C.). Over his tomb at Hsien-yang, near Ch'ang-an, was erected a powerful sculpture representing a Chinese horse trampling a barbarian underfoot.

But these Chinese expeditions into the uncultivated wastes of Upper Mongolia represented only punitive or preventive raids. It was in the direction of Central Asia that China turned her gaze for preference. There, in present-day Sinkiang, lived sedentary populations who, as recent discoveries have shown, belonged to the Indo-European language family. The oases which lay along two arcs to the north and to the south of the Tarim Basin were the natural stages of the caravan route which was to put China in communication with the Greco-Roman world. As early as 108 B.C. Wu-ti's generals imposed Chinese suzerainty on two of the principal oases in this area, those of Lob Nor and Turfan. In 102 B.C. one of the Chinese commanders, Li Kuang-li, in a march of unparalleled audacity, advanced with sixty thousand men as far as Ferghana, on the threshold of present-day Soviet Turkestan. The object of this expedition is significant. The Chinese were at a disadvantage against the formidable cavalry of the Huns, despite the spectacular exploits of such commanders as Huo Ch'ü-ping and Wei Ch'ing. The Huns, besides being born horsemen, had the small Mongolian horses whose fire and endurance are proverbial. The Chinese were not such good horsemen, and were forced to rely on a breed of similar height, but far less hardy. Now Persia, Transoxiana, and Ferghana were the home of a breed of Arab coursers similar to our present-day English Arabs; these were the "Nicaean stallions" whose qualities were celebrated by Greek historians. It was in order to obtain this breed and to gain over the Huns a decisive superiority in their remounts, that the Chinese in 102 B.C. compelled Ferghana to send a given number of stallions as annual tribute. This event, it may be added, has left its traces in the history of art. For while the bas-reliefs from Han tombs chiefly depict the ancient thickset Chinese horse, a sort of miniature *percheron* with heavy croup and breast, the terra-cotta figures of the same period found in China and Korea show a courser of far more elegant lines and nearer to the Greek model, which is doubtless none other than the horse imported from Transoxiana in the year 102.

Meanwhile in Mongolia the Huns had not disbanded, and towards the end of the reign of Wu-ti the Chinese had reason to regret their own overconfidence in this respect. In the year 99 B.C., a young Chinese captain called Li Ling undertook to lead a column of five thousand foot-soldiers from the Great Wall into the heart of Mongolia. He left China by way of the Edsin Gol, and plunged into the Gobi, marching north towards the Ongun River and the Khangai Mountains; but he soon found himself surrounded by Hun cavalry, whose circling horsemen riddled his little force with their arrows. He realized his imprudence, decapitated all the trollops whom the soldiers had concealed in the baggage waggons and who were slowing down the pace, and beat a retreat, harassed by the pursuing nomads. After having lost a third part of his effective strength, used up his arrows, and abandoned his waggons, he had come within fifty kilometres of the frontier when he was surrounded in a gorge, where during the night the Huns rolled down enormous rocks on to his men. Only four hundred Chinese managed to escape. All the rest, including the impetuous Li Ling himself, were taken prisoner.

Notwithstanding the rage which shook the emperor Wu-ti on hearing these tidings, this was in no way comparable with the disaster that overtook the Roman general Varus. The safety of the frontiers was not at stake. At worst the system of counter-raids in Mongolia might have to be abandoned for the time being. The most serious consequence of this episode was that it served the Confucian literati as a pretext for protesting against the policy of armaments and expansion. "However great a country may be, if it loves war it will perish. Arms are ill-omened instruments. The territories which have been wrested from the Huns are unsuited for cultivation; and furthermore, these brutes are incapable of assimilation. It is better to ignore them, and leave them to pasture their flocks in the solitary wastes." Throughout Chinese history we find these declamatory speeches by the literati. They represented the permanent doctrine of the mandarinate, which ultimately prevailed over the warrior temperament of ancient China. The day was to come when an army career, despised by the literati, was to be considered an inferior occupation, and when any preventive war was to be rendered impossible by their utopian pacifism.

With rulers such as Wu-ti these declamations had little effect. Not content with tracing the pattern of Chinese expansion in Central Asia, the emperor accomplished a work of even greater importance, the final annexation of South China.

We have seen that in ancient times Chinese territory was confined to North and Central China, that is to say the basin of the Yellow River and the northern basin of the Long River. Southern China remained in the same class as Indo-China, a foreign country, a land of mountains, or at least of wooded hills which contrasted with the low lying alluvial plains and loess terraces of primitive China. Ch'in Shih-huang-ti, a pioneer in this as in other things, was the first to give a definite impetus to the movement towards the south. He undertook a tour of inspection as far south as Ch'angsha, in the centre of present-day Hunan, and sent an expeditionary force to occupy the Cantonese region. After his death, however, the chiefs of this army declared their independence and founded at Canton a Chinese-native kingdom which drew the Annamites of present-day Tonking into its orbit. In the year 111 B.C. the emperor Wu-ti put an end to this dissidence and Canton was definitely attached to China; an event which was to have an incalculable influence on the course of history. In the following year he likewise assumed control of the province of Chekiang (to the south of Shanghai); an annexation of no less importance when one realizes that this new and still colonial China was much later, at the time of the great invasions, to become the real China, the last stronghold of the empire. Lastly, to the northeast Wu-ti established Chinese domination over a part of Korea, and to the southeast, over the Annamite country, which at that period comprised Tonking and the northern provinces of present-day Annam as far south as Huê.

The emperor Wu-ti's achievement may be summed up as follows. At home, Chinese autocracy was put on a firm basis through the support of the literati and the ruin of the last of the feudal lords. The bounds of China proper were defined; they extended south to the harbours of Chekiang and to Canton. Abroad, the historic domain of Chinese imperialism was likewise marked out across Central Asia to western Turkestan, across the Korean peninsula to the heights of Seoul, and across Indo-China to the approaches of Huê. If the Chinese of today are still proud of the name "sons of Han", truly it is because of the great emperor who ruled from 140 to 87 B.C. This was the period when the victories of Marius and Sulla established Roman domination over the Mediterranean world. The armies of Wu-ti established a *Pax Sinica* in Central and Eastern Asia, the Far Eastern equivalent of the *Pax Romana*.

The next emperor to resume the work of this great monarch was his great-grandson Hsüan-ti, who ruled from 73 to 49 B.C. This clear-headed prince had occasion to discern the subversive tendencies of the literati—professional pacifists and covert opponents of Chinese expansion.

"The Han", he exclaimed on one occasion, "have their own code, which is the code of conquerors. We are no longer living in the times of Chou, the age of government by virtue and education. The literati fail to understand the different needs of different times. They speak always of the virtues of antiquity and the evils of the present age. They impress the simple-minded, filling their ears with high-sounding and empty phrases. How is one to give positions of responsibility to men living in a utopian world and thus devoid of practical sense?"

The conquest of Central Asia continued. Under Hsüan-ti the Chinese armies occupied the principal strategic points in the Tarim basin, including Turfan, Karashar, and Yarkand. To the north, Chinese policy gained a decisive victory. By fomenting the quarrels between two rival Hun pretenders, it managed to provoke a schism in the Hun empire. One of the rival chiefs, the one who was destined to obtain control of Mongolia, sought Chinese support. He became a vassal and in 51 B.C. (the year of the final subjection of Gaul by Julius Caesar) he came to the court of Ch'ang-an to kowtow ("knock the head" on the ground, indicating submission and respect) before the emperor Hsüan-ti. His ousted rival departed into the steppes of western Turkestan to found a new Hun kingdom to the west of Lake Balkhash. But in 35 B.C. a Chinese army came to hunt him out, surprised his camp, and cut off his head. This bold step arrested the expansion of the western Huns, and, incidentally, doubtless saved Europe for more than four centuries. It was not until the year A.D. 347 that these same Huns, regrouped around the family of Attila, started once more on their conquering march across the Germanic and Roman world.

TRANSLATOR'S NOTE

There are a few points worth noting about the nomenclature of Chinese emperors.

"The First Emperor of Ch'in" (Ch'in Shih-huang-ti) himself took this title; but from Han to Sui the rulers are usually known by their *shih*, or posthumous epithet, plus *Ti* (Emperor). For example, Han Wu-ti ("Mighty"), Han Ming-ti ("Bright"), and so on. Strictly speaking, it is tautological for us to say "The *emperor* Wu-*ti*".

From T'ang to Sung the rulers are usually known by their *miao-hao* or posthumous "temple name", which consists of an epithet plus *Tsu* or *Tsung* (Ancestor). For example, T'ang Kao-tsu ("High"), T'ang T'ai-tsung ("Great"), and so on.

From Yüan to Ch'ing official historians again refer to the emperors by their "temple names". However, the rulers of the foreign Yüan dynasty are also commonly known by their Mongol names and title: Grand Khan Kublai, Grand Khan Temur, and so on.

Moreover, the Ming and Ch'ing rulers are sometimes referred to as being of such and such a "reign-title" or era (*nien-hao*, literally "years-name"). The use of reign-titles began with Han Wu-ti in 140 B.C., which was proclaimed the first year of Chien-yüan. Thus 135 B.C. was "Chien-yüan year 6". The reign-titles were changed, usually within some ten years or less, according to the best astrological advice; such a change was almost certain to be made in the event of natural or political disasters. But the Ming and Ch'ing dynasties abandoned this means of protecting the national welfare; hence there was only one reign-title for each emperor (except in the case of Ming Ying-tsung, whose reign was interrupted for eight years). Therefore it is possible to refer, for instance, to Ch'ing Sheng-tsu as K'ang-hsi-ti, "The Emperor of the period K'ang-hsi". Most Western historians refer to him as "The emperor K'ang-hsi" or simply "K'ang-hsi", which is a little misleading in that K'ang-hsi by itself means the period 1662–1722, not the emperor who reigned during this period.

Another point of importance is that the reigning emperor was always referred to as (His) Highness, or by other terms meaning the Emperor. When he succeeded to the throne his personal name became tabu, like the names of one's parents; his historical title, as mentioned above, was conferred posthumously.

CHAPTER IX

THE TRIUMPH OF THE LITERATI

IN the last chapter we suggested a certain parallelism between the formation of the Roman Empire and the empire of the Han dynasty. The solidity of the Roman conquest was shown by the fact that it was never imperilled during the long period of almost permanent civil war which raged throughout the Latin world from the crossing of the Rubicon (49 B.C.) to the Battle of Actium (31 B.C.). Some years later, China too underwent a crisis of such magnitude that the dynasty all but disappeared; but in spite of this, Chinese rule in Asia was able to survive.

The decadence of the earlier branch of the Han dynasty was evidently brought about by the peculiar atmosphere of court life, for it is not only in France that courts like Versailles prepare the fall of dynasties. In addition there was the growing influence of the literati, whose ideas were out of touch with practical affairs. The history of the last rulers of this branch is a recital of intrigues between the camarilla of the eunuchs and the Confucian literati, both equally incapable of envisaging, from an objective point of view, the permanent requirements of Chinese greatness. The emperor Yüan-ti, who came to the throne at the age of twenty-seven and died at the age of forty-three (48–33 B.C.), was a timid and irresolute intellectual who allowed himself to be shut in by his eunuchs. The degeneration increased with the emperor Ch'eng-ti, who came to the throne when nineteen years old and died at the age of forty-five (32–7 B.C.); he was at once a scholar and a debauchee (at night he would go out incognito to visit the pleasure-houses of the capital, at the risk of being set upon). His successor Ai-ti, likewise proclaimed emperor at the age of nineteen, who reigned from 6 B.C. to A.D. 1, lived in the company of catamites and appointed his Antinous commander-in-chief. This depravity finally brought the dynasty into disrepute. The old dowager empress, the widow of Yüan-ti, took advantage of this to have the power entrusted to her own nephew, the celebrated Wang Mang, a politician of unbridled ambition. For several months he maintained a phantom emperor, a child nine years old, and had him drink a cup of poison when he had served his purpose. He then proclaimed himself Son of Heaven (on 10, January A.D. 9).

Wang Mang, who thus usurped the power, was not simply a man of ambition. Certainly the official history, written later in praise of the restored branch of the Han dynasty, condemns the usurper. What it fails to say, or at least what it tries to dissemble, is that this reign (from A.D. 9 to 22) marked the triumph of the party of the literati. Wang Mang was well schooled in their teaching and shared their theories about patriarchal government, the so-called government of the earliest (mythical) rulers and of the first kings of the Chou dynasty, which in China played somewhat the role of that state of nature so dear to Jean Jacques Rousseau. In this spirit Wang Mang decreed a series of reforms, of extreme interest in that they corresponded to an undeniable social crisis.

Since the advent of Chinese autocracy the latifundia had increased and the class of small landowners had diminished, thus adding to the numbers of dependants and slaves. In times of famine especially, the poor people were reduced to selling all their patrimony, and even to selling themselves and their children into slavery. Wang Mang sought to combat this enslavement of the rural population and to bring back "the times when each man possessed a hundred measures of land and paid the state a tithe in kind". "But now", he added, turning the sword in the wound, "one sees the fields of the rich stretching in hundreds and thousands, while the poor have not land enough to plant a needle. Furthermore slave markets have been established where men are sold like horses and cattle; a thing manifestly contrary to the wishes of Heaven and Earth, Who have given man a nature nobler than that of the animals." In the year A.D. 9, emulating the ancient utopia of the philosopher Mencius, Wang Mang granted a property of five hectares to each family of eight people. At the same time he obliged people with larger domains to distribute the residue among their relations and neighbours. In order to prevent the reconstitution of large estates, he declared as a principle that the state was the sole proprietor of the soil. He forbade any modification of this statute, thereby preventing all buying and selling of land; in the same way he forbade all traffic in slaves, the state alone having the right to possess them.

In the following year (A.D. 10) Wang Mang created a body of officials whose duty it was to regulate the economy of the state. Overseers of markets were assigned the quarterly task of fixing the maximum price of each commodity. "Stabilizers of prices" were to buy at the current price merchandise (such as grain, silk, and cloth) which had been brought to the market and failed to find a buyer; these unsold goods were to be stored by the agents and put back on the market when the scarcity of a commodity threatened to raise the price. Official bankers were to lend money at a rate of interest of three per cent per month. On the other hand, taxation was based on a tenth part of all profits. With the exception of the farmers, for whom the reckoning at each harvest was a simple one, a statutory declaration was demanded in the various trades—hunters and fishermen, raisers of stock or of silkworms, spinners and weavers, metalworkers, merchants, doctors, diviners, and magicians—all had to declare their earnings and hand over a tenth part to the state. Wang Mang also authorised successive new coinages (which account for the surprising number of coins bearing his name), in the course of which he repeatedly debased the currency. To this end he decreed a monopoly of gold and laid an embargo on copper.

These reforms reveal not only a man of spirit, preoccupied with finding radical solutions for the crisis of his time, but also a rather utopian intellectual, more of a theorist than a judge of human nature. His vexatious state control soon brought about a general revolt. The monopoly of gold had ruined the nobility. The fixed rates of exchange for fresh issues of inferior money, in conjunction with the obligation to return the older money of better alloy to the state at the same nominal value, was ruining commerce. Finally, the state monopoly of timber and fisheries seriously affected the peasantry. The economy being disorganized, bad harvests caused famine to ravage the provinces. Peasant revolts broke out, notably in Shantung, an overpopulated region whose natural fertility is insufficient to withstand several months of drought or floods, and which for that reason has always been a hotbed of social unrest and a centre for sects of Taoist fanatics. In 3 B.C. Shantung suffered from a drought of such proportions that crowds of the starving were to be seen wandering about the country and invoking the Taoist deities. In A.D. 11 the Yellow River broke its banks and flooded the plains of Shantung and Hopei. In A.D. 14 the famine was so intense that the peasants took to cannibalism. A brigand chief organized the peasant insurgents in disciplined bands, instructing them to paint their eyebrows red as a means of recognition. The Red Eyebrows, supported by the sympathies of the people, routed the regular troops and soon made themselves masters of the lower basin of the Yellow River (A.D. 18).

Meanwhile legitimism was not dead and the Han dynasty still had its partisans. With the collapse of Wang Mang's reforms, and amid the disorder resulting from the peasant revolts of the Red Eyebrows, the legitimists rose in revolt. Two Han princes, Liu Hsiu and Liu Hsüan, appeared as leaders, the first in the province of Honan, the second in the province of Hopei. In A.D. 22 the two groups had the good sense to unite; recognizing Liu Hsüan as their leader, they stormed Ch'ang-an, the imperial capital. Deserted by his followers, Wang Mang took refuge on the top of a tower built in the middle of a pool in the imperial park. He was assassinated there and his head was brought to the Han princes. Thus perished the man who had dreamed of changing the foundations of Chinese society in accordance with the ideals of the Confucian literati.

Although the usurper had been overthrown, order was not yet

re-established. Liu Hsüan, the Han prince in whose name the restoration had been accomplished, was a mediocrity who, once in power, showed himself incapable. He interested himself solely in his pleasures and made his cook a high official. Meanwhile the Red Eyebrows still held the eastern provinces, and now, encouraged by the incapacity of Liu Hsüan, they marched on the capital. They captured it without any great effort and Liu Hsüan took to flight. Once masters of the city, the peasant insurgents indulged in an orgy of looting. Having captured Liu Hsüan, they had him strangled.

There remained the second Han pretender Liu Hsiu, a man of a very different calibre, clever and energetic, a good soldier and a popular leader. Before the destruction of Ch'ang-an he had set up headquarters at Loyang, where he now proclaimed himself emperor (A.D. 25). The Red Eyebrows, after thoroughly pillaging Ch'ang-an, ebbed back towards the east. Liu Hsiu's army surrounded them between Ch'ang-an and Loyang, massacred an immense number, and made prisoners of the rest, in all some eighty thousand bandits and their trollops. In addition Liu Hsiu, who was shrewdly aware how to end a revolution, took the sturdiest among the revolutionaries and enrolled them in his own regiments (A.D. 27). Three years later his reforming administration had already produced such good results that the tax could be lowered from one-tenth to one-thirtieth of harvests and profits.

CHAPTER X

THE SILK ROAD

THE Han dynasty was restored. The fortunate Liu Hsiu, who was now emperor (Kuang-wu-ti), was to devote the thirty-two years of his reign (A.D. 25–57) to repairing the ravages of war in his own country and re-establishing Chinese hegemony in eastern Asia.

During the years of unrest China had naturally lost the larger part of her foreign dependencies. Revolution was contagious, and certain possessions which had remained loyal during the troubled years became the centres of belated revolts. Such was the case of the Annamite country in Indo-China, which at that period comprised only Tonking and Annam, north of Huê. The southern and central provinces of modern Annam were then in the power of a Malayo-Polynesian people, the Tcham. Moreover the Annamites really occupied only the delta of Tonking and the narrow coastal strip of northern Annam; for the Annamite is essentially a cultivator of the paddy fields of the coast—a way of life that distinguishes him from his neighbours of the same race, the Muong, hunters in the wooded inland hills. A common way of life brought the Annamite closer to the Chinese, and when about 110 B.C. Chinese domination was imposed on the country, it was accepted in a docile manner. In the tombs of Thanh-hoa both "Indonesian" implements of the Proto-Annamites and purely Chinese articles are found at the same sites. In the year A.D. 40, however, as the result of a series of Chinese administrative blunders, the Annamites, inspired by two heroines later celebrated in local legend, shook off the Chinese yoke. The emperor Kuang-wu-ti entrusted the task of putting down this rebellion to a veteran commander called Ma Yüan, whose exploits on the Indo-Chinese coast, the farthest point reached by the Chinese navigators of those times, were to earn him the title of "Pacifier of the Waves". Entering Tonking in A.D. 42, Ma Yüan put down the Annamite revolt at the beginning of the following year. Tradition attributes to him the erection of a bronze column at Quang-nam (in the region of Tourane) to mark the frontier between Chinese territory and the uncivilized lands of the Tchamps.

Ma Yüan went from Indo-China to the other end of the empire in order to repulse the Huns of Mongolia, as well as other Turco-Mongolian hordes leading a nomadic existence further to the east, towards the Great Khingan Mountains (A.D. 45). Shortly afterwards the Huns became divided among themselves. In the year A.D. 46 there was in Upper Asia a drought of such magnitude that for three years the steppes were denuded of any trace of vegetation, and half the cattle and even some of the nomads themselves perished from hunger. As always among the Huns, dissension followed on famine. The nomads of Inner Mongolia revolted against the chief who reigned on the upper reaches of the Orkhon in Outer Mongolia, and accepted Chinese suzerainty (A.D. 48). They were established as allies along the frontier in the Ordos Loop, to guard that section of the Great Wall and the Yellow River. These Hun allies remained loyal to China as long as the Chinese were able to maintain their supremacy, that is for more than two centuries. At the death of Kuang-wu-ti Chinese hegemony was thus restored in the Far East. It remained for his son, the emperor Ming-ti (A.D. 58–75), to complete his achievement by restoring the protectorate in Central Asia. During his reign the Chinese attempted a final settlement of the problem of the Tarim region.

The basin of the River Tarim is, like others in Central Asia, a region of interior drainage. The watercourses which flow down from the T'ien Shan and the Pamirs mostly fade away before joining the main river, the Tarim, which in turn is almost dry when it loses itself in the salt marshes of Lob Nor. But its basin is largely composed of a rich soil similar to the loess of North China, with the result that where irrigation is possible, cultivators and gardeners find their slightest efforts rewarded. In fact it is a case of a dying Nile or Euphrates flowing through a Mesopotamia in the process of desiccation. Life has slowly receded from the banks of the river and subsists only along the two semicircles of mountains which surround the Tarim Basin; the arc of the T'ien Shan in the north and the arc of the Pamirs and Altyn Tagh in the south. There, on the mountain slopes where the still living streams descend, a string of oases forms the last refuge of cultivation. These oases are spaced out from Kashgar in the west to Lob Nor in the east; in the north—going east from Kashgar—are Kucha and Karashar, whence the Turfan group extends towards the northeast; in the south—again starting from Kashgar—are Yarkand, Khotan, Niya, and Miron, the latter oasis situated at the approaches of Lob Nor.

The main interest of these oases lies in the fact that they constitute two lines of caravan stages between China on the one side, and India, Persia, and the Mediterranean world on the other. They were the indispensable intermediaries between the Far East and the West. These oases, moreover, have always been intensively cultivated, with irrigation works which have transformed them into garden cities where maize, wheat, melons, watermelons, apples, apricots, pomegranates, and grapes grow in profusion. The peasants who cultivate these oases differ from the Altaic nomads who surround them (although they now speak a Turkish language), and are more like the agricultural populations of western Asia. Their physical appearance, even today, is not Mongolian, but is very similar to the Iranian variety of Caucasian. The explorer Fernand Grenard describes them as having "abundant dark hair and beards, fair rosy skins, when they are not tanned by the sun and air, long oval faces with fine, prominent, and often straight noses, and brown eyes which are not slanting". Chinese travellers of antiquity and the early Middle Ages have left us similar pictures of them.

Excavations in the region confirm this ethnographical evidence, and show that up to the ninth century A.D. the people of Turfan, Karashar, Kucha, and Kashgar, spoke not Turkish but purely Indo-

European languages, closely related to Iranian, Sanskrit, and the European tongues.

The importance of the oases of the Tarim Basin on the main route between China and the West did not fail to attract the attention of the two great military powers of the Far East and Upper Asia. Both the Huns, from the heights of the Khangai, and the Chinese, from the frontier marches of Kansu, kept watch on the two caravan routes and laid claim to the control of them. The Chinese, under the Former Han dynasty, about the year 100 B.C., had already imposed their suzerainty on the little kingdoms of the Tarim Basin; but there as elsewhere, the civil wars in China during the first twenty-five years of the Christian era had lost them a good deal of ground.

The court of the Later Han dynasty was fortunate in having a team of outstanding soldiers to reconquer this area, to "open up the Western Regions". In the year A.D. 73 two of these generals, Tou Ku and Keng Ping, "the commander of swift horses", led a preliminary expedition into Mongolia and put the Northern Huns to flight. In order to block their path, a military colony was established at the oasis of Hami, in the heart of the western Gobi. In A.D. 74 Tou Ku and Keng Ping set out to attack the oasis of Turfan. "The king came out of the town, removed his head-dress, and embracing the hooves of Keng Ping's horse, made his submission."

The boldest of these Chinese captains was a general of cavalry called Pan Ch'ao. He belonged to a highly cultivated family. His brother and his sister—the latter one of the most celebrated literary women in Chinese history—were the authors of the history of the Former Han dynasty. He preferred the glory of arms to that of the pen, and above all the adventurous life of the West. Moreover, he considered that "only he who penetrates into the tiger's lair can carry off the cubs". Sent with a detachment to obtain information in the region of Lob Nor, he guessed from the unfriendly attitude of the local king that the latter had been won over by some emissary of the Huns. Meeting one of the natives, he suddenly asked him: "A messenger has come from the Huns. Where is he to be found?" The other, disconcerted, revealed the whole truth. Pan Ch'ao then gathered his officers together. "He drank with them, and when they were heated with wine he explained the position: 'If the emissary persuades the king to give us up to the Huns, our remains will be food for the wolves. Let us profit from the darkness and take the barbarians by surprise.' " They asked how he was to take this initiative without first obtaining permission from the Chinese civil commissioner who was accompanying the army; an objection which exasperated Pan Ch'ao. "Our life or death is to be decided today; what do we care for the opinions of a common civil servant? If we inform him of our plan he will certainly take fright and our projects will be divulged." He finally won them over. Night had fallen and the wind was blowing up a gale. "Pan Ch'ao ordered some of his men to take their drums and hide behind the barbarian camp. It was agreed between them that as soon as they saw flames rising they would all start beating their drums and shouting loudly. The remainder of his men were concealed, fully armed, before the gates. Then Pan Ch'ao started a great fire in the direction of the wind, while at the same time a wild clamour of war cries and drums broke forth. The barbarians were taken by surprise and in complete confusion. Pan Ch'ao killed three of them with his own hands, his soldiers decapitated thirty others and amongst them the Hun envoy, while another hundred or so perished in the flames." This done, Pan Ch'ao summoned the king of Lob Nor into his presence and without a word showed him the head of the Hun emissary. The king, who had been on the point of betraying them, in abject fear renewed his vassalage to China.

In the south of the Tarim Basin, the king of Khotan was also lending an ear to the emissaries of the Huns. This was an equally serious matter; for, while Lob Nor was able to intercept the arrival of the caravans, Khotan controlled the whole of the southern route. Pan Ch'ao, being warned of this defection, arrived unexpectedly at

Khotan. The king treated him with scant respect, for he had been incited against the Chinese by a local sorcerer who was in league with the Huns. "The Chinese envoy possesses a bay horse", declared the royal sorcerer, "which our gods are desirous that I sacrifice to them." Intimidated by this message, the king made bold to ask Pan Ch'ao for his horse. The latter feigned consent, on condition that the sorcerer should himself come and take delivery of the animal. As soon as the sorcerer arrived, Pan Ch'ao cut off his head and sent it to the king. The latter made his submission and handed over the Hunnish agents.

In the year A.D. 75 a general revolt against the Chinese protectorate broke out in the Tarim region. Pan Ch'ao was besieged in Kashgar, while the other Chinese generals were blockaded near Turfan. They were reduced to eating the leather of their equipment, but they held out to the end. Meanwhile Chinese court circles were becoming frightened by these continuous wars. The emperor Ming-ti had just died and was succeeded (A.D. 75) by his son, Chang-ti, who was only twenty years old. An order was given to evacuate the Tarim region. Pan Ch'ao made a show of obeying, or at least he beat a retreat as far as Khotan; then he changed his mind and deliberately, despite the orders that he had received, turned about and re-established himself in Kashgar, decapitating all those who had shown disloyalty in the interval. In the meantime the Chinese legions from Kansu were regaining the Turfan region from the Huns. "They cut off three thousand eight hundred barbarian heads and captured thirty-seven thousand head of cattle. The Northern Huns (from Mongolia) fled in terror."

In a memorial addressed to the new emperor, Pan Ch'ao strove to reconcile the timorous attitude of the court to his own methods in the West. The Chinese hero showed that these distant campaigns, which the literati condemned as a useless waste of life and money, were really a far-sighted defensive policy. It was a question of sheltering China from the periodic attacks of the Huns: "To capture the thirty-six kingdoms of the West is to cut off the right arm of the Hun." His method was the truly colonial policy of "setting barbarians to catch barbarians". Indeed, he was able to achieve the conquest of the Tarim region only by forcing each newly-conquered oasis to furnish troops, which he used against the others still in revolt. The genuinely Chinese elements in his armies were negligible, apart from a handful of adventurers and deportees who came to retrieve their honour in the eventful life of the marches. They all of them lived off the lands which they were protecting against a renewed offensive by the Huns. "At Yarkand and Kashgar", Pan Ch'ao explained to the emperor, "the cultivated soil is fertile, and the soldiers who are garrisoned there cost the empire nothing." He judiciously contrasted this area, kept verdant by the proximity of the Pamirs and with a hinterland of forests, with the stony salt-clay desert which stretches from Lob Nor to Tun-huang.

All colonial policy is based on a knowledge of native psychology. Pan Ch'ao was a past master at this game. In the year A.D. 87 the king of Kashgar, who had recently come out in revolt, feigned submission and asked for an interview. He arrived with a strong contingent of cavalry, intending to carry out a surprise attack. Pan Ch'ao for his part pretended to believe in his visitor's good intentions, and gave a feast for him. When the wine had circulated freely, he seized the king and cut off his head. At the same moment the Chinese troops dropped the mask and fell upon the enemy, who were massacred. At Yarkand, in the year 88, being forced to rely on an army inferior in numbers both of Chinese and of Khotan auxiliaries, Pan Ch'ao pretended to beat a retreat during the night, then returned by a forced march and at cockcrow fell on the people of Yarkand, cut off five thousand heads, and forced the town into submission.

To the north, in Mongolia, the Chinese commanders intent on emulating Pan Ch'ao were no less resolute. In A.D. 91 the Chinese legions advanced into the heart of the Hun country, probably as far as the banks of the Orkhon, and made prisoners of the Hun chieftain's entire family. In the Tarim region, the large oasis of Kucha, losing all hope of further help from the Huns, surrendered in the year 90. Karashar alone remained in revolt. In 94, with a troop of auxiliaries from Kucha and Lob Nor, Pan Ch'ao marched against the rebel city. The inhabitants cut down the bridges across the river Yuldus, but all in vain, for Pan Ch'ao forded the waist-deep river and appeared out of the marshes in front of Karashar. Some of the inhabitants were able to escape across Lake Bagrach, but the rest were forced to surrender. The king of the country was decapitated on the exact spot where he had executed the Chinese Resident. "Pan Ch'ao allowed his soldiers to pillage freely. They cut off more than five thousand heads, and carried off more than three hundred thousand horses, oxen and sheep." Honoured by the court with the title of "Protector of the Western Regions", the Chinese conqueror was virtually viceroy of Central Asia. "He kept order as far as the Pamirs and the Hanging Passes"; as far, that is, as the gateways to Persia and India.

In the direction of India and Afghanistan lay the kingdom of the Indo-Scythians, a people of whom we shall have occasion to speak more fully later on, for it was through them that Buddhism reached China. Persia belonged to the Arsacid Parthians, who by reason of Pan Ch'ao's conquests had come, if not into actual contact, at least into commercial relations with the Chinese, while on the Euphrates they were neighbours of the Roman Empire. The Parthians, masters of the greater part of present-day Iraq and Iran, were doubtless separated from the Chinese conquests by Transoxiana and Indo-Scythian Afghanistan. Yet while the Romans menaced them in Mesopotamia, the march of the Chinese legions seemed to be advancing from the eastern slopes of the Pamirs. In A.D. 94, the Parthians deemed it prudent, "making use of numerous successive interpreters", to send to the Han court an embassy with gifts which may have been described as tribute. In 97 Pan Ch'ao commissioned one of his aides, a man called Kan Ying, to go and establish regular relations with these Parthians, and also with the Roman Empire beyond.

The Roman Empire was already known to the Chinese under

the name of Ta-ch'in.[1] They even knew the names of the capitals of the Roman Orient; Antioch under the transcription of Hsien-tu and Alexandria under that of An-tu. If the envoy of Pan Ch'ao had succeeded in reaching the Roman Empire, it would have been at the time when the emperor Trajan was ascending the throne; the emperor whose reign (98–117) was to mark the zenith of Roman expansion in Asia, and who in the course of a memorable campaign (A.D. 116) entered the Parthian capital Ctesiphon as its conqueror. One imagines an alliance between the Chinese legions and the Roman legions for the joint sovereignty of the Middle East, or on a more modest scale, of a series of agreements uniting the Romans of Trajan, the Indo-Scythians of Kanichka, and Pan Ch'ao's veteran forces against the Parthians. Vain dreams; for the Chinese envoy Kan Ying, having reached the Parthians, allowed them to dissuade him from pushing on to the Roman frontiers. This would appear to show how much the Parthians feared a possible understanding between Rome and China.

Pan Ch'ao retired from active service in A.D. 102. On his return to the capital, Loyang, he was loaded with honours; but he was worn out by twenty-nine years of campaigning and died a few months later. After his death his great task, as was inevitable, suffered new setbacks. His successors in the government of the Tarim region, honest commanders of garrisons in the interior, knew nothing about the colonial environment. Yet before leaving, Pan Ch'ao had warned them what to expect: "Officers who serve in these distant regions are not necessarily pious sons and obedient grandsons. They have all been deported for some offence, this is the reason that they are sent to serve in the frontier marches. On the other hand, the barbarians are as changeable as birds and wild beasts. Learn to be lenient with minor faults, and content yourselves with controlling the general discipline." These wise counsels fell on deaf ears, with the result that in 106 a general revolt broke out in the Tarim region.

[1] Which could mean "Great Ch'in" (Ch'in being the same word as the old state of Ch'in); the derivation of the name is uncertain.

Once more the Chinese court became discouraged. The literati had their chance to demand the evacuation of the colonies and the abandonment of the protectorate in the name of their ancient pacifist theories. The theme was always the same; in the days of the first dynasties—which figured in the speeches of Chinese literati as a golden age—China had no foreign possessions: "Confined within their proper bounds, the people lived happily. Why then persist in maintaining these distant garrisons, which cost so much, and which prove powerless against periodic revolts?" The opinion of the literati was about to prevail in the council, when Pan Yung, the son of Pan Ch'ao, asked permission to speak. "If you abandon the Tarim region", he said, "you abandon it to the Huns. This would be to give them back their stores and their treasure, to refix their severed arm! The day would soon come when the barbarians once more treated our frontiers with contempt and the gates of our cities were kept closed in broad daylight." He won the support of the council, and (between A.D. 123 and 127) re-established the Chinese protectorate in Central Asia.

The establishment of the Chinese protectorate in these regions had a considerable bearing on the history of civilization. It was the time when, by the opening up of the two routes across the Tarim Basin—the north road by way of Lob Nor, Karashar, Kucha, and Kashgar, and the south road by way of Lob Nor, Niya, Khotan, Yarkand, and Kashgar—China entered into commercial relations with the Roman world. It was by these routes that the Chinese exported their products to Roman Asia, the chief commodity being silk. The road across the Tarim Basin, with its two routes, was the Silk Road.

Chinese sericulture goes back to far distant times. The *Yü-kung* and the *Chou-li*, texts which date, the one from between the ninth and sixth centuries B.C., the other from the fourth century B.C., speak of silk as one of the principal sources of wealth in the regions which correspond to present-day Shantung and Honan. Under the Han dynasty, rolls of silk were used as currency in official trade with foreign courts.

When the Greco-Roman world became acquainted with silk, there was no product in greater demand. Alexandria and Rome quarrelled over the destination of the various cargoes. Lucan tells us that Cleopatra, wishing to dazzle her guests at a banquet, appeared resplendent in a silken gown. In his *Georgics* (II, 120–1) Virgil sings of the silkworm cocoons, "the delicate wool that the Seres comb from the leaves of their trees". This name Seres for the Chinese is revealing; it is derived from the word for silk, for to the Romans China was above all the "Silk country", or Serica. The fashion for silk became so popular that the sumptuary laws enacted by Tiberius forbade men to wear silken garments, in order to keep enough for the women. Pliny and Martial also speak of the silk trade, which was carried on in the most fashionable quarter of the capital. The whole trade had of necessity to pass through the Parthian Empire and the Chinese annals observe that the Parthians meant to preserve their monopoly of Chinese silks; therefore they prevented all direct communication between China and Rome, as we saw in the case of Kan Ying.

In the first century A.D. a Greco-Roman merchant called Maes Titianos, a native of Macedonia whose chief dealings appear to have been in Syria, had the bold idea of overcoming the obstacle of Parthia by having his agents explore the Silk Road from Syria as far as China. The result of his investigations have been handed down to us by Marinos of Tyre (about A.D. 110) via the geographer Ptolemy (about A.D. 170). The route, which evidently started from Antioch, crossed the Euphrates at Hierapolis (the present-day Menbij, to the east of Aleppo), entered the Parthian Empire, where it passed through Ecbatana (Hamadan) and Hecatompylos (Shahrod); thence by Antioch of Margiana (Merv) it reached Bactra (Balkh) in the Indo-Scythian Empire. From there it turned to the north, "as far as the ascent to the mountainous country of the *Komedoi*", at the foot of the Pamirs, "then, crossing the mountains, it turned to the south, as far as the ravine which opens into the plain", where one came to a place called "the Stone Tower" (*Lithinos Pyrgos*), which has been variously located at Tashkurgan, to the southwest of Yarkand, and in the upper valley of the Alai, to the west of Kashgar. From there the route described by Marinos of Tyre and Ptolemy passed through "the country of *Kasia*"—which may (despite all that has been said to the contrary) have been Kashgar (*Kacha* in Sanskrit)—then by *Issedon Scythica*, which may have been the oasis of Kucha; *Damna*, which was probably the oasis of Karashar; and *Issedon Serica*, probably in the region of Lob Nor. The route then passed by *Daxata*, which was probably the Jade Gate (Yü-men), the entrance to China from the marches of Tun-huang, and *Thogara*, which might be the present town of Kan-chou in the province of Kansu, where to this day arrive all the caravans from Central Asia. The route terminated at *Sera Metropolis*, probably the earlier capital of the Han dynasty Ch'ang-an (present-day Sian), the first great Chinese city to be reached when coming from the west.

The Silk Road was not the only route by which the empire of the Han dynasty was in communication with the Roman Empire. The Alexandrian geographers Marinos of Tyre and Ptolemy also describe a sea route—the future "Spice Route"—ending in the port of *Kattigara*, which may have been situated in present-day Tonking, somewhere near Haiphong. The *Circumnavigation of the Erythraean Sea* (A.D. 90) states that by sailing towards the north beyond the *Golden Chersonese* (the peninsula of Malacca), one may come to an inland city called by the name of *Thina*, from which the silks of Serica are exported to Bactra. It is probable that at this date the *Thina* of the Greek geographer, a Hellenic transcription of the name China, was Loyang, the new capital of the Han dynasty.[1] Finally, we learn from the Chinese annalists that in the year A.D. 166 a personage arrived in China who claimed to be an envoy of the emperor Marcus Aurelius (in Chinese, An-tun, a faithful transcription of Marcus Aurelius

[1] "China" appears to come from an ancient Sanskrit name for the regions to the east, and not, as often supposed, from the name of the state of Ch'in. When necessary the Chinese would distinguish the centre of the world, where they lived, from the peripheral regions; one of the ancient expressions has become the modern name for China: Chung-kuo, literally "central country".

Antoninus). This stranger had travelled by the sea route from "beyond Jih-nan"—a Han commandery which corresponded to present-day southern Annam.

By these two routes—the transcontinental road and the sea route—Buddhism was to enter China, an event of capital importance for the destiny of the Far East.

CHAPTER XI

THE REVELATION OF BUDDHISM

BUDDHISM is essentially an Indian religion and was confined to India for some six hundred years. Its founder Sakyamuni, who earned the title of the Buddha (that is to say, the Enlightened), lived in the eastern valley of the Ganges between the years 563 and 483 B.C. He was a young noble of the Nepalese jungle who renounced the world to lead the life of a hermit. After a long period of mortification he discerned that this was unavailing, and in the shade of the *Bodhi* tree at Gaya (to the south of present-day Patna) he attained Enlightenment. He understood the law of universal suffering, which shows that the world is but a torrent of change, resolving into sorrow. It should at once be said that this pessimism arose from a belief universally held in India, the belief in metempsychosis or the transmigration of souls. Western religion offers the reward of eternal life. The eternal life of the Indian doctrines took the form of a nightmare, for with all the hazards of transmigration—birth, suffering and death—to be reborn for eternal suffering and dying was like a sentence of hard labour for eternity.

To this nightmare the Buddha offered a solution. To escape from the eternal cycle of rebirth in a world of transmigration, it was necessary above all to extinguish the "thirst for personality" which brings about rebirth, to extinguish the self; and this extinction was the true *nirvana* or beatitude. To this end the Buddha preached not suicide (which could only plunge one back into the most hideous reincarnations), but struggle against the passions, immolation of the individual for the benefit of all life, and universal charity carried to the extent of constant self-sacrifice on behalf of all creatures, both men and animals. His doctrine, while metaphysically negative, resulted in the practice of a morality of renunciation, chastity, charity and meekness.

In order to understand the immense expansion of Buddhism, one should first realize the attraction that such a spiritual climate was bound to have for truly noble souls. In particular one may point out the poetic element, of an almost Franciscan tenderness, which informs the legends of the "former lives" (*djataka*) of the Buddha under various human and animal shapes, legends which found expression in literature and in art. They include the king of the stags who sacrificed himself for his herd, the hare who hurled himself into the fire to feed a starving Brahmin, the elephant who offered his tusks to his murderer, and many other tales.

During the life of its founder, Buddhism was preached in the provinces of the eastern Ganges, in Magadha (South Bihar), at Benares and in Oudh, whence it spread progressively through the rest of India. The church which he founded consisted of an order of monks, gathered together in monasteries around which were grouped the lower orders of lay enthusiasts. Buddhist doctrine naturally became modified in the course of the next five centuries. On the somewhat frigid morality of its founder was superimposed a theology which satisfied the needs of the human heart. The historic Buddha, having attained to *nirvana* (that is, "extinction"), was almost inaccessible to prayer. Later Buddhism obviated this difficulty by creating a number of future Buddhas—the *bodhisattvas*—who awaited the hour of their incarnation in a wonderful paradise, and spent this waiting period in the salvation of earthly creatures. Certain of these bodhisattvas eventually won away popular devotion from the historic Buddha. This was the case with Maitreya, the bodhisattva whose incarnation is imminent, and who for that reason has been called the "Messiah of Buddhism". Then there was Avalokiteshvara, whose Sanskrit name designates a sort of Buddhist Providence, and who under the form of a "Buddhist Madonna", the "goddess" Kuan-yin, was to play so considerable a part in Chinese Buddhism. Closely associated with Avalokiteshvara was Amitabha ("infinite light"), who assumed a role no less important in the Sino-Japanese pietist sects. The creation of this pantheon, which was apparently constituted in northern India during the first centuries of our era, completed the main features of Buddhism just at the time when it was about to undertake the conversion of the Far East.

The newly created bodhisattvas were to contribute much to this conversion. These lofty spiritual figures, full of compassion and mercy, produced around them an atmosphere of trust and love, a devotional and personal religion to which eastern Asia could offer no equivalent. In particular China (where Confucianism and Taoism had nothing similar) was to find therein the revelation of a new spiritual world with an appeal to all levels of Chinese society. Philosophical speculation found in it an inexhaustible source of nourishment, thanks to the metaphysics with which, towards the first century of our era, Indian Buddhism had been crowned. In general, the systems thus elaborated taught an absolute idealism based on the unreality of both the self and the outside world. The universe became a realm of "nothing but thought", an "ocean of ideals"; a doctrine which had a certain resemblance to ancient Chinese Taoism. Again, the affections of the people could not fail to be won by the innumerable legends about each bodhisattva, by the tender and wonderful images that were set up for their adoration, by the lives of the saints —"the golden legend of Buddhism", by the changing colours of its paradises and hells, and finally, and not least important, by Buddhist art itself.

Up to the Christian era Indian Buddhism produced an art full of charm and inspired by the timeless naturalism of India. The artists of these first and purely Indian schools of sculpture never ventured to portray the likeness of Buddha, any more than a Moslem would paint a picture of Allah or Mahomet. Doubtless it was more than a question of respect; it was a question of logic: for surely it would have been contradictory to wish to revive, through an image, the one who had finally attained nirvana, that is to say who had become de-personalized. Even in the scenes of his life the image of Buddha was replaced by a number of conventional symbols. The point of view changed, however, when Hellenism took root in Northwest India (first under the Greek successors of Alexander the Great, and then under the Indo-Scythian kings who succeeded them, and who were themselves decidedly hellenophile. The Greeks who were converted to Buddhism felt a need to represent the Buddha realistically, and drew their inspiration from the model of their god Apollo. Thus the first statues of the Buddha (modelled about the beginning of the Christian era in the Peshawar region, the ancient Gandhara) were of a pure Apollo to whom were simply added the ritual characteristics of the Buddha: the mark of wisdom between the eyes, the lengthening of the lobes of the ears (caused by the heavy earrings that the Buddha had worn when he was a prince), and finally the chignon for the flowered turban, which later, when this style of headdress was forgotten, developed into a protuberance of the cranium.

Hundreds of these Greek Buddhas, with their classic profiles and Hellenic drapery, have been discovered in the excavations carried out in ancient Gandhara and farther west at Hadda, between Peshawar and Kabul. And it was this same type of Greek Buddha which, century by century and step by step, was to be handed on across the whole of Central Asia to China and Japan, giving birth to the innumerable Buddhas of the Far East. Needless to say, during the course of this immense journey across time and space, the original Greek Buddha became modified. It was to end by becoming Chinese, but even then it retained, in the straightness of profile and arrangement of drapery, a distant reminder of its Hellenic origins.

Indian Buddhism adopted this Greek iconography shortly before it undertook the conversion of Central Asia (the Tarim Basin) and China.

It might seem that the Buddhist missionaries were singularly tardy in their efforts to preach the gospel in China. Sakyamuni died in 483 B.C., and it is not until A.D. 60–70 that the first Chinese Buddhist community is reported. In fact it was only then that the evangelization of China by Buddhist missionaries was made possible by the concurrence of two great political events. In the first place, Northwest India and Afghanistan (a region at that time as deeply Buddhist as the Ganges Valley) had become part of a great empire. This was the empire of the Indo-Scythians, a people who originated in Central Asia and had for this reason kept up relations with the Chinese, while, once installed on the borders of India and Persia as successors to the last Indo-Greek kings, they came at the same time into contact with Indian beliefs—Buddhism in particular—and Hellenism. The most famous of these Indo-Scythian kings, Kanichka, who was perhaps the contemporary of Pan Ch'ao and Trajan, has left some fine coins, bearing the image of Buddha treated in the Greek manner, and inscribed with the name *Boddo* in Greek lettering. Apart from a brief quarrel in A.D. 88, when the Indo-Scythians had tried to intervene in the Tarim Basin and had been frustrated by Pan Ch'ao, their relations with China were excellent; this assured the safety of communications between India and the Chinese protectorate of the Tarim region.

It would be hard to exaggerate the religious consequences of the western conquests of Han China—the second historical factor which favoured the spread of Buddhism across eastern Asia. The formation of the "world-wide" empire of the Han dynasty, its extension as far as the Pamirs, that is to say to the gates of India, and the opening-up of the Silk Road made China the neighbour of the Indo-Scythian Empire. Buddhism, a catholic religion, soon benefited from this unprecedented situation. In the same way, and during roughly the same period, the Roman conquests made possible the propagation of Christianity in the West. In this respect the *Pax Sinica* in the Far East had somewhat similar spiritual consequences to those of the *Pax Romana* in the Mediterranean world.

The course of the Buddhist apostolate commenced, as dictated by geography, with the region of Khotan in the southern part of the Tarim Basin, as is shown by the discovery there of Greco-Buddhist sculptures. Sculptured bas-reliefs in the courtyard of an ancient Buddhist *stupa* (shrine mound) at Rewak, to the northeast of Khotan, date from the first two centuries A.D. and have a purely Greek rhythm in their draperies. The path of Buddhist evangelization followed the caravan routes of the silk trade. On the site of ancient Khotan (at Yotkan) and farther east near Niya have been found intaglios of Roman workmanship, showing the ancient gods —Pallas Athene, Zeus, Eros, Herakles—or quadrigae (chariots drawn by four horses abreast). Apparently most of these intaglios could have been carved on the spot by itinerant lapidaries; Asiatic Greeks, Syrians or Bactrians whom the lure of profit or a taste for travel had drawn as far as the country of the Seres. At Miron, to the south of Lob Nor, in an ancient Buddhist sanctuary of about the third century A.D. have been found frescoes which, apart from their Buddhist inspiration, might have been discovered in Roman Asia or at Pompeii. One is surprised to find a Buddha escorted by his monks, with winged spirits, beardless men in Phrygian caps, female lute players, and finally quadrigae which derive directly from the Roman art of Syria. One of these frescoes bears an inscription in Indian characters giving the name of the painter: Tita, which may possibly be an Indianized version of the name Titus. There are few things more revealing than these Buddhist and Roman paintings, found in the heart of the Lob Nor desert, at the last stages of the caravan route before the first Chinese frontier station of Tun-huang.

But for the Buddhist missionaries from Northwest India the Tarim Basin was only the gateway to China. In the years A.D. 60–70, one of the first Buddhist communities was formed at the court of a cadet prince of the Han dynasty whose fief lay in the present province of Kiangsu. It is interesting to note that this prince was a Taoist. Indeed Buddhism, when it was first preached in China, appeared to the Chinese as a Taoist sect; rather in the way that to the Romans Christianity was at first nothing but a Jewish sect. The Buddhist missionaries, consciously or not, profited from this initial misapprehension. Having to create an entirely new vocabulary to translate Indian concepts into the Chinese language—one might say, into Chinese thought—it was naturally from Taoist terminology that they borrowed their equivalents, and on its pattern modelled their newly coined expressions. Similarly the Jesuit missionaries of the seventeenth century, in order to render Christian theological concepts into Chinese, were obliged to borrow part of their vocabulary from the Confucian intellectuals. Thus too the Christian apologists of the third century borrowed their philosophical terminology from Plato and Philo. The first Buddhist communities in China were, as Henri Maspero puts it, followers of "a Taoism of an increasingly Buddhist flavour".

The most important Buddhist community was naturally the one which grew up in the latter half of the second century A.D. at Loyang, the imperial capital. It was founded by a Parthian who arrived in China in 148 and died in A.D. 170. It may seem curious that a Parthian should be found among the first Buddhist missionaries to China, but it is in no way an isolated case. Among the ranks of the Buddhist apostles in China at this period and in the first half of the third century A.D. may be found other Parthians, and also Indo-Scythians, natives of the Indo-Scythian Empire which dominated Afghanistan and Northwest India. The presence of these ranians among the newly established Buddhist communities in the Han Empire gives an additional interest to the introduction of Buddhism into this country, since the religion of Buddha brought to the Far East not only Indian thought and Greek art, but also certain influences from ancient Persian civilization.

Despite these local successes, Buddhism enjoyed no general vogue in China during the Han period. Although at first it benefited from its confusion with Taoism, the Taoists were not slow to denounce this fundamental error, and pursued the Buddhist missionaries with unappeasable sectarian hatred. As for the Confucian intellectuals, they pronounced a final verdict against "the foreign religion": Buddhist monasticism was anti-social, because it destroyed family life and jeopardized the cult of ancestors, while the Buddhist monk, selfishly pre-occupied with his individual salvation, showed himself indifferent to the destinies of the state. This was the beginning of a quarrel which was to last until modern times. Throughout the centuries Confucians and Buddhists fought one another with unequal arms, for Confucianism—in the widest sense of the word—was to remain the official doctrine of the state; while Buddhism, even under emperors who personally favoured it, only represented an unofficial movement, a particular religion which, however widespread in times of religious fervour, always remained foreign to the Chinese family and the Chinese state.

Under the Han dynasty Buddhism, although it was never persecuted, played a part of no greater importance in China than did Christianity in the Roman Empire at the time of Trajan and Marcus Aurelius.

CHAPTER XII

THE SPLENDOUR AND DECADENCE OF HAN

THE long peace which China enjoyed under the Han dynasty brought her unprecedented wealth; to this the art of the period bears witness.

The art of Han China is of especial interest to us because it represents the culmination of the artistic evolution of earlier periods just before the foreign influences introduced by Buddhism upset all the traditional standards.

We have already described the principal stages in the development of ancient Chinese bronzes. First there was the Shang dynasty, a period of prodigious creative activity, with a vital power, a spontaneity and a variety of motifs unequalled at any later date. Then the beginning of the Chou, a period of heaviness and impoverishment of both form and decoration. Finally the age of the Warring States and the Ch'in dynasty: a renewal of creative activity, with decoration enlivened by a vibrant rhythm. With the advent of the Han dynasty forms were simplified to such an extent that Chinese bronzes of this period, through the purity of their lines, sometimes have the sobriety of a Greek vase. In their decoration (where decoration, apart from the *t'ao-t'ieh* which hold the ringed handles, was not entirely suppressed) the exuberance and complexity of the Warring States bronzes was replaced by an equally striking simplicity. All overloading—carried to an extreme in certain ancient bronzes—disappeared. From now on the elegance of the motifs lies in "decorative symmetry, a skilful use of line and symbol, and the sobriety of the modelling in the round". Decoration in relief was often replaced by engraved designs or by inlaid turquoise, malachite, gold or silver. "In this manner marvellous adornments were achieved, either in geometrical designs or enlivened by real or fantastic scenes: figures of monsters, dancing genii, and scenes of hunting or warfare, all remarkable for their prodigious vigour." Similar incrustations of turquoise and precious metals are found on buckles of the Han period (and on others doubtless dating from the time of the Warring States), ornaments of clothing which may, as already indicated, be of Hunnish origin. And it is not impossible that the technique of inlay, so widely developed in China during the Han period, may have been imported from the Greco-Iranian world.

Under the Warring States and the Han dynasty bronze mirrors first made their appearance and rapidly spread throughout the country. These mirrors, which were for magical rather than utilitarian purposes, had decoration characteristic of the two periods. The Han mirrors show the same geometrical simplicity found in the bronze vases, a simplicity which in no way detracted from the magical power which the Taoists ascribed to mirrors.

The elegant decoration of interlacings, scrolls and spirals which we find on the inlaid bronzes of the Han period was also employed on lacquerwork of the same period, which has been found not only in China proper, but also in Chinese tombs in Korea, as well as in the Hunnish tomb of Noin Ula, near Urga in Mongolia, and at Begram, near Kabul in Afghanistan.

The stone engravings and bas-reliefs from the small burial chambers found in Honan and Shantung are probably copies, made by craftsmen working with the chisel, of palace frescoes long since vanished. It is an art of line, graphic, full of speed and movement with its cavalcades and processions of chariots or its fantastic dancing gods and monsters. This art is doubly interesting, because in the scenes of noble and military life it attempts to reconstruct the history of ancient times as the Han intellectuals imagined it, while in the scenes of fantasy it evokes a mythology which has partially disappeared through being banished by official Confucianism, a mythology of which we should know even less had it not survived in Taoist legends. We shall have occasion to see the effects of Neo-

Taoism towards the end of the Han period and the part it played in the religious movement involved in the downfall of the dynasty. The funeral reliefs of Honan and Shantung help us to understand the undercurrents of this stream which was to undermine the apparently secure Confucian society of the age.

The sculptures on the burial columns of Szechwan, notably those on the celebrated "Column of Shen", are of a higher standard and in a style which approaches more closely to Greco-Roman classicism. Be that as it may, these are the works of artists, not of mere craftsmen. Note, by the way, that certain of the sculptured reliefs of the Han period, for example those of Shensi which depict lions (animals not found in China), seem to have been inspired by models which if not (as some have said) purely Persian, were at least Greco-Persian. This is quite likely an example of the influence of the Silk Road.

Sculpture in the round, which seemed to have disappeared from China after the Shang marbles, reappeared during the period of the Warring States in the shape of the dragons and animals such as tigers and oxen which often surmounted the lids of bronzes of that period. The sober realism of these figures was developed under the Han. Sculpture in the round was no longer employed only as a decorative motif, but was treated as an end in itself. There appear a multitude of terra-cotta funeral statuettes, including figures of people, animals and mythical beings. We have here, as in ancient Egypt, the substitutes of living things which were made in order to enable the dead to continue their normal everyday existence. The dominating quality of these little sculptures, more particularly in the statuettes of animals, is again a sober and vivid realism, without excessive muscular development and full of movement.

While the art of the Han dynasty had not yet felt the influence of Buddhism, certain of its techniques remained linked with the animal art of the steppes, as had been the case during the preceding period of the Warring States. We have indicated the characteristics of this art of the steppes, represented by small articles of bronze used for equipment and harness—buckles, clasps and plaques—decorated with stylized motifs of fighting animals, more or less entangled and frequently placed in asymmetrical opposition. We have also seen that, despite many variations according to time and place, the art of the steppes extended from the Scytho-Sarmatian domain in southern Russia to the Hun dominions of the Ordos and Outer Mongolia. The continuity of this art was shown by the excavations at Pasyryk in the Russian Altai; the objects from the beginning of the first century B.C. look as much Scytho-Sarmatian as Hunnish. The tumulus of Noin Ula, near Urga in Outer Mongolia, which dates from the first years of the present era, is of even greater interest. In this tomb of a Hun chieftain were found side by side a dated Chinese lacquer (of the year 2 B.C.), Chinese silks, and a magnificent woollen carpet embroidered with fighting animals in the purest style of the steppes; clear proof of the interpenetration of the two cultures. As further evidence, in the Musée Cernuschi in Paris there is a Han bronze, where the subject, a fight between animals of the steppes, is treated in a purely Chinese manner. We have seen how in the first century B.C. the Han dynasty established one section of the Huns as barbarian allies and guardians of the Ordos frontier. In the frontier marches of the Ordos the interpenetration between Chinese art and the art of the steppes was to continue until the time of Genghis Khan.

The establishment of these Hun allies at the foot of the Great Wall showed the confidence that China had in her own strength. This confidence was not misplaced; and down to the fourth century A.D. the Huns of the Ordos were to prove tractable auxiliaries. Meanwhile the Huns of Upper Mongolia (the Orkhon Basin) in about A.D. 150 lost their hegemony over eastern Mongolia to other nomad hordes, the Hsien-pi, natives of the northern Khingan, who appear to be the ancestors of the historic Mongols.[1] The Hsien-pi, like every other new horde, naturally attacked the frontiers of the Chinese Empire, but these attacks, which were intermittently renewed throughout the second half of the second century, particularly in the

[1] The name Siberia (Russian *Sibir*) is traced to Hsien-pi or Hsi-pi (two readings).

south of present-day Manchuria, were repulsed on every occasion. Unlike the Roman Empire, the Han empire was not to succumb to invasion. Its fall was to be the result of an internal crisis at once political, social, and intellectual.

From a purely political point of view, the Han dynasty, which seemed to have obtained a new vigour after the restoration of A.D. 25, soon relapsed into decadence and even degeneracy. Its princes came to the throne at an early age and died in the prime of life, worn out by youthful excesses. In the artificial atmosphere of the court the camarilla became all-powerful, and the influence of dowager empresses, concubines and eunuchs predominated. Yet just when the central power was thus weakening, the Confucian literati strove to consolidate its foundations by providing an official doctrine of empire and society. In the year A.D. 79, a commission of scholars compiled a definitive edition of the works attributed to Confucius and his school, which from then on had canonical authority. Previously the texts and explanations had varied from one "book" and one teacher to another. Between 175 and 183, in order to perpetuate this edition, the text was engraved on a series of stone slabs, and the ink rubbings made from them were an anticipation of the art of printing—indeed Chinese printing must have had an analogous origin.[1] The establishment of the Confucian texts as a canonical doctrine resulted in the establishment of the literati as an organized class. Strongly conscious of being trustees of the official doctrine, they tended to become an official body—the leading body of the state—and sought to assure themselves of power at court. They came up against the camarilla represented by the eunuchs, and after desperate political struggles were for the time being defeated. Between 175 and 179 several of them lost their lives endeavouring to stem the decay of the Han dynasty.

[1] In this first engraving of the texts, the characters were cut into the stone right way round, so that in rubbings they came out white on a black background and reversed. Engraving in the "real" sense first appeared, not in inscriptions, but (from the early sixth century) on seals, which were then carved in relief and in reverse; when printed, they came out in black or red on a white background.

About the same time the Taoist sects began to form themselves into organized "churches".[1] Taoism, as we have seen, originated in the ancient schools of sorcerers, and despite the loftiness of its metaphysics it had never broken away from magic. Up to this time it had been confined to small circles of illuminati; but towards the end of the Han period, as a result of a serious social crisis and the increasing poverty of the rural classes, it gained large numbers of converts. We have seen the earlier manifestations of this crisis, which the reforms of Wang Mang had attempted to resolve, and which since his defeat had continued to grow. "Rural society of the Han period", says Maspero, "was composed of a small number of rich landowners above, mostly officials or the descendants of officials, and underneath a genuine proletariat of landless peasants or small landowners, of whom the most fortunate cultivated allotments of village land, while others emigrated, became soldiers or pirates, hired themselves out as agricultural labourers, or became tenants on the estates of the great landowners; but never, with rare exceptions, did they succeed in escaping from destitution." The times favoured political agitators. In Szechwan and the upper valley of the Han River, a family of Taoist magicians named Chang organized a secret society which played an active part in politics during the second half of the second century.[2] The Chang worked wonders, healed the sick, remitted sins, and earned public gratitude by taking over from the negligent authorities such public works as the repair of roads and bridges, as well as the free distribution of rice to the starving. In a few years they

[1] Primitive Taoism was based on small and doubtless highly exclusive sects of initiates, for the fathers of the Taoist system were quite unconcerned with any kind of popular preaching. It was in imitation of Buddhism (although they were carrying on a bitter struggle against it) that the Neo-Taoists of the late Han period thought of forming a sort of ecclesiastical organization which was to be occupied with propaganda and political and social problems.

[2] A twelfth-century author, Hung Mai, thus formulated the law governing Chinese revolutions: "Since the days of antiquity, the appearance and cessation of brigandage has been dependent on famines brought about by floods and droughts. Driven by cold or hunger men gather together with loud cries intent on pillage. . . . When there are rascals who practise doctrines of sorcery to seduce the people, and having waited for a suitable time come out in revolt, the harm that they can do is incalculable."

gained hundreds of thousands of followers, whom they armed and organized into military detachments under regular commanders and recognizable by their yellow turbans. They then announced that, according to the conjunction of the stars, the year 184 corresponded to the opening of a new millennium.

At a given signal the revolt broke out in the south of Hopei, the neighbouring districts of Shantung, and in the Huai River basin. The authorities were completely taken by surprise and everywhere overwhelmed. The court was forced to raise large numbers of troops to reconquer the country. When the Yellow Turbans had been chased out of Shantung they reformed in the valley of the Han, and the revolt was only subdued with the capture of its last stronghold at Nan-yang, in the southwest of Honan. All the rebel peasants who could be found were relentlessly put to death. But after such horrors, the sufferings of the people grew even worse. The poet Wang Ts'an (117–217) paints a poignant picture of these terrible years:

The Western Capital lies in sad confusion;
The wolf and tiger come to plague her people.

. . . .

Whitened bones were strewn across the plain.
Upon the road I saw a starving woman
Abandoning her infant in the grass;
She looked round when she heard its piercing wail,
But brushing away her tears would not turn back:
"I do not know at what place death may take me,
What can I do to help the two of us now?"
I spurred my horse and left behind that scene;
I could not bear to hear the woman's words.

. . . .

I turned about to gaze back on Ch'ang-an,
And thought how many had gone to the underworld,
Sighing a heavy sigh and my heart in pain. . . .

CHAPTER XIII

THE THREE KINGDOMS

WHILE the peasant revolt of the Yellow Turbans laid waste the provinces, at court the camarilla of eunuchs continued to keep control over a series of apathetic regents and child emperors. In the year 189 the chief officers, exasperated beyond endurance, planned a thoroughgoing massacre of the palace eunuchs, but General Tung Cho, whom the conspirators had called to their aid, took the opportunity to establish a dictatorship. This was the signal for an outbreak of military anarchy, for the levying of a provincial militia to combat the Yellow Turbans had led to the formation of local armies owing loyalty to nobody but their own commanders. While Tung Cho installed himself as master in the capital, other generals seized power in the provinces. Tung Cho, a coarse and brutal old soldier, proved himself incapable of mastering the anarchy. In the year 190, deciding to transfer his residence to Ch'ang-an, he set fire to the imperial palace of Loyang and allowed his soldiers to pillage the capital. Thus the art treasures which the Han dynasty had accumulated over the last two centuries were destroyed. Tung Cho's tyranny and his bloodthirsty fits of temper finally alienated his own generals, who assassinated him and threw his naked corpse to the people. (He was a huge man, swollen with fat; they inserted a lamp wick in his navel and lit it—it burned for several days.)

These events were followed by a period of confusion worse than all that had gone before.

Taking advantage of China's internal troubles, the Huns resumed their plundering. The poetess Ts'ai Yen, who was captured by them, has left a poignant picture of these raids in her *Song of Distress:*

. . . They cut and felled, and not a man was left;
The sprawling corpses piled up into heaps.
Upon the shafts they hung the heads of men,
And in the carts they loaded up the women.
For long they drove and crossed the western border;
The homeward road was dangerous and barred.
We saw behind us only empty distance;
Our spleen and gall were eaten up by fear.
Those carried off devised a thousand plans,
But never were allowed to meet together;
Some of them there were closest of relations,
Wanted to talk but did not dare to speak,
If anyone were rash enough to murmur,
Then it was said the prisoners would be killed:
"And when it comes to chopping with the sword
We shall not be the ones to spare your lives! . . ."

Meanwhile at court the different factions went on contending for power until the day in 196 when one of the commanders of armies, Ts'ao Ts'ao, arrived at Loyang at the head of his troops and there proclaimed himself protector of the empire, while the young emperor became a puppet in his hands, as he had earlier been in the hands of Tung Cho.

In contrast to the gross soldier who had not long been overthrown, Ts'ao Ts'ao had the makings of a leader. A good captain and disciplinarian, unscrupulous certainly, and given to brutality, but politically adroit, he was also a scholar of considerable talent, and his poems have been preserved in anthologies; most of them are strongly lyrical, with a masculine vigour.[1] Had it been in the power of any one man to reunite the empire, Ts'ao Ts'ao would have been the most likely candidate for the task. As it was, after eight years of incessant struggles (A.D. 196–204) he only succeeded in becoming master of the Yellow River basin, the northern provinces which, however, constituted the richest and most thickly populated part of the empire. In the Long River basin other army chieftains had carved out kingdoms for themselves. One of them, Sun Ch'üan, asserted his independence on the lower Long River, and in a short

[1] See note on next page.

time the whole of southern China recognized his authority. He was a curious figure who was attracted by new doctrines and favoured Buddhist missionaries.

At the same time a third pretender, Liu Pei, appeared on the scene. He was a man of noble birth, a prince of Han, but he came of a younger branch of the family which had fallen into such dire poverty that he was forced to work for his living and keep his old mother by making straw sandals. Seeing the decadence of his cousins, the weakling emperors of Loyang, who were no longer anything but puppets in the hands of the dictator Ts'ao Ts'ao, Liu Pei felt his imperial blood boiling in his veins. He found three peerless companions to help him, three paladins who were later to be immortalized in history, legend, romance, and drama. The first of these was Kuan Yü, who was to be canonized in popular religion as the god of war. The second was Chang Fei, a man of humble origin (he had been a butcher), who became renowned for his dauntless

---

[1] For example his much quoted *Short Song*, which he improvised at a banquet given to the literati of his party:

When drinking wine we ought to sing;
Short is the span of human life,
Passing as the morning dew,
Many, alas, the days that have gone.

When things go wrong we should be great;
Secret thoughts will not be stilled.
What do we have for sorrow's balm?
Nothing so fine as Tu-k'ang's * gift.

"Blue was the dress of my fellow-disciple,
Sad is my heart now he is gone."
All because of absent friends
We still repeat those lines to-day.

"Yu, yu! calls the browsing deer
Feeding on the heathland grass."
Here I have the finest guests,
The pipes are blown, the zither sounds.

Bright and lustrous is the moon,
Who shall ever pluck it down?
Sorrow rises from within
And you cannot cut it off.

We travel east, we travel west,
And cherish memories in vain.
When far apart we talk and drink,
The heart remembers ancient kindness.

The moon is bright and stars are few,
Southward flies the magpie black,†
Circles thrice about a tree,
What branch can he settle on?

A mountain cannot be too high,
An ocean cannot be too deep;
The Duke of Chou spat out his food,‡
The hearts of all were turned to him.

* A legendary brewer. † A bird of good omen.
‡ In his haste to welcome worthy followers.

courage. He and Kuan Yü were both to give their lives for their master. Finally there was Chu-ke Liang, at once warrior and diplomat, who abandoned his fields to devote himself body and soul to the cause of the pretender whose principal counsellor he became. Indeed, it was on the advice of Chu-ke Liang that Liu Pei chose the province of Szechwan, where he finally succeeded in establishing his authority..

The struggles between the three pretenders—Ts'ao Ts'ao, Sun Ch'üan and Liu Pei—still enjoy an extraordinary popularity in China; for their history has been preserved and amplified by legend. The *Romance of the Three Kindgoms*—which is in fact no older than the fourteenth century—and the innumerable plays which have been derived from it, have dignified these struggles with the importance of an epic and have made the *Romance* a Chinese equivalent of the western medieval chronicles of heroes. Take for example the Battle of Chiang-ling in 208, when Liu Pei, encircled by Ts'ao Ts'ao's army, forces his way through the enemy ranks with a handful of horsemen. Then Chang Fei, as soon as his master is safe, goes back to the rearguard, and like Bayard defends a bridge alone. "Holding his lance across the withers of his horse, he cried: 'It is I, Chang Fei! If anyone wishes to make my acquaintance, let him approach!' " And he held his ground for some time, in order to intimidate the enemy. A little further on Chang Fei finds his master's young son, whom the enemy were on the point of carrying off. He lays his precious burden across the front of his saddle and gallops through the midst of the enemy ranks to the banks of the Long River, where a boat is waiting. Meanwhile Ts'ao Ts'ao and his army were making preparations to cross the Long River, with the intention of conquering the south of China as they had conquered the north. Their fleet was already in position to protect the army during the crossing of the river, when Liu Pei launched a series of fire ships which, carried along by the wind, set fire to the enemy craft. The flames spread until they reached the straw huts of the camp which Ts'ao Ts'ao had erected on the farther bank. Countless men and horses perished in the flames or in the waves. The dictator of the north was forced to abandon his project of conquering southern China.

Meanwhile Han legitimism had remained alive in men's hearts. Liu Pei, who had become the incarnation of this dynastic sentiment, seemed on the point of exploiting his victory and forcing the usurper back into the northern provinces. But he had reckoned without Sun Ch'üan, the third pretender. The latter, who until now had been his ally (they had even become brothers-in-law), began to grow apprehensive lest the legitimist party become too successful. Aided by the civil war, he was busy carving out for himself a vast kingdom comprising the provinces of the lower Long River and the Cantonese region. Fearing for the future of his possessions, in 217 he suddenly broke off his alliance with Liu Pei and leagued himself with Ts'ao Ts'ao. This defection dashed the legitimists' hopes of reconquering China, and it also caused the death of Kuan Yü, Liu Pei's old companion in arms and the bravest of the brave. Kuan Yü was fighting against the northerners, when Sun Ch'üan's men attacked him in the rear. Abandoned by his troops and retreating with a handful of loyal followers, he fell into an ambush, was captured and summarily beheaded (219).

Strengthened by this change in the balance of power, Ts'ao Ts'ao, the dictator of northern China, was preparing to take the final step and dethrone his sovereign, the weakling emperor of the Han dynasty, when he himself died in 220. He left the power to his son Ts'ao P'ei, who inherited his father's ambitions and also his talents (he too was a gifted poet). The new dictator's first concern was to realize his father's imperial ambitions. In the same year (220), at Loyang, he was proclaimed emperor and founder of the Wei dynasty.

The usurpation had been accomplished, at least in the provinces of the north, but there was a strong legitimist reaction in favour of Liu Pei. From then on he was the acknowledged heir and representative of the Han dynasty. In his territory of Szechwan, he too was proclaimed emperor, and indeed had a far greater claim to the title than his rival. It is even possible that if he had taken advantage of the general sentiment in his favour to attack Ts'ao P'ei before the latter had had time to consolidate his position, he might have been able to reunite China and re-establish the legitimate dynasty through his line. But, as a point of honour, he felt himself obliged first to avenge the death of his faithful follower Kuan Yü, who had been put to death by the third pretender, Sun Ch'üan, the king of the lower Long River. And so it was against Sun Ch'üan that he turned his forces; a strategic error for which historians, novelists, and dramatists have never ceased to reproach him, for he thus strengthened the coalition of his enemies instead of trying to separate them. Moreover, during the campaign he lost his other faithful follower Chang Fei, who was murdered in his tent by traitors who carried his severed head to Sun Ch'üan. Liu Pei, discouraged by the train of events, died shortly after his return from this disastrous campaign (223), leaving the tutelage of his son in the hands of the magnanimous Chu-ke Liang.

China was now divided into three distinct kingdoms. The first was the kingdom founded by Liu Pei in Szechwan; the only one whose imperial character was recognized by later historians, since Liu Pei, being a Han prince, was the only legitimate pretender. The second—the "illegitimate empire"—was the kingdom founded by the usurpers named Ts'ao; it had the imperial capital Loyang together with all the northern provinces. The third kingdom was that founded by Sun Ch'üan on the lower Long River; it took the name of the Kingdom of Wu, and from 229 had its capital at Chien-yeh (Nanking). It included nearly the whole of southern China.

It is interesting to note how closely this partition of China followed the lines of geographical division. The opposition between North and South China is a fact of nature. Everything makes them different. The former is conditioned by the climate of the steppes, whereas the latter is sub-tropical; the one joins the outskirts of the Gobi, while the other meets the Asiatic monsoon belt. The north of China, comprising the great plain of loess and alluvial soil and the loess plateaux which forms its hinterland, is a land of wheat and millet; the south, formed of successive ranges of highlands—for long forest-covered—and bathed in the monsoon rains, is a country of tea and rice, where the water buffalo takes the place of the horse in agricultural work. The north, where the Yellow River remains untamed, is the country of land transport; the south, where the Long River forms a marvellous navigable waterway, is the land of water transport. One may add that in the third century A.D. the difference must have been no less marked from an anthropological point of view. North China, overpopulated, with its intensive cultivation, was the true China. The South, with the exception of the provinces of the lower Long River, was still only a land for colonization; a new China, mostly forest, and peopled by a different race, the Chinese immigrants established by the Han dynasty being still in scattered groups. Even neglecting the still half-savage, scantily populated and scarcely colonized Cantonese region, the area of the middle and lower Long River (where the kingdom of Wu had its capitals—Wuchang and Nanking), though more Chinese in character, had been so only since the reign of Ch'in Shih-huang-ti, who had been the first to work systematically for its colonization and assimilation.

It was not without good reason that the supporters of Han legitimism had chosen Szechwan as an inviolable refuge. Indeed Szechwan (*ssu ch'uan*—"four rivers") constitutes one of the most strongly defined geographical units of the Chinese "continent". Separated by great distances from the main historical centres of China, it is further isolated by the formidable alpine network which protects it to the north and east, while the rapids of Yi-ch'ang protect it from fleets attempting to sail up the Long River. Its remoteness obliges it to be self-sufficient and the richness of its soil makes this possible. In the heart of Szechwan lies the famous "Red Basin" of soft tertiary sandstone, which in area of cultivated land almost equals the "Central Plain" of the northeast. The altitude of this region, combined with a mild and humid climate, makes it possible to cultivate both rice and wheat. The natural autonomy of Szechwan has been emphasized by geographers, economists, and historians. It played a prominent part at every turning-point of Chinese history.

To sum up, at the time when the great united empire of the Han dynasty disintegrated, its partition was effected in accordance with permanent geographical factors; North China and South China—China old and new, metropolitan and colonial—and to the west Szechwan, remote and with a life of its own.

The period of the Three Kingdoms began like an epic. The first generation of its protagonists resembled heroes of medieval legend, but after the second generation there were none but blighted scions. In the north in particular, the Ts'ao family, kings of the Wei dynasty, degenerated very rapidly. Becoming mere figureheads, they allowed the real power to fall into the hands of the family of Ts'ao Ts'ao's major-domo Ssu-ma Yi. His son, the energetic Ssu-ma Chao, seemed to have raised to their highest point the fortunes of the Wei dynasty, whose affairs had been placed in his hands; in 263 he overthrew the Han kingdom in Szechwan and annexed it to his master's possessions. In reality the conquest served principally to increase the authority of this all-powerful minister. In 265 his son and successor, Ssu-ma Yen, took the obvious and final step: he deposed the last figurehead of the Wei dynasty, and ascended the throne at Loyang as founder of the Chin dynasty. In 280 he completed his task by annexing Wu, the last of the Three Kingdoms, and so brought the south back into a united China.

After sixty years of division, the empire had been reunited under the house of Ssu-ma, the new dynasty of Chin. It seemed as if the great days of the Han had returned, but in fact no dynasty ever degenerated so rapidly as the Chin. Their history is one of kinsmen who butcher one another in horrible palace dramas, without a single political idea or sign of greatness to set against these monotonous killings, and there emerges no personality of any importance.

It was at this point that the Turco-Mongolian hordes invaded the empire.

CHAPTER XIV

THE GREAT INVASIONS

WE have seen how the Han empire, at a time when it was all-powerful, allowed certain clans of Huns to establish themselves, as allies of China, in the great loop of the Yellow River, along that part of the Great Wall. For a long time these Hun allies had proved faithful auxiliaries. But during the civil wars which in the last years of the second century A.D. marked the death throes of the Han dynasty, they profited from the general chaos to start their encroachments. Crossing the Great Wall at a time when, through the weakness of the central power, no one troubled to prevent them, they were able to establish their camps in the heart of Shansi (195). China was on the eve of the fall of the Han dynasty. The chief of these Huns opportunely recalled that one of his ancestresses came of that illustrious house. With an effrontery that was not devoid of cunning he adopted the family name of the great Chinese dynasty for his own house. Thus when the claim of legitimacy had been extinguished in China proper by a series of usurpers, it was revived in the yurts of a Hun clan. In a large gathering held at Taiyüan in Shansi in 308, the Hun chieftain, thenceforth known as Liu Yüan, was solemnly proclaimed the legitimate heir of the Han dynasty, and arrogantly laid claim to the "heritage of his ancestors", that is to say, the Han empire.

Liu Yüan's son, Liu Ts'ung, was to carry these threats into execution. Like many of the young barbarian allies, he had been brought up at the court of Loyang, and according to the dynastic history he had even become a good Chinese scholar. At all events the scholar had not forgotten the military qualities of his own people, for he was still able to bend a hundred-pound bow. He had, moreover, acquired some valuable information during his stay at the capital. The pomp and ceremony of the imperial court might conceal from a casual observer the decadence of the dynasty, the imperfections of the men who directed it, the rotten nature of its institutions, and the true weakness of the colossus with feet of clay; but this Hun prince was not deceived. In 311 he launched four columns of cavalry against the imperial capital of Loyang. The Huns burst into the town, swept down on the imperial palace, and took the emperor prisoner. The crown prince was killed, and thirty thousand inhabitants of the town massacred. The palace was set on fire, and the imperial tombs looted of their treasures. The emperor himself was carried off as the captive of Liu Ts'ung, who forced him to serve as cup-bearer, until one day in a fit of cruelty he had him executed.

Another prince of the imperial family was then proclaimed emperor at the western capital of Ch'ang-an (the present Sian, in Shensi), amidst the ruins which a recent invasion of Hunnish cavalry had left in its wake. "In the ruins of Ch'ang-an, where he sat enthroned, the population had dwindled to less than a hundred families. Weeds and brushwood had sprung up everywhere." During the winter months of the year 316 the Huns reappeared without warning in front of the city. As their army was made up of cavalry and incapable of undertaking a regular siege, they took to riding in an endless procession round the walls. This persistent merry-go-round had the effect of a strict blockade, and the city was forced by famine to surrender (December 316). Once more the Hun king, Liu Ts'ung, seated on his throne, received an emperor of China as his prisoner and "forced him to rinse out the cups during feasts." Then one day when one of the other Chinese captives, moved by this sad spectacle, gave way to tears, the enraged Hun ordered the execution of his unfortunate prisoner.

After this succession of disasters the imperial dynasty of Chin, abandoning the whole of northern China to the invader, took refuge in southern China, beyond the Long River, and established its capital at Nanking (318). For nearly three centuries (318–589) there endured in the south an empire comparable, both in its imperfections and its paradoxical vitality, with the Byzantine Empire. Nanking took the place of Ch'ang-an and Loyang in the same way that Byzantium, in the Roman world, replaced Rome and Milan.

During the same period in northern China, the Turco-Mongolian hordes jostled and destroyed each other in a perpetual overturning of ephemeral hegemonies. After the death of Liu Ts'ung, his family was overthrown by one of his former lieutenants, another Hun chieftain called Shih Lei (329). This illiterate Hun was enlightened enough to enjoy having the Chinese classics explained to him; but his successors combined their native savagery with all the vices of a decadent civilization. Shih Lei's nephew, Shih Hu (ruled 334–349), was a monster of debauchery whose own son tried to assassinate him (and was duly executed by his father). This Tartar Bluebeard used to have the most attractive of his concubines roasted and served at table: "From time to time he used to have one of the girls of his harem beheaded, cooked and served to his guests, while the uncooked head was passed round on a plate to prove that he had not sacrificed the least beautiful." With the contrast of character not uncommon among barbarians perverted by their first contact with civilization, but capable of being reformed by the preaching of a saint, Shih Hu was one of the most zealous protectors of Buddhism.

In fact Buddhism, it must be admitted, gained ground as a result of the barbarian invasions. At a time when savagery was rife, it was only natural that men who were tormented in spirit should turn to the spiritual consolations dispensed by Buddhism. Moreover, rough barbarians like the Huns were not likely to have the same inflexible prejudice against this religion as did the Confucian intellectuals. Despite the opposition of the latter, Shih Hu published an edict formally authorizing Buddhist preaching. The famous Fu Chien (ruled 357–385), another barbarian king who for a time was master of the whole of northern China, adopted the same attitude. Moreover, time had begun to do its work and this was no longer a case of the tribal chieftain who looked on the Indian miracle-workers merely as shamans of a superior variety who could bring luck to his enterprises; Fu Chien was a barbarian in the process of adaptation, a sincere supporter of Chinese culture who was both a genuinely pious Buddhist and a humane and merciful administrator. Yet, despite the personal goodwill of certain chieftains, the measures they took were soon rendered ineffective as one horde was destroyed by another. We shall not attempt to enumerate all the barbarian tribes who contested for the Yellow River basin and the Peking region during these terrible decades. It is sufficient to say that the struggle was in general between the Huns—probably a "proto-Turkish" people—and the Hsien-pi clans—probably "proto-Mongol". The former, as has been seen, came down from the Ordos, the latter from the Manchurian borders northeast of Peking; and both alternately exercised hegemony over the north of China.

In the long run the installation of nomads in the heart of this ancient agricultural country caused incalculable damage. Not only were great historic cities like Ch'ang-an sacked, burnt and depopulated, but the fields themselves lay fallow, abandoned by the peasants. Thus emptied of its inhabitants, the rich valley of the Wei around Ch'ang-an became the haunt of wolves and tigers. The barbarian chieftain Fu Sheng, who ruled in Shensi from 354 to 357, was besought by his terrified Chinese subjects to deliver them from the wild beasts. He refused, and in doing so his manner would suggest that he felt more in sympathy with the wolves than the farmers: "These animals are hungry," he said: "when once they are replete they won't eat anyone else." Beneath his brutal humour one can divine the secret satisfaction of the barbarian chief; this invasion of the country by the wild animals of the steppes seemed to consummate its occupation by the Turco-Mongolian hordes. The Hun kings installed whole tribes in districts which had become depopulated, a measure which must have had a permanent effect on the ethnical composition of North China.[1]

[1] There is a famous ballad of this period (fifth century?) which recounts the life of a heroine named Mu-lan. She disguised herself in men's clothes and went to war,

While these calamities were descending upon North China, which for two centuries became little more than a dependency of the Mongolian steppes, decadence was ever more apparent in the Chinese Empire of the south, at the Chien-k'ang (Nanking) court of the last of the Chin dynasty, those Byzantines of the Far East. At the beginning of the fifth century a soldier of fortune named Liu Yü, a former cobbler turned general, gave a transitory vitality to the old empire. Emboldened by a few successes against the barbarians, he dethroned the Chin and proclaimed himself emperor of the Sung dynasty (now called Liu Sung, to distinguish it from the great Sung dynasty founded in the tenth century). His family, which occupied the throne of Nanking from 420 to 479, lapsed into a state of degeneracy worse than ever before. The third emperor of this line was assassinated at the instigation of one of his sons (453). The parricide was afterwards put to death by his own brother (454), who became emperor (454–465) and, fearing a similar fate, took the precaution of massacring the majority of the other princes of royal blood. The next emperor, who only reigned for six months (465)—he came to

taking her aged father's place under the colours of one of the barbarian chieftains contending for North China:

> . . . In the eastern market she bought a fine horse,
> In the western market she bought saddle and blanket,
> In the southern market she bought bridle and reins,
> In the northern market she bought a long whip.
> At dawn she set out from her parents' house,
> At dusk she camped on the Yellow River shore.
> She did not hear her father and mother calling to their
>   daughter; she only heard the hissing voice of the
>   Yellow River's flowing waves.
> At sunrise they set off and left the Yellow River,
> At dusk they camped beside the Black Water.
> She did not hear her father and mother calling to their
>   daughter; she only heard the Hunnish horsemen
>   shout across the hills of Yen.
> Ten thousand li she rode on army duties,
> Borders and mountains crossed as swift as flight.
> Through the northern night there sounded out the kettle-drum,
> In the winter daylight soldiers' armour gleaming. . . .

We do not know whether she was the daughter of one of the barbarian colonists or of a Chinese who had acquired Hunnish habits. At all events it is a curious example of how northern China was in process of assimilating the manners of the steppes.

the throne at sixteen and was assassinated at seventeen—was a sort of Nero who ordered the execution of his regents, close relations and concubines. It was not long before he was murdered himself, but his uncle and successor (465–472), nicknamed "The Pig" because of his obesity, was no less bloodthirsty, and he in turn had all his brothers and nephews executed. When he was dying, "The Pig" bequeathed the empire to the son of his favourite. This emperor-by-chance was a precocious youngster (crowned at ten, killed at fifteen) and showed such ferocity that he had to be beheaded, which was done during a night of drunkenness (477). Liu Yü's family was already decimated and dishonoured when, in the year 479, one of the state officers deposed it and founded a new dynasty called Ch'i.

The Ch'i occupied the throne of Nanking from 479 to 502. They in their turn were soon demoralized by the taste of power. Their history, like that of the dynasty which preceded them, is little more than a series of assassinations; each of the rulers taking the precaution of getting rid of all the other members of his family, until some relation that he had overlooked took the opportunity of doing away with him. During this period the power was exercised by court favourites, while the throne was occupied by adolescent emperors, frequently assassinated before attaining maturity because of their ferocious cruelty. In the year 502 a general, the future Liang Wu-ti, seized the throne and, although he was related to the imperial family, attempted to dissociate himself from that odious house by founding a new dynasty, that of Liang.

Liang Wu-ti, who reigned in Nanking from A.D. 502 to 549, was a sovereign of a certain greatness who made a radical break with the corrupt tradition of his predecessors. Leading a life which was almost austere in its simplicity, honest and humane, he combined the virtues of a soldier with a respect for culture and men of letters. So great at first was his respect for Confucianism that he built a temple to Confucius at Nanking and reinstated the study of the classics in the place of honour that it had once occupied. In the same spirit, he reorganized the mandarin class and formed it into a hierarchy. After the abominations of the preceding dynasties, this was a praiseworthy effort to bring back to the state and to the family those traditional moral ideas on which Chinese society was based. But soon Liang Wu-ti's sympathies shifted; under the influence of some Indian monks, who had come by the sea route to Nanking, he was converted to Buddhism. He first of all showed his respect for the Buddhist doctrine of non-violence (*ahimsa*), by forbidding the immolation of animals in sacrifices to the ancestors, a prohibition which gained him the disapprobation of the Confucian intellectuals. In the year 527 he went still further; he professed himself a monk, and the state was obliged to ransom its ruler from the clergy. While his Buddhism seems to have been sincere and enlightened, it must be conceded to the intellectuals, thenceforth his unrelenting critics, that the monk in him ended by destroying the statesman. He was so deeply imbued with the spirit of Buddhist mercy that even in the case of a conspiracy he could not bring himself to order capital punishment. Relapsing into a somewhat senile devotion, he allowed himself to be tricked by a rebellious general who arrived without warning and laid siege to Nanking. He died at the age of eighty-six amidst the ruin of his house—and of his illusions. The Liang dynasty, weakened by his errors, only survived him by a few years; while the Ch'en dynasty which followed (557–589) did not have time to demonstrate its capacities, for in 589 the rulers of North China captured Nanking and put an end to the "Byzantine" empire of the south.

During the period which we have outlined, the existence of that empire was simply a prolonged decadence. It was in the north that history was being made, and it is to this history of the Sino-Turkish China of the north that we shall now turn.

CHAPTER XV

THE ART OF THE WEI DYNASTY

WE have seen that throughout the fourth century in North China, successive hordes of Turco-Mongolians destroyed each other in a continual overturning of ephemeral kingdoms. Out of this chaos emerged at last a more permanent government, that of the T'o-pa (Tabghach), a people who played a significant part in the history both of civilization and of art. Their dynasty was called Wei (often referred to as T'o-pa Wei to distinguish it from the Three Kingdoms Wei).

The T'o-pa were a Turkish tribe who had settled in the most northerly part of Shansi at the beginning of the period of the great invasions. Between 396 and 439 they destroyed or absorbed all the other tribes that had become established in the north of China, and united the area under their own domination, just as in Europe the Franks, having survived the Burgundians, Visigoths, and Lombards, founded the Carolingian Empire on their ruins. And just as the Franks were able to reconcile Germanic culture with Latin, so too the T'o-pa were long able to preserve their Turkish strength, while at the same time they increasingly shared in the Chinese tradition. Moreover, they gained merit in the eyes of the Chinese as the defenders of the north of China against new invaders, in particular against the Mongol horde of the Avars (Jou-jan) who were then masters of the Gobi. By a series of preventive expeditions and crushing counter-raids they succeeded thoughout the fifth century in forcing these nomads back into the heart of Mongolia.

The king T'o-pa T'ao (T'ai-wu-ti, ruled 424–452), who finally established the greatness of his house, devoted his life to a twofold struggle; campaigns in the Gobi to protect Chinese soil against fresh nomadic invasions from the north, and a constant pressure against the southern Chinese empire of Nanking. In a curious speech, which the annalists have preserved, he himself suggests the advantage he enjoyed by being half-Chinese in relation to the barbarians and half-barbarian in relation to the Chinese. "The Chinese (meaning the men of the empire of Nanking) are foot-soldiers and we are horsemen. What can a herd of colts and heifers do against a tiger or a pack of wolves? As for the nomads, in summer they put their flocks to pasture in the north of the Gobi, and in winter they come to make raids across our frontiers. All that is necessary is to attack them in their steppes in the springtime. At that season their horses are good for nothing; the stallions are taken up with the mares and the mares with their foals. One need only surprise them at that time, cut off their access to the pastures and water holes, and in a few days they are at our mercy!" In the year 425 he acted on his words. Four columns of light cavalry crossed the Gobi from south to north; their progress was unhampered by supply trains, and each man carried rations for fifteen days. The Avars, completely taken by surprise, were driven back from the Mongolian steppes into the mountains near Lake Baikal or along the Orkhon. A further raid in 429 was conducted by T'o-pa T'ao in person. Once again surprised and thrown into disorder, the nomads were forced to surrender hundreds of thousands of their horses, carts, cattle, and sheep. The last descendants of these same Avars were to be exterminated in Hungary nearly four hundred years later by another defender of civilization, Charlemagne.

A further comparison can be drawn between the way in which Charlemagne harmonized Germanic and Latin culture, and T'o-pa T'ao's efforts to harmonize the Turkish beliefs of his people with the tenets of Chinese thought. *Tengri*, the god-heaven of the Altaic tribes, was easily transformed into *T'ien*, the Heaven that surmounted Confucian philosophy, while the goddess-earth and the various divinities of the springs and mountain-tops were identified with the deities of Chinese nature worship, just as the Romans had assimilated the gods of neighbouring countries into their own gods. But T'o-pa T'ao went further than his predecessors by abandoning such Altaic cults as could not be made to tally with the beliefs of Confucianism. Nevertheless, while endeavouring in this way to sinicize his people, he did not allow them to lose their military qualities. It was for this reason that he refused to abandon the encampments of his forbears on the furthermost frontier of Shansi, on the edge of the steppes, for the historic Chinese capitals of Ch'ang-an and Loyang which his armies had conquered. Furthermore, he retained the barbarous though prudent ancestral custom that before the accession of a new T'o-pa king his mother should be put to death, thus avoiding any rancour or ambition on the part of the future dowager or members of her clan. Finally, unlike many other barbarian chieftains, he mistrusted the enervating influence of Buddhism and the increase in monastic celibacy. In 438 he promulgated an edict of secularization directed against the Buddhist monks, and this was reinforced in 444 and 446 by real measures of persecution. Confucian annalists have maliciously insisted that the edict of 446 was due to the discovery of alcohol and women in one of the most famous Buddhist monasteries. But the chief complaint that the Confucian literati brought against the great Indian religion was more serious: Buddhist monasticism "did away with the family" and consequently struck at the roots of the cult of ancestors; and in addition (a telling argument to a soldier like T'o-pa T'ao) it gave men an opportunity to evade military service.

The persecution came to an end with the assassination of T'o-pa T'ao and the eventual succession of his grandson, T'o-pa Chün (Wen-ch'eng-ti), during the year 452. The next ruler, T'o-pa Hung (Hsien-wen-ti, 466–471), openly declared himself a Buddhist. In 471 he abdicated in favour of his son—a child of five—and became a monk. "He retired to a pagoda built in the royal park, where he lived in the company of contemplative monks, and refused to listen to any news apart from events of exceptional gravity." His son the young king showed an equal enthusiasm for the great Indian religion.

Under its influence he humanized the harsh legislation of the T'o-pa; the punishment of mutilation was replaced by imprisonment. The Buddhist spirit of compassion towards all living creatures even led to the suppression, or at least to a considerable diminution, of animal sacrifices to Heaven, Earth, ancestors, and genii. In the year 494 the same king completed the sinicization of his realm by removing his capital from P'ing-ch'eng (in the extreme north of Shansi) to Loyang, the ancient eastern capital, and by requiring his officials to use the Chinese language and wear Chinese dress.

From 515 to 528 the T'o-pa kingdom was governed by the dowager queen Hu. This heiress to the old barbarian chieftains was the last great ruler of the dynasty. An unscrupulous woman of great energy, she stopped at nothing in order to conserve her power. Fearing a former rival, she forced her to enter a convent, and there had her put to death. She likewise ordered the execution of those of her lovers who had ceased to please her. In the year 528 she poisoned her son, who was beginning to grow weary of submitting to the tutelage of her lovers; but at this the indignant state officers began a revolt. Perceiving herself lost, the ruthless queen cut off her hair and hastened to make her vows in a Buddhist nunnery; but the insurgents dragged her out and hurled her into the Yellow River. In spite of her crimes, the dowager Hu, like the kings who preceded her, was a most devout Buddhist. The famous Buddhist caves of Lung-men owe part of their construction to her, and it was she who sent the pilgrim Sung Yün on his mission to India (518–521).

Ages of bloodshed are often ages of faith. It is to the T'o-pa Wei that China owes her greatest religious sculpture, that of the Buddhist grottoes of Yün-kang in the north of Shansi (452–512), and of Lung-men near Loyang (from 494).

Wei sculpture has been called the Far Eastern equivalent of the Romanesque and Gothic sculptures which developed six and eight centuries later in Europe. The starting-points—the Greco-Buddhist style in China, and the Gallo-Roman style in Europe—are analogous. And just as the Gothic or Romanesque makers of images adapted the traditions of Greco-Roman plastic art to purely spiritual ends, so the art of the Wei period resorted to the Gandhara technique of drapery and the Apollo-like features, with no other purpose than to render more perfectly the pure spirituality of Buddhism. This was all-important. The classical modelling, when it has not disappeared; the drapery, when it is not stylized into great angular folds or into little rounded waves; and the human charm of the features, when they are not almost entirely emaciated—all these are subservient to metaphysical thought. Here nothing remains but tells of piety, fervour, and unalloyed faith. A certain bodhisattva of Yün-kang is meditation personified. Another Yün-kang image, with a piercing smile like that of the angels at Reims, expresses detachment from worldly things, and also, perhaps unintentionally, a secret irony—yet an irony full of indulgence towards the spectacle of universal folly and vanity. But more often this transcendent irony seems to fade away, so that through the profound contemplation shines only the immeasurable peace of Deliverance.

It is possible to trace the evolution of the art of Yün-kang. First the Greco-Buddhist influence was brought from Afghanistan by the Gandhara missionaries who were so numerous at the court of the T'o-pa kings. Thus the colossal statues which dominate the grottos recall in their severe treatment the giant Buddhas of Bamiyan in Afghanistan. More remarkable is the way in which the smaller statues in the cliff-niches break away from the lessons of Gandhara art. These thin, elongated, and often angular figures, which have drapery in nervous folds, but which preserve a soothing simplicity and a youthful grace, offer something which was lacking in the purely "formal" sculpture of Gandhara; an art of pure spirituality. As Hackin wrote: "The forms, characterized by a pleasing severity, bear witness to a rapid adaptation of art to the exigencies of faith. They betoken a high level of spiritual life; their plastic appearance is discreetly attenuated and ceases to attract attention, and the smile of tender humanity remains the only concession made to this world by the Blessed One." This is a harmony which could never have been achieved all at once. According to Sirèn, the art of Yün-kang developed from an extreme mystical spareness towards a relative restoration of plastic form. "The art of Yün-kang, on attaining maturity, seems to a certain extent to depart from its earlier stylization. The forms become rounder and fuller, the folds of the dress become less stiff, and the interplay of line is more supple. Nevertheless, the figures retain a relatively severe appearance, and an indescribable air of introspection and detachment which places them on a high level among religious sculptures."[1]

The sculpture of the caves of Lung-men is a continuation of that at Yün-kang. Often, as for example in images which date from the years 509 and 523, the mysticism and stylization are carried even further. The great elongated rigid figures, with their fixed smiles and their draperies breaking harshly into great folds or subsiding trivially into little waves, are antipodal to any preoccupation with modelling. These are no longer the shapes of material beings under the pointed arch of the huge nimbus whose flame surrounds them, forming a stylized symbol of the cloak of monasticism. This priestly quality endows the bodhisattvas of Lung-men (those from the sixth century, that is) with a most striking mysticism.

It is permissible to draw a comparison between the art of this period and Romanesque art in Europe, providing it is understood that this is done from the point of view of comparative philosophy, that it is for the purpose of analysing and comparing human values. If across the bounds of time and space there is a relationship between Wei and Romanesque art, it is because both are derived from the classical canon, albeit a classical canon freed from convention and renovated by a great mystical force, and thenceforth called upon to express purely spiritual values instead of bodily beauty. A similar distance separates the art of Yün-kang and Lung-men from Greco-Buddhist art to that which separates Roman art from the European cathedrals. Epochs of great religious art are rare. The Wei period was one of them.

[1] One of the finest of these bodhisattvas is in the Musée Cernuschi in Paris.

CHAPTER XVI

YANG-TI, SON OF HEAVEN

IN course of time the T'o-pa became too thoroughly sinicized and too completely blended into the Chinese population to avoid becoming decadent. In 534 the dynasty split into two branches which shared the north of China; subsequently each of these royal houses was replaced by its respective major-domo. In 581 the two kingdoms were reunited by an energetic minister, Yang Chien, who founded a new dynasty, the Sui. Yang Chien completed his task in the year 589 by conquering the Chinese "Byzantine" empire (then under the Ch'en dynasty) with its capital at Nanking, that is to say the whole of South China. After being divided for two hundred and seventy-one years (318–589), China was again united. Ch'ang-an (modern Sian), the ancient western capital, became once more the seat of government.

Yang Chien (the emperor Wen-ti) was a man of sterling qualities who, although comparatively uneducated, was a careful administrator and gave everything his personal attention. He was a cautious and thrifty man who dealt severely with dishonest officials and succeeded in restoring strict order in society and the state, though the methods he employed in doing so were sometimes distasteful. In foreign affairs he reaped the benefit of Chinese unification.

Since the middle of the sixth century an event of primary importance had occurred in Upper Asia. This was the foundation of the Turkish Empire. In fact it is only towards this period that the Turks first appear in history, at least under that name (in Chinese, T'u-chüeh). In the Turkish language it signifies "the strong", and was probably the name of a Hun tribe originating in the Khangai mountains of Outer Mongolia. During the first half of the sixth century the Turks were still subordinate to the Avars (Jou-jan), the Mongolian horde who were masters of the Gobi and of Outer Mongolia. In 552 the Turks revolted against the Avars, overwhelmed them, and drove them out of Mongolia. One section of the Avars fled as far as Europe and in Hungary founded a khanate which was to terrorize Byzantium until destroyed by Charlemagne two and a half centuries later.

The Turks thus became masters of the whole of Mongolia. Their chieftains, who bore the title of Kaghan, or Grand Khan, dwelt near the present Karakorum, in the region of the Upper Orkhon. In 565 the Turks doubled their possessions by capturing what is now Soviet Turkestan (Tashkent, Bukhara, and Samarkand) from the Mongolian horde of the Hephthalites. They then controlled all Upper Asia, from the Great Wall of China to the frontiers of Persia. A Turkish inscription at Kocho Tsaidam in Mongolia, which dates from the year 732, tells of these conquests in a magnificent poem: "When the blue sky was created above and the dark earth below, between the two were created the sons of men. Above the sons of men rose up the kaghan my ancestors. After becoming masters, they governed the institutions and the empire of the Turkish people. In the four corners of the earth they had many enemies, but making expeditions with armies they enslaved and pacified many peoples in the four corners of the earth. They forced them to bow the head and to bend the knee. They enabled us to dwell between the Khingan Mountains in the east and the Iron Gates in the west. All the way between these two outposts stretched the dominion of the Blue Turks!" This immense empire was divided up between two branches of the leading Turkish clan almost immediately after it was formed. The khanate of the Eastern Turks retained their headquarters on the Orkhon and ruled over Mongolia. The Western Turks established headquarters near Issyk Kul and held western Turkestan. The former waged war against China, the latter against Sassanid Persia.

As soon as he had restored Chinese unity, Yang Chien made it the object of his diplomacy to stir up discord between the Eastern and Western Turks. At the time of his death in 604, the Turks, paralysed by their own civil wars, were allowing China to re-establish her supremacy in Central Asia.

Yang Chien's son Yang Kuang (the emperor Yang-ti) was a great sovereign, or rather, his was a great reign (605–616). He was a temperamental and unstable character whose life was divided between periods of consuming activity and others of depression and inertia. For all his faults and vices, he was fully aware of the renewed greatness of the imperial throne and of China's mission as a dominating power in Asia.

Yang-ti was famous for his love of pomp and luxury. Besides his father's capital at Ch'ang-an, he made Loyang a second capital. "He embellished its surroundings with a park one hundred and twenty kilometres in circumference, where he made a lake nine kilometres long, out of which rose three Islands of the Immortals, adorned with magnificent pavilions. Along the banks of a waterway which opened into the lake he constructed sixteen villas for his favourites, and these houses were reached by boat. All the known refinements of luxury were displayed in these dwellings and in the gardens which surrounded them. In autumn, when the leaves had fallen from the maples, the trees and bushes were decked with leaves and flowers made of glistening fabrics. In addition to real lotuses, the lake was adorned with artificial lotus blossoms which were continually renewed. The emperor enjoyed sailing on the lake or riding in the park on moonlight nights, with a band of beautiful girls who improvised verses or sang songs." But besides this private magnificence, Yang-ti was also responsible for great public works, including canals which connected Loyang with the Long River.

In foreign affairs Yang-ti continued his father's policy of stirring up discord between the rival Turkish chieftains, which enabled him to play the role of arbiter between their various khanates. By 608 Chinese prestige was restored to such an extent that the emperor was able to make a tour of inspection along the frontier of Kansu, where he received homage from several western oases, notably from the people of Turfan. In Korea, Yang-ti was less successful. In the years 612, 613, and 614 he directed three great expeditions against that country which all ended in failure. The retreat of the imperial army turned into disaster. With the object of restoring Chinese prestige among the Turks, Yang-ti made a tour of inspection along the Great Wall, on the edge of the Gobi. There he was surprised by a Turkish attack, and besieged for a month in a frontier post from which he escaped only with difficulty (615).

People had grown weary of Yang-ti's taxation, of his construction schemes, and of the excessive forced labour. In 616 began a general revolt. The Chinese Xerxes, as he has been called because of the Korean disaster, ended his days like the legendary Sardanapalus. In 616 he retired to Chiang-tu (Yangchow) on the lower Long River, where he sought to forget his misfortune in a life of pleasure. In April of 618 his bodyguard broke into the palace, massacred his favourite son before his eyes—the blood gushed out over the imperial cloak—then one of them strangled the emperor. He was only fifty years old.

History has been severe in its judgment of the two Sui emperors, but it was they who restored the unity of China and began the restoration of Chinese hegemony in Central Asia. The truth is that they have been eclipsed by their successors, the T'ang emperors. The latter were to complete the task undertaken by Yang Chien and his son, and to make China once more the arbiter of Eastern Asia.

CHAPTER XVII

T'AI-TSUNG THE GREAT

THE fall of the Sui dynasty seemed destined to plunge China into another period of division and anarchy. In each province arose military leaders who fought for supremacy. Then appeared the soldier of genius who was destined to restore the empire and to impose a new course on the history and civilization of China for three centuries.

He was called Li Shih-min. His father Li Yüan, Count of T'ang and governor of a military district in Shansi, was a gentleman of good family, a respected general, and an official as honest as was possible for one in so important a position; he was a timorous individual, always afraid of compromising himself, and was loyalist enough to break his oath of office only in the last extremity. In addition he was full of Confucian wisdom and learned maxims. Li Shih-min too, despite his youth (he was born in 597 and was now little more than twenty years of age), had been brought up on historical anecdotes and fine sayings. But his experience of camp life—for his father's fief was situated on the frontier and constantly exposed to Turkish raids—and also his experiences at court—the court of the Sui emperors, the most magnificent, corrupt and bizarre that had ever been known in the Far East—had taught the young man how to make use of Confucian wisdom instead of becoming its slave. Throughout his career (on which lie some strange shadows) he always made sure of having conventional morality on his side. In addition, a prodigious vitality, an almost infallible power of decision, bravery, cunning, audacity and good sense were all blended to perfection in his character; he was the ideal man of his times.

The empire was in the throes of military anarchy. The emperor

Yang-ti, who had retired to Yangchow, led a life of debauchery while his generals fought each other for the provinces. The young Li Shih-min, assured of strong military backing in his domains in Shansi, strengthened by his friendly relations with several Turkish khans, and having moreover formed valuable connections with various palace officials, grew impatient at his father's old-fashioned loyalism. In order to force the latter's hand, he had recourse to a typically Chinese stratagem. He was in league with one of the palace eunuchs. At the instigation of Li Shih-min, the eunuch offered Li Yüan a girl intended for the imperial harem. The damsel must have been attractive, for, without reflecting on the consequences of his action, the worthy Li Yüan accepted this dangerous gift. Afterwards Li Shih-min had it pointed out to his father that they had made themselves outlaws, the abduction of one of the women of the palace being a capital offence. Li Yüan was struck with consternation—but what was to be done? It was too late to draw back. He therefore summoned his followers to his residence at T'aiyüan, and mobilized the troops under his command. At the same time he allayed his conscience by announcing that he was taking up arms only as a loyalist, in order to deliver the emperor from the other pretenders.

Everything went exactly as Li Shih-min had intended. As by intrigue he had obtained assistance from within the imperial harem, so by his military directness he had won the sympathy of the Turks, and these dangerous neighbours placed at his disposal five hundred picked mercenaries and two thousand horses. Meanwhile his sister, a young heroine who rode on horseback as well as he did, sold her jewels and with the money enrolled ten thousand men and brought them to him. Li Shih-min soon had sixty thousand tried soldiers under his command, men whose hardships he shared, whom he could inspire by his example, and who would willingly die for him. For over four years (618–622) he led his soldiers from province to province, encountering army after army and restoring order out of chaos.

His father's scruples were quickly appeased by circumstances. At the imperial court, down on the Long River, the imperial guard took advantage of the general chaos to assassinate the legitimate emperor, Yang-ti. Thereupon the Count of T'ang declared himself the avenger of the dynasty and, in the name of a last representative of the Sui imperial line, assumed the military command of the empire. Some months later, at the instigation of Li Shih-min, he deposed this phantom sovereign and had himself proclaimed emperor (618).

The imperial capital of Ch'ang-an (a city which has played a part in Chinese history similar to that of Rome in the West) was the first to open its gates to the new emperor—for was he not a native of this province of Shensi, which since the time of Ch'in Shih-huang-ti had seen the rise of all the great dynasties? Li Shih-min then moved on to lay siege to Loyang, which was under the command of one of his father's most formidable rivals. It was a difficult task, since the city was a particularly strong one and the other pretenders, disquieted by the successes of the T'ang forces, lost no time in coming to its aid. The young hero was accompanied by one of his former adversaries, Yü-chih Ching-te, whom he had won over to his cause after taking him prisoner. With his habitual generosity, and against the advice of his followers, Li Shih-min put him in command of one of the armies.

As soon as they came in sight of the city, Li Shih-min with a body of eight hundred horsemen went on ahead to reconnoitre its approaches, but the garrison, observing this, sallied forth and surrounded the little force. As the T'ang leader, sabre in hand, was trying to open up a way of retreat, one of the enemy officers recognized him and rushed at him with lowered lance. The future emperor nearly paid for his rashness with his life, but Ching-te, who had never lost sight of him, darted forth and killed the assailant. At that moment the T'ang battalions entered the battle and rescued their leader. Meanwhile, an enemy army commanded by one of the pretenders was coming down from Hopei to relieve Loyang. When it was only a few miles distant from the city, Li Shih-min took the pick of his cavalry and set out in the morning twilight. He galloped to the enemy camp, took their defences by surprise, and cut his way to the tent of the general, who amid the confusion received a lance wound and was captured. Several days later Loyang capitulated.

Li Shih-min returned to Ch'ang-an in triumph (621). The Chinese annalists give an unwontedly colourful picture of the young conqueror's return. They describe him riding slowly through the streets of the capital on a richly caparisoned courser; he wore his coat of arms and a golden breastplate, with a helmet on his head, his bow in a sling, and a quiver of arrows across his shoulder; and his sword was in his hand. The vanquished pretenders walked on either side of his horse, close to the stirrups. The scene described in the *T'ang History* can be pictured all the more vividly in the light of recent archaeological discoveries. In terra-cotta funeral figures are to be found the cavalry of T'ang, their horses prancing and pawing the ground. We even have the images, the names, and the records of Li Shih-min's favourite mounts, those sturdy horses with plaited manes which he had sculptured in relief on the walls of his tomb. The courser that took part in the triumph at Ch'ang-an was undoubtedly "Autumn Dew", famous as its master's faithful companion throughout the campaign in Honan. As for the armour that the conqueror wore, there are exact replicas of it on the stalwart shoulders of warriors portrayed in the funeral images, or on guardian *lokapala* in the Buddhist statuary.

Chinese unity was restored none too soon. The Turks were on the march.

The military anarchy in China had seemed to the Turks to offer an ideal opportunity for intervention. The khan of the Eastern Turks, Hsieh-li Kaghan, with his nephew Tu-li led a large column of cavalry which swept past the frontier posts and arrived at the suburbs of the imperial capital, Ch'ang-an. The old emperor, Kao-tsu (the erstwhile Li Yüan), took fright and talked of evacuating the city. Li Shih-min left him to talk, while he himself went out with a hundred picked horsemen to take up the Turkish challenge. He boldly rode up to them, entered their ranks and addressed them all:

"The T'ang dynasty owes nothing to the Turks. Why then do you invade our realms? I am ready to try my strength against your khan!" At the same time he made a personal appeal to certain chieftains, such as Tu-li, who had been bound to him by ties of military comradeship, and reawakened in them the feelings of brothers in arms. His resolute bearing and his knowledge of the workings of the Turkish mind overawed the fickle nomads. The chieftains of the various hordes talked together for some time, and then they all turned their horses' heads and rode away. Some hours later the country was deluged by torrential rain. Li Shih-min straightway summoned his captains and, according to his biographer, addressed them as follows: "Comrades, now is the time to show our mettle. The whole plain has turned into a sea of mud. Night is about to fall and it will be very dark. The Turks are only to be feared when they are able to shoot their arrows. Let us charge them with our sabres and lances. We shall destroy them before they can prepare their defences!" And so it was done. The Turkish camp was stormed before dawn and the Chinese cavalry cut its way as far as the khan's tent. The latter asked for terms and retreated into Mongolia (624).

As time went on Li Shih-min increasingly asserted his authority as the protector of the empire. His two brothers, growing jealous of his glory, resolved to get rid of him. Even his father, who owed his throne to Li Shih-min, gradually began to take umbrage at his popularity and ceased to entrust him with public affairs. So began one of those savage dramas which occurred as frequently in the Forbidden City as in the Sacred Palace of Byzantium; when following the account of those tragic days in the *T'ang History*, one might well be reading a page in the history of Byzantium. His brothers gave Li Shih-min a banquet to celebrate his victories and poisoned him. He took an antidote and recovered. Then they hired assassins and lay in wait for him near one of the palace gates. But a traitor warned him (the whole story is as full of treachery as it is of bloodshed and virtuous declamations), and Li Shih-min forestalled them. Forewarned of his enemies' designs, his faithful supporters posted horsemen at suitable spots. At the hour appointed for the ambush, he advanced against the enemy in this war of assassination as against an enemy on the field of battle. "He buckled on his breastplate, donned his helmet, took his quiver and arrows and set out for the palace." As soon as his two brothers saw him approaching, they let fly a volley of arrows, but missed. Li Shih-min shot down one of them with his first arrow, while his lieutenant killed the other. At this moment appeared the soldiers whom the lieutenant had placed in concealment, and, according to the *T'ang History*, "nobody dared to make any further movement". Meanwhile the palace servants and the local populace were beginning to gather round. Li Shih-min then took off his helmet, made himself known and, standing before the bloody corpses of his brothers, addressed the crowd: "My children, have no fear for my safety; those who wished to assassinate me are dead!" Then Li Shih-min's faithful follower Ching-te struck off the heads of the two princes and showed them to the crowd.

It remained to announce this execution to the emperor, who had always shown a marked partiality for the two victims. Li Shih-min entrusted Ching-te with this task. The latter, disregarding the most sacred rules of etiquette, entered the emperor's apartments fully armed, his hands possibly still red with the blood of the two princes. One can read between the lines of the official account and imagine what must have happened; a fine spectacle of Confucian hypocrisy, with the murderers, still hot from the fight, quoting moral maxims for the one purpose of justifying their action without loss of face.

On learning the news, the old emperor was unable to restrain his tears and his anger. His first action was to order a strict inquiry. He had failed to understand that he was no longer master of the situation. One of his courtiers discreetly reminded him of the real state of affairs. "There is no need to make any further inquiry. . . . No matter how these events came about, the two dead princes were guilty and the Prince of Ch'in is innocent." Words worthy of Tacitus, which add the final touch to this Neronian drama! The courtiers then detailed various monstrous crimes committed by the two murdered princes. Had they not been carrying on intrigues with several of their father's wives? That in itself was more than sufficient to legalize their execution.

Li Shih-min himself was then announced. The fratricide presented himself with every token of the most moving filial piety, and the aged monarch, in tears, embraced him and even congratulated him on having saved their family. It was a touching scene. "The emperor", writes the annalist calmly, "had always hesitated to choose between his sons. The death of the two eldest put an end to his perplexities, and his former affection for Li Shih-min took full possession of his heart. When he saw him at his feet like a criminal begging for mercy, he was unable to restrain his tears. He raised him up, embraced him and assured him that, far from thinking him guilty, he was convinced that Li Shih-min had acted only in legitimate self-defence." After making this announcement the emperor, as was expected of him, abdicated in favour of his son. This was not accomplished without further edifying scenes: Li Shih-min, in conformity with the rules of etiquette, refused the throne; in vain the Grand Council pronounced unanimously in favour of the master of the hour—he refused once more, and "weeping and throwing himself at his father's feet besought him to retain the power until his death". But the old man commanded and Li Shih-min, as a dutiful son and loyal subject, had to obey. Thus compelled, he finally ascended the throne on September 4, 626. In order to put an end to any possible vendettas and pacify the empire, the new monarch had all his sisters-in-law and nephews put to death without delay. The former emperor retired to one of his palaces where, we are told, "he lived in the enjoyment of all honours and tranquil pleasures, while his son never gave him the slightest occasion to regret the step he had taken in abdicating the throne".

In the meantime this palace coup had given the Turks fresh grounds for hope. The new emperor was hardly on the throne when one hundred thousand Turkish horsemen from Outer Mongolia crossed the Gobi and advanced on Ch'ang-an. On September 23, 626, they appeared before the Bridge of Pien, beyond the north gate of the city. Once again the courtiers besought their young sovereign to abandon so exposed a capital. But Li Shih-min—whom we shall henceforth call by his canonical title of T'ai-tsung—was not a man to let himself be intimidated.[1] The Turkish leader, Hsieh-li Kaghan, insolently sent one of his men to demand tribute, and threatened that if it were not paid a million nomads would lay waste the capital. T'ai-tsung replied by threatening to cut off the ambassador's head. He was taking a grave risk, for it seems that he had very few troops in Ch'ang-an at the time. In order to deceive the enemy, he ordered his troops to march out through various gates and deploy themselves beneath the walls, while he in his usual manner went off with a handful of horsemen to reconnoitre the enemy army. Despite the protests of his companions, he rode along the river Wei opposite the Turkish squadrons, at the mercy of their arrows. He had a better knowledge of the psychology of the nomads than had his followers. "The Turks know me," his biographer credits him with saying. "They have learned to fear me. The mere sight of me is enough to strike terror into their souls; and on seeing my troops march out they will believe them to be far more numerous than they really are." And he continued to ride towards the enemy "with the same confidence as if he had been going to visit his own camp". On seeing him, "the Turks, impressed by his grand and fearless bearing, got down from their horses and saluted him in the manner of their country". At the same moment the Chinese troops took up their positions on the plain behind him so that their armour and their standards glittered in the sunshine. T'ai-tsung continued towards the Turkish camp, then, reining in his horse, he made a sign to the Chinese army to draw back and remain in battle order.

The emperor, raising his voice, called on the two Turkish leaders, Hsieh-li Kaghan and Tu-li, and offered to fight in single combat, as was customary among the warriors of the steppes: "Li Shih-min has not forgotten the use of arms since he became emperor!" And in

[1] Concerning titles of emperors, see note, page 62.

the name of military honour, speaking in their own language and appealing to their warrior spirit, he vehemently reproached them with having broken the truce and betrayed their oath. Defied to their faces, subdued by this impressive show of courage, and surprised by the deployment of the Chinese army, the Turkish khans asked for peace. Next day peace was concluded on the bridge across the Wei, after the traditional sacrifice of a white horse. This time the Turks had learned their lesson. They never came back.

His councillors advised T'ai-tsung to reinforce the Great Wall so as to prevent the recurrence of similar alarms. He smiled and replied: "What need have we to fortify frontiers?" And in fact the authority of the Orkhon Turks was being undermined by internal dissensions and revolts purposely fostered by the emperor. After a rash provocation by Hsieh-li Kaghan, T'ai-tsung threw the entire Chinese army against him. The imperial forces came upon the kaghan near Kuei-hua (Kueisui) in Inner Mongolia, surprised his camp and dispersed his hordes. They then drove him into Outer Mongolia, towards the Orkhon and the Kerulen, where he was forced to take refuge with a tribe who handed him over to the Chinese. After this the khanate of the Eastern Turks remained subject to China for over fifty years (630–682).

The *T'ang History* complacently describes the imposing spectacle of the Turkish chieftains prostrate at the feet of T'ai-tsung. At a public audience the emperor liked to see them all together, both the khans recently conquered and those who had come over long ago. "As soon as they had arrived in the audience chamber, they performed the respectful ceremonial of knocking their foreheads on the ground, three times at each of three prostrations". The chieftains of the loyalist hordes took precedence over Hsieh-li Kaghan, who was treated as a prisoner of war. However, after humiliating him, the emperor shrewdly granted him a pardon and assigned him a palace at the court, where he was kept in a state of semi-captivity.

The entire khanate of the Eastern Turks that is to say the area of present-day Mongolia, was joined to the T'ang empire (630).

A Turkish inscription at Kocho Tsaidam reads as follows: "The sons of the Turkish nobility became slaves of the Chinese people and their virgin daughters became bondmaids. The Turkish nobles abandoned their Turkish titles and received Chinese ones in their place. They submitted to the Chinese kaghan, and for fifty years worked and strove on his behalf. For him they undertook expeditions towards the rising sun, and to the west as far as the Iron Gates (in Turkestan). But to the Chinese kaghan they surrendered their empire and their institutions."

With the help of these auxiliaries, during the next twenty years T'ai-tsung brought the Turks of Turkestan and the oases of the Gobi within his sphere. With his advent an unexpected and epic China was revealed to the astonished peoples of Asia. Far from coming to terms with the barbarians and buying them off with gold, T'ai-tsung made them tremble at the sound of his name. This spirit is well expressed in the realistic art of the period, in the forceful animal and military themes of the reliefs, statues and terra-cotta funeral figures, with their almost excessive vigour (for instance the athletic *lokapala* of Lung-men) and their taste for accentuation that frequently attained the violence of caricature. Even the T'ang ceramics, with their rather violent colouring of orange-yellow and bright green, reveal the taste of this epoch.

If T'ai-tsung ever compared his achievement with that of the great conquerors of the past, he must have evoked the name of that most famous emperor of Chinese antiquity, Han Wu-ti. The Han empire which existed before the barbarian invasions of the fourth century was, in effect, restored, and the exploits of the T'ang cavalry even surpassed those of the Han. Even Pan Ch'ao, the conqueror of ancient Kashgar, did not carry off as many herds of cattle, break up as many barbarian hordes or cut off as many thousand heads as did the T'ang generals. For during the three intervening centuries, when China had been the victim of barbarian invasions, she had absorbed the blood of the victorious hordes, and now, nourished and strengthened by it, she was able to turn against the men of the steppes the strength she had drawn from them, and to add to it the immense superiority of a civilization more than a thousand years old.

Look at the funeral statuettes, those images of horsemen and foot-soldiers with battered faces of a half-Tartar appearance, their features hardened almost into a grimace; they wear either the caps of Turkish auxiliaries or the helmets of T'ang legionaries. There they are, roughly encased in their hardened leather armour, the breast- and back-plates reinforced with metal, the skirts of leather or of metal scales, and they carry large round or rectangular shields decorated with monstrous faces—men ready to cross the Gobi or to climb the Khangai. Even in objects of Buddhist workmanship, such as the temple guardians (*lokapala*) or the guardian-genius Vajrapani, we come across this same crustacean armour and a similar formidable and surly appearance. The horses of this terra-cotta cavalry still neigh and snort and paw the ground as they impatiently await the beginning of a raid against Kashgar or Kucha! The Western Turks, who made the Sassanid Empire tremble and later caused anxiety to the young Arab power, were to bow before the T'ang cavalry which was so similar to their own. Before long they were to see it sweeping down on their camps, burning their carts and scattering their felt tents, as far west as the gorges of Tarbagatai—and to find it still pursuing them across the flat Kirghiz Steppe.

Once he had defeated the Eastern Turks in Mongolia, T'ai-tsung had his hands free to deal with the Western Turks in Turkestan. The latter were united under a powerful sovereign whose rule extended from the Altai Mountains to the Aral Sea. In summer he lived in the T'ien Shan, and in winter near the "hot lake", the Issyk Kul. He is fairly well known because of a description by the Buddhist pilgrim Hsüan Tsang. It was at the beginning of the year 630, near Tokmak, to the west of the Issyk Kul (in the present-day Kirghiz Republic), that the pilgrim met the khan with his immense cavalry forces, then moving towards the west. "All of them were mounted on horses or camels. They wore furs and woollen garments, and carried long lances, bows, and banners. Their masses stretched over so great a distance that it was impossible to see the end of them." The emperor T'ai-tsung, who believed it wise "to ally oneself with those who are far off against those who are near at hand", had spared these western hordes as long as he had those of Mongolia to deal with. But in 630, the year which had brought the subjugation of Mongolia, chance—perhaps not entirely unsolicited—played into his hands. The khan of Turkestan whose power had so greatly impressed the pilgrim was murdered under somewhat mysterious circumstances, and his kingdom broke up into several hostile groups of tribes. Thus the khanate of the Western Turks did not long outlast that of the Turks of Mongolia. In 642 a Chinese expeditionary force operating near Urumchi wiped out one by one such tribes as offered resistance. The remainder accepted Chinese hegemony.

Having annihilated the Turks, the emperor T'ai-tsung was able to re-establish the Chinese protectorate over the Tarim Basin.

In order to understand the important part played during the early Middle Ages by these now wretched oases of the Tarim Basin, we must recapitulate what has been said earlier with regard to the Han period. From the ethnological point of view, at least some of these oases—Turfan, Karashar, and Kucha—were inhabited by people speaking Indo-European dialects closely related not only to the Aryan languages of Asia (Iranian and Sanskrit), but also to the European languages (Slav, Latin, Celtic etc.), to say nothing of the "Eastern Iranian" language spoken in the region of Kashgar. From a cultural point of view, from the third to the eighth century present-day "Chinese Turkestan" (Sinkiang) was, as a result of Buddhist evangelization, virtually a province of Outer India, where Sanskrit and Prakrit literature and philosophy were held in as much honour as they were on the banks of the Ganges. From the artistic point of view, this land was a posthumous conquest of Alexander the Great—again as a result of Buddhism, which had acquired an Alexandrian iconography. While Greece may be said to have died at Byzantium, yet its artistic influence, thenceforth inseparably linked to Buddhist dogma, continued until well into the seventh century to make itself felt posthumously from Kashgar east to Turfan and Lob Nor—and it may perhaps be that we can trace this influence in the free classicism of some Chinese mirrors of the T'ang period.[1] So the light of a dead star may continue for many centuries to reach us across the bounds of time and space. Today nothing remains of the brilliant commercial, religious, and artistic activity of the Tarim Basin. The advance of the desert has killed the soil, and Islam has smothered the ancient centres of Buddhist culture. One finds there—and realizes the mortality of civilizations—the ruined walls of a whole social edifice which collapsed; but without which, not so long ago, the thoroughfare between the worlds of India and Europe and the world of China would have been impossible.

There is an animated contemporary description of the oases of the Tarim Basin, written by the Chinese pilgrim Hsüan Tsang in the account of his travels to India (he made the westward journey in 629 and 630, and returned in 644). To this period belong also most of the archaeological discoveries made between 1902 and 1914.

The art of the Tarim Basin at that time derived directly from the Buddhist workshops of Afghanistan, with their double current of Greco-Indian and Irano-Buddhist influences. The discovery of the modelled wall sculptures of Fondukistan, between Kabul and Bamian, has thrown light on these influences. The sculptures are dated by coins of the Sassanid king Khosroes II (590–628) found on the same site, and they show the Buddhist art of Afghanistan still reproducing Hellenistic models for the images of Buddhist divinities, but together with these using purely Hindu types for the images of women, and Sassanid Persian types for those of men. This same association of types is found in the frescoes of the Buddhist grottoes of Kyzyl, near Kucha in the northern part of the Tarim Basin, frescoes which Hackin regards as belonging to two periods, the

[1] Many Chinese mirrors of the T'ang period simply carry on the indigenous tradition of the Six Dynasties; some, however, ornamented with their dance of horses, stags, and lions chasing each other among scroll patterns and clusters of grapes, seem reminiscent of Greco-Roman or, occasionally, Iranian workmanship.

earliest dating from between 450 and 650, and the others from between 650 and 750. Together they show that while the spiritual civilization of an oasis such as Kucha was, thanks to Buddhism, purely Indian, its material civilization indicated considerable Sassanid Persian influence. Indeed the pictures of lay nobility, and here the princesses as well, betray a direct imitation of Persian models. Nothing could show more clearly the important part played by these oases of the caravan routes, not only as stages in the pilgrimage from China to India, but also as commercial halts between China and Persia. What we have said of the frescoes of Kyzyl is equally true of the sculptures of Shorchuk, near Karashar, the frescoes and sculptures of the Turfan oases, and—in the south of the Tarim Basin—the paintings of Dandinalik, near Khotan.

T'ang China, aspiring to dominate Upper Asia, could not fail to interest itself in the oases of the Tarim Basin, the protectorate over which was indispensable for controlling the caravan routes to India and Persia. The emperor T'ai-tsung hoped to draw them into his orbit by peaceful means. Turfan, the nearest of the western oases, was most directly influenced by Chinese culture, as is shown by the Buddhist frescoes of the region, in which T'ang style is intermingled with copies of Indian and Iranian work; moreover, the reigning dynasty was of Chinese extraction. In 629 the Chinese Buddhist Hsüan Tsang, passing through Turfan on his pilgrimage to India, received an enthusiastic welcome from the local king (so enthusiastic in fact that he had the greatest difficulty in tearing himself away from this hospitality in order to resume his journey). In the following year this king came to tender his homage to the emperor T'ai-tsung. But in 640 he was foolish enough to ally himself with Turkish rebels to cut the caravan routes between China, India, and Persia. He relied on the distances across the sands of the Gobi to protect him, but a corps of Chinese cavalry crossed the Gobi and arrived unexpectedly at Turfan. When he heard this news, the king died of shock. The Chinese army besieged the town and soon a shower of stones was falling on the oasis. The new king, a very young man, came out to the imperial camp. "His apologies did not amount to abject humility, and one of the Chinese generals got up and said: 'Our first duty is to capture the town! What is the use of arguing with this child? Let the signal for the assault be given!' The young king, drenched in sweat, prostrated himself on the ground and surrendered unconditionally. The Chinese generals took him prisoner and later presented him to T'ai-tsung in the great ceremonial hall. The rite of the libation for the return of the warriors was celebrated, and for three days wine was distributed." The king of Turfan's jewelled sword was given by the emperor to the Turkish *condottiere* A-shih-na She-erh.

The people of Karashar—the next important oasis on the road to the west—had helped the Chinese to defeat the men of Turfan, with whom they were at enmity. As soon as Turfan had been annexed, they took fright and allied themselves to the dissident Turks. T'ai-tsung sent a fresh army across the Gobi under the command of a highly resourceful warrior called Kuo Hsiao-k'e. "The site of Karashar had a circumference of seventeen kilometres. It was protected on all four sides by the T'ien Shan and Lake Bagrach; the inhabitants were convinced that it could not be taken by surprise. But Kuo Hsiao-k'e, advancing by forced marches, crossed the river and arrived by night at the foot of the ramparts. He waited till dawn before storming the city amid the cries of the multitude. The drums and horns sounded with a great noise, and the soldiers of T'ang were given free rein. The inhabitants were panic-stricken. A thousand heads fell." T'ai-tsung directed all the operations from his capital. "One day the emperor said to the ministers by his side: 'Kuo Hsiao-k'e left Turfan for Karashar on the eleventh day of the eighth month, he should have arrived there during the second ten days of that month and destroyed the kingdom on the twenty-second day; his envoys ought soon to be arriving'. At this moment a courier entered to bring news of the victory" (644).

The most prosperous of the cities of the Tarim Basin was Kucha, whose Buddhist frescoes show that it enjoyed a high level of civilization and refinement. The king of Kucha was called Swarnatep, which in the local Indo-European language meant "God of Gold". In 630 he gave the Chinese pilgrim Hsüan Tsang a warm welcome, and recognized the suzerainty of the T'ang dynasty, but in 644 he turned round and allied himself with Karashar against the empire. He died shortly afterwards, and was succeeded by his younger brother, who was called by the Buddhist Sanskrit name of Haripushpa or "Divine Flower" (646). The new king, sensing the approaching storm, hastened to send an envoy to the imperial court with his protestations of devotion. But it was too late. A-shih-na She-erh, the Turkish *condottiere* in the service of the Chinese, had already left for the west with an army of Chinese regulars and Tartar mercenaries.

The inhabitants of Kucha were expecting an attack from the southeast, from out of the Gobi. It came instead from the northwest, A-shih-na She-erh having followed the track which leads from Urumchi by the headwaters of the Yuldus and over the high passes of the T'ien Shan. Instead of their allies from Karashar, the terrified people of Kucha saw the Chinese squadrons deploying in the stony desert which stretches to the north of the town. When King Haripushpa came out of the city to face the enemy, the Chinese, employing a tactic of the old wars in Mongolia, pretended to give in, lured the brilliant knights of Kucha into the desert, and there destroyed them. It was the Cressy and the Agincourt of the fine lords pictured in the Buddhist frescoes of Kyzyl. A-shih-na She-erh entered Kucha in triumph; then, as the king with the remains of his army had taken refuge in the fortified town of Yaka-arik, he followed him thither and captured the place after a siege of forty days. At Kucha, A-shih-na She-erh cut off eleven thousand heads. "The Western Regions were stricken with terror."

The fall of Kucha was a death blow to the independence of the cities of the Gobi; it marked the end of a charming and cultivated world which had survived from other times. The brilliant civilization recalled by the frescoes of Kyzyl never completely recovered from this catastrophe. Researches carried out at Kyzyl by J. Hackin show that at this date (648–650) there was a break between two styles of painting, the second of which used stronger colours to compensate for a diminution in relief. In this style a fresh wave of Sassanid Persian influence is also perceptible, but this is in fact the work of Persian refugees who, after the Arabs had conquered their country in 652, escaped and took refuge in the new Chinese protectorate.

After gaining control over the northern oases of the Tarim Basin, the Chinese turned their attention to the southern group. The king of Khotan had accepted the suzerainty of the emperor T'ai-tsung in 632, and in 635 he sent his son to serve in the imperial guard. However, these proofs of goodwill do not seem to have satisfied the Chinese, and after they had conquered Kucha in 648, they felt that the time had come to enforce a stricter control over the southern oases. "After this blow the Western Regions are stricken with terror," they said. "Now is the time to take the light cavalry and go and slip a halter on the king of Khotan!" This was no sooner said than done. The Chinese squadrons arrived unexpectedly at the oasis of Khotan, and the king trembled. The Chinese commander "explained to him the prestige and supernatural power of T'ang, and exhorted him to come and present himself to the Son of Heaven". The king followed his advice; moreover he lost nothing by it, for after a sojourn of several months at the court of Ch'ang-an, he was allowed to return home with a ceremonial robe and five thousand rolls of silk.

In Tibet, which until then had remained barbarous, an energetic chieftain was forming a kingdom in the Lhasa region. After having waged war against China, he finally entered the T'ang orbit, and in 641 the emperor T'ai-tsung bestowed on him the hand of a Chinese princess. So it was that civilization began to infiltrate among these savage mountaineers. T'ai-tsung even sent an ambassador to India, to the court of the North Indian emperor Harcha (643). But China's best ambassador to that country was the famous pilgrim Hsüan Tsang, who left Ch'ang-an in 629, and did not return until 644, after having travelled all over Central Asia and India. We have already referred to his outward journey by way of Turfan, Karashar, Kucha, the T'ien Shan, the Issyk Kul, Tokmak, Samarkand, Balkh, and the Kabul Valley, and his return journey by way of the Pamirs, Kashgar, Yarkand, Khotan, Lob Nor, and Tun-huang. In fact he followed the two routes of the ancient Silk Road. The peace imposed by the T'ang dynasty reopened the transcontinental routes from China to India and Persia which had been blocked at one point or another ever since the fall of the Han dynasty. On occasion the might of T'ai-tsung even followed in the steps of the pilgrims. In 647 a Chinese embassy was attacked on its way to India, and the ambassador, Wang Hsüan-ts'e, went to seek reinforcements from Tibetan and Nepalese chieftains who were vassals of the empire. With their contingents, he returned to India and took vengeance on his aggressors, whom he led back in chains to Ch'ang-an.

As a result of her conquests, China exercised direct rule as far as the Pamirs. One can understand T'ai-tsung's legitimate pride. "In olden times the only rulers who subdued the barbarians," his biographer credits him with saying, "were Ch'in Shih-huang-ti and Han Wu-ti. But taking my three-foot sword in my hand, I have subjugated the two hundred kingdoms and made quiet all within the four seas, while the far-off barbarians have come one after another to make their submission!"

This extension of Chinese power towards India and Persia had its effects in the spiritual sphere.

Since the fall of the T'o-pa Wei dynasty, which towards the end had zealously promoted Buddhism, that religion had undergone numerous attacks. In 574 one of the short-lived dynasties in the north of China had issued an edict which proscribed both the "foreign religion" and Taoism, but after six years this persecution came to an end. The two Sui emperors started out as orthodox Confucianists—for like every other new dynasty they required the support of the mandarinate to establish their legitimacy—but as time went on they showed a greater sympathy for Buddhism. As for the rough soldier who became T'ang T'ai-tsung, at the time of his accession he felt nothing but suspicion towards this Indian religion of surrender and renunciation. "The emperor Liang Wu-ti," he remarked, "preached Buddhism to his officers with such success that they were incapable of riding on horseback to defend him against the rebels." He regarded Taoist "non-action" in an equally unfavourable light. "The emperor Yüan-ti used to explain the texts of Lao-Tzu to his followers; he would have been better occupied in marching against the barbarians who were invading the empire." T'ai-tsung's private adviser in these matters was an elderly Confucian scholar who naturally abhorred Buddhism. He submitted a memorial which has remained famous to this day, and which lists all the complaints of state Confucianism against the monks of Sakyamuni. The following extract throws light on the battle of ideas which was being fought out in China.

"Buddhism", this pamphlet says in substance, "first reached us by way of the Tarim Basin, in a foreign form which could not be highly injurious. But since the time of Han the Indian scriptures have been translated into Chinese. Their diffusion undermines filial piety and loyalty to the imperial house. Young men take to a monastic life so as to escape their public duties. They shave their heads, live on alms and refuse to make due obeisance to their prince and to their parents." Moreover, "the doctrine of Buddha is full of absurdity and extravagance. His disciples pass their life in idleness and never take the trouble to do anything. If they wear clothes which are different from our own, it is in order to influence the public authorities and to free themselves from all care. By their fanciful ideas they persuade simple people to chase after illusory happiness, and inspire them with contempt for our laws and the wise institutions of our forefathers." And further on: "This sect numbers more than one hundred thousand monks and the same number of nuns, all vowed to celibacy. It would be in the state's interest to marry them off to each other. They would form a hundred thousand families and provide soldiers for the future." Down to modern times one finds repeated accusations against the anti-social and anti-national character of Buddhist monasticism. This anti-clericalism had become a tradition among the Confucian literati, that is to say among almost the entire mandarinate.

Since his accession in 626, the emperor T'ai-tsung, who shared this point of view, had greatly reduced the number of monks and monasteries. But the establishment of Chinese domination over a land so deeply imbued with Buddhism as the Tarim Basin, and the consequent political relations with India herself, were in the long run to modify the emperor's attitude. This is shown by the story of Hsüan Tsang. When in 629 the celebrated Buddhist scholar sought permission to leave on a pilgrimage to the holy land of the Ganges, the authorities refused to give him the necessary passports. He was obliged to cross the frontier in secret, avoiding the frontier post of Tun-huang and setting out without a guide into the middle of the Gobi, where he nearly lost his life on the first stages of his journey. The combination of Chinese prestige and the Buddhist piety of the local rulers protected him while crossing the Tarim Basin, and he was able to reach India through Turkestan and Afghanistan. In India he was given the warmest welcome, not only by his co-religionists, but even by Hindu princes, curious to see this traveller who had come all the way from China to study Sanskrit philosophy in their country.

Hsüan Tsang was not only a devout Buddhist inspired by a desire to behold the holy places connected with the birth, preaching and death of the Buddha. He was also a most remarkable philosopher who made a thorough study of the various metaphysical systems of Brahminism and Buddhism. The system which he finally evolved, and which he expounded in a synthesis of singular penetration, is one of absolute idealism, a little after the manner of Berkeley and Fichte. He allows the negation of both the personal self and the external world, or rather their common reduction to what he calls the "nothing-but-thought" or, if one prefers, the "plane of ideals". It is a subtly shaded philosophy which oscillates between subjectivism and monism; but it cannot properly be defined as either of these intellectual attitudes, since unlike monism it denies all notion of substance, while unlike Western subjectivism it denies the self, or at least the substantial self.

In reality it was far more than such systems that translators like Hsüan Tsang revealed to China. It was a whole treasury of concepts, points of view, metaphysical constructions and intellectual analyses. It was indeed the entire heritage of Indian thought which was thus made accessible to the subjects of the T'ang dynasty. Despite the opposition of the Confucian intellectuals, there took place an invasion of dynamic ideas which it was impossible to resist. A proof of this is that the orthodox Neo-Confucianism of the Sung period, elaborated by Chu Hsi, was unconsciously permeated with these ideas. There was a "mental transfusion" which can only be compared with the sudden invasion of Western ideas in the twentieth century. Hsüan Tsang's most remarkable achievement was perhaps not so much the crossing of the Gobi, the T'ien Shan, the Pamirs and the Hindu Kush, as the exploration of this unknown world of Indian thought, this luxuriant and apparently impassable forest through which he traced safe and unerring paths. It was a prodigious labour, in which, doubtless following many precursors but surpassing them all, he succeeded in translating the most complex, delicate and subtle Indian metaphysical concepts and in fashioning a Chinese vocabulary adequate for the purpose—almost a new language—with that imperfect tool, the Chinese written character. Only those Catholic missionaries who have had to translate Thomist philosophy into Chinese characters can appreciate such an achievement.

In addition to being a pious pilgrim and the translator of metaphysical works of astonishing power, Hsüan Tsang was also one of the most clear-sighted of explorers and one of the most accurate of geographers. The account of his journey is a survey, country by country, mile by mile, of the physical, political and economic geography of Central Asia and India during the first half of the seventh century. He lists the agricultural and commercial activities of all the regions that he passed through, from the Chinese frontier to the approaches of Persia, and from Afghanistan to Assam. He also enumerates the languages (including a summary of Sanskrit grammar), the institutions and customs (with a rapid sketch of the caste system), the superstitions, religions, and philosophies of all the different peoples that he encountered on his journey. Finally, he gives an extremely precise account of the various political powers, with the characters of the different rulers.

These last observations must have been particularly valuable for the *Weltpolitik* of the emperor T'ai-tsung. In 629 he had wished to prevent the pilgrim's departure, but when the latter returned to China in 644 the emperor accorded him the most flattering and friendly welcome. He questioned the traveller at length about the various Indian kingdoms, and was so well satisfied by his replies that he wished to entrust him with the duties of a minister. Hsüan Tsang, fully occupied with his works on religion and philosophy, declined the offer. However, he took up residence at Ch'ang-an, at the Great Benevolence monastery, which was still in process of completion and whence T'ai-tsung, who had taken a liking to him, often had him summoned to the palace. The consecration of this monastery was celebrated by a solemn procession witnessed by the emperor, who out of friendship for Hsüan Tsang had consented to make an appearance. Hsüan Tsang's biography describes this magnificent procession which accompanied the banners and Buddhist statues brought back from India. Recent archaeological discoveries confirm the Indian origin of some of the Chinese Buddhist sculpture of this period. In the grottos of T'ien-lung-shan, in northern Shansi, have been discovered statues of bodhisattvas, apparently contemporary and certainly of the T'ang dynasty, which are a direct imitation of Indian Gupta art. They have a softness of modelling, a rounded charm and a blending of forms which seem arrestingly un-Chinese, and which represent the whole Indian sense of beauty with its inherent tropical sensuousness. There was, moreover, a general rehabilitation of plastic form during the Sui and early T'ang periods. Buddhist sculpture, forsaking the aridity of "Chinese Romanesque", gradually restored an emphasis on modelling. There is no doubt that this change was partially due to the example of the Indian models brought back by pilgrims such as Hsüan Tsang.

The extension of the T'ang Empire as far as the borders of India and Persia not only brought about a closer contact with Buddhist India, but also made it possible for Christian missionaries to travel from Persia and Transoxiana, and led to the establishment of Nestorian Christianity in the heart of the empire. In 635 a Nestorian priest known as A-lo-pen—a Chinese transcription of the Syriac religious title of Rabban—arrived in Ch'ang-an. In 638 this missionary erected a church in the capital, an event recorded in the Syriac and Chinese inscription of 781 which also tells of the emperor T'ai-tsung's benevolent attitude towards Christianity.[1]

In his fifty-third year, and after twenty-three years of one of the most glorious reigns in Chinese history, T'ai-tsung died in his palace at Ch'ang-an on the 10th of July, 649. He was buried nearby at Li-ch'üan. He had had carved around his tomb the statues of kings he had conquered and images of the war horses that he rode during his campaigns. His veterans were so devoted to him that one of them, the old Turkish captain A-shih-na She-erh, wanted to kill himself over the mortal remains of his master in the ancient fashion, "so as to be able to keep guard over the tomb of the Emperor".

[1] Chinese expansion into Central Asia also had its repercussions on the economic life of China. For example it was during the T'ang period that the Chinese, in imitation of the Indians, first learned how to make sugar from sugar-cane (an event whose importance can be judged from the present sugar-cane plantations of Szechwan and the Cantonese region). They also learned how to make wine from grapes. During the period of the first Han emperors China first entered into direct relations with the oases of Kashgar, Turfan, Karashar, and Kucha, and with Ferghana, all of them places famous for their grapes. According to tradition, the grape was first introduced into China about 125 B.C. But it was not until the T'ang dynasty, in the seventh century, that the Chinese, doubtless following the example of the wine-growers of Turfan, first took to making wine from grapes in addition to the brews of rice, millet and other grains known to them since time immemorial. The use of tea, a plant which grows in the south, had been known in North China since Chou times, but under the Han it was still a luxury drink, reserved for the upper and middle classes. It was not until the T'ang dynasty, in the middle of the eighth century, that it became a national drink, available to all classes.

CHAPTER XVIII

DRAMAS AT THE T'ANG COURT

THE emperor Kao-tsung, son of the great T'ai-tsung, was only twenty-two when he succeeded to the throne. His reign lasted for thirty-three years (650–683). He was diligent and naturally benevolent, of a well-meaning though regrettably weak character. He paid observance to all the different religious cults, at one time ascending the sacred mountain of T'ai-shan to offer sacrifices to the Sovereign Lord of August Heaven, and on other occasions accompanying pilgrimages both to the tomb of Confucius and to the most ancient Taoist temples. According to the Sino-Syriac stele of Ch'ang-an, he also patronized Nestorian Christianity. During his reign, or at least during the earlier part of it, Chinese expansion continued, thanks to his father's veteran officers. In the conquest of Korea Kao-tsung succeeded where both the great T'ai-tsung and his predecessor the Sui emperor Yang-ti had failed. Between 660 and 665 his generals conquered Paikche, one of the three Korean kingdoms, situated on the southwest coast of the peninsula. In 668 they seized Kokuli (Korea), the most important of the three kingdoms, which lay to the northwest of Seoul. Since the third Korean kingdom of Silla, which was on the east coast, had spontaneously recognized Chinese suzerainty, the whole peninsula thus passed into the Chinese orbit. In Turkestan, the imperial army had to put down a revolt of the Western Turks northeast of the Issyk Kul. At the approach of winter the Chinese general Su Ting-fang marched against the rebels. "Winter was coming on, the ground was covered with snow. The Turks never imagined that the Chinese would start a campaign in such desolate lonely country at such a season." Su Ting-fang surprised the nomads on the River Boratala, a tributary of the Ebi Nor. He defeated them a second time on the River Chu, to the west of the Issyk Kul, and finally forced their khan to take refuge in Tashkent, where he was betrayed to the Chinese (657). The Western Turks had to accept as their khans men who were nominees of the empire.

It seemed that the emperor Kao-tsung had succeeded in completing his father's lifework when suddenly the situation was reversed. Beginning in 665, the Western Turks came out in open rebellion. In 670 the Tibetans, who were still almost savages, overran the Tarim Basin and captured Kucha, Karashar, Kashgar, and Khotan—the "Four Garrisons" of the Chinese. Still more serious, the khanate of the Eastern Turks in Mongolia, which had its centre on the Upper Orkhon and which had been destroyed by the emperor T'ai-tsung in 630, was now reconstituted under a descendant of the former ruling clan, the kaghan Kutlugh. The empire again fell on evil days. For thirty-nine years (682–721) the Mongolian Turks, "who were like wolves", came from beyond the Great Wall to lay waste the lands of the Chinese, who were "like sheep".

Meanwhile at the capital Kao-tsung's reign came to a disastrous end through the empress Wu Tse-t'ien.

Wu Tse-t'ien was a former favourite of the emperor T'ai-tsung. She entered the imperial harem in 637, at the age of fourteen, and was outstanding for her wit and beauty. When the future Kao-tsung was still Crown prince, he had seen her among his father's flock of wives, and from that day had nursed a silent love for her. On T'ai-tsung's death his wives and concubines had to cut off their hair and enter a convent. As soon as the official period of mourning came to an end, the new Son of Heaven gave orders for the young woman to be brought out of retirement, and gave her back her position at court. But a secondary role was not enough for this ambitious concubine. According to her enemy the poet Lo Pin-wang, "her eyebrows, arched like the antennae of a butterfly, would never consent to yield to other women. Hiding her face with her sleeve, she applied herself to slander. Her vixen charms had the power of bewitching her master." She was prepared to commit any crime, however monstrous, in order to attain her ends. With her own hands she strangled the child she had borne to the emperor and caused the legitimate empress to be accused of the heinous crime.

The account of this drama in the T'ang annals is reminiscent of Tacitus, with an additional *mise en scène* of hypocritical politeness. After the birth of the child, a girl, the empress came to pay a visit to Wu Tse-t'ien. She caressed the infant, took it in her arms and congratulated the young mother. As soon as she had left, Wu Tse-t'ien suffocated the newborn child and replaced it in its cradle. The arrival of the emperor was announced. Wu Tse-t'ien received him, her face glowing with pleasure, and uncovered the cradle to show him his daughter. A horrid sight met his eyes; in the cradle lay the dead body of his child. Bursting into tears, Wu Tse-t'ien was careful not to bring any direct accusation against the woman whose ruin she was determined to bring about. Finally, when questioned, she contented herself with incriminating her attendants. As was to be expected, the latter, so as to divert suspicion from themselves, described the visit which the empress had made a few minutes earlier. The scene had been so cleverly contrived that Kao-tsung was convinced of the empress's guilt. She was degraded and Wu Tse-t'ien promoted to her place (655). Despite the opposition of his father's old comrades, the emperor fell completely under the control of his new consort. Like Agrippina in ancient Rome, she attended the deliberations of the council hidden behind a curtain. Since Kao-tsung continued to pay secret visits to the former empress, Wu Tse-t'ien gave orders for the unhappy woman to have her hands and feet cut off.

From 660 onwards it was Wu Tse-t'ien who directed the affairs of state in the name of the weak Kao-tsung. Through a system of informers which she had established, she was able with impunity to terrorize the court, giving full rein to her jealousy and vindictiveness, and to annihilate her enemies even when they happened to be members of the T'ang imperial family. After bringing about the destruction of the mandarins who opposed her, she forced their widows and daughters to become her slaves. The emperor, weak and helpless, realized the innocence of her victims but did not dare to take any action. It is said that remorse affected his health, but it is possible that his enfeeblement was assisted by the ministrations of his wife. The annalists relate that during the latter days of his life, "his head swelled up and he became like a blind man. His doctor offered to tap the swollen part, but Wu Tse-t'ien cried out that to lay hands on the imperial face was a crime of *lèse-majesté* which was punishable by death. The doctor held to his opinion and punctured the swelling, whereupon the emperor's eyesight was greatly improved. . . . The empress, pretending that she was delighted, went to fetch a hundred pieces of silk, which she personally gave to the doctor. A month later, however, it was learned that the emperor had suddenly fallen ill and that he had died without witnesses" (December 27, 683). Acting in the name of her son, Wu Tse-t'ien remained absolute mistress of the empire for twenty-two years (683–705).

Despite her unscrupulous behaviour, Wu Tse-t'ien was a woman of superior ability, and more skilled than her unhappy husband in the management of affairs of state. The administrative machinery of the T'ang empire continued to function under her energetic guidance, despite the tragedies that were taking place in the seraglio; and the veteran soldiers almost everywhere held back the barbarians. It was under her government that in the Tarim Basin the Chinese recovered the "Four Garrisons" of Kucha, Karashar, Kashgar, and Khotan (692). She was less successful in her relations with the Turks of Mongolia, and hardly a year passed without their making sudden raids and pillaging the frontier districts of Kansu, Shensi, Shansi, and Hopei. "In those times", says the Turkish inscription of Kocho Tsaidam, "we had so many victorious expeditions that our slaves became slave-owners themselves."

In internal affairs Wu Tse-t'ien overcame all obstacles. Everyone gave way before the will of this indomitable woman. So great was her audacity that in 684 she went to the length of deposing her own son, the young emperor Chung-tsung, and had herself proclaimed "emperor" in his place (690). The princes of the blood, ashamed of being ruled over by a former concubine and spurred into action by an appeal from the poet Lo Pin-wang, made an abortive attempt at revolt. Their revolt was put down and their severed heads were brought to the empress. Meanwhile Wu Tse-t'ien realized the necessity of conciliating the Turks of Mongolia so as to put an end to their raids and at the same time gain their support against her enemies. She sent an embassy to their kaghan Bekchor (Mo-chüeh) to ask for the hand of his daughter in marriage to her nephew. The Turk refused this offer with disdain. He did not intend to marry his daughter to the nephew of a usurper, but to the legitimate emperor whom the latter had set aside. Setting himself up as an arbiter between the factions at the imperial court, he declared himself the champion of legitimacy and threatened that, if the T'ang dynasty were not restored, he would come at the head of his hordes and effect the restoration himself. Wu Tse-t'ien was alarmed, and formally recognized the rights of Chung-tsung, although in reality she continued as sole ruler herself.

Assured of her power, she satisfied her every whim. Although well on in years, she took a young monk as her favourite and arranged for him to be appointed abbot of one of the principal monasteries of Loyang, "with leave to enter the palace at any hour of the day or night". Moreover, quite apart from the personal attractions of her young chaplain, the old dowager was deeply interested in Buddhism. In the character of this extraordinary woman a strong feeling for religion was neighbour to all the impulses of cruelty and lechery, and she had phases of manifesting the deepest devotion. Thus between 672 and 675 she ordered and superintended the sculpture of the famous rock Buddha of Lung-men with his entourage of bodhisattvas, monks and guardian kings. Such works, in which the idealism and mysticism of former times was replaced by a startling realistic violence, doubtless throw some light on the type of Buddhism which was likely to appeal to Wu Tse-t'ien. They also bear witness to the special protection which the sovereign accorded to this faith. A noted recipient of this protection was the pilgrim Yi Ching, a monk from Hopei, who in 671 embarked for India by way of Sumatra. In 695, after twenty-four years in the sanctuaries of India and Outer India, he returned by the sea route, bringing back a large number of Sanskrit texts. On his arrival at Loyang, Wu Tse-t'ien went to meet him with an immense retinue; she accorded him every facility for the work of translation to which he dedicated the rest of his life.

Meanwhile Wu Tse-t'ien's reign was drawing to its close. Hostile public opinion and the threat of Turkish intervention had decided her to effect at least a nominal restoration of the emperor Chung-tsung. In reality she continued to govern alone, aided by her new favourites, the brothers Chang. But a plot was being hatched against her. One night, in the year 705, the conspirators took up arms and invaded the palace. They met the timorous Chung-tsung, the powerless sovereign, acclaimed him emperor and dragged him by force into the apartments of Wu Tse-t'ien. The aged empress, awakened from sleep, alone and defenceless, her favourites slaughtered at her feet, was still capable of resistance. She made one final attempt to intimidate Chung-tsung, and would perhaps have attained her end if the conspirators had given her time, but they held a dagger to her throat and forced her to abdicate (February 22, 705). She died of chagrin some months later, at the age of eighty-two.

The emperor Chung-tsung, once again placed at the head of the state, showed himself the same good and weak man as before. His favourite relaxation was to go and converse with the Buddhist monk Yi-Ching while the latter was working at his Chinese translation of the Sanskrit scriptures which he had brought back from India. Chung-tsung must have remembered, moreover, how when he had been persecuted by his terrible mother he had long prayed to the Bodhisattva, the good physician of both body and soul, and how his prayers had been answered. After his restoration to the throne in 705 he had no wish to show himself ungrateful to his celestial protector, and he would frequently summon the most saintly monks in the capital to his palace. His special favourite was Yi Ching, who spent the summer of 707 with him. The emperor even went to the monastery where the pilgrim worked, sat on his mat, and with his own hand assisted in the translation of the Indian scriptures.

Unfortunately this friendly collaboration between the gentle emperor and the saintly monk was shortly to be interrupted by another palace drama. Chung-tsung's wife, the young empress Wei, was a woman of deplorably loose morals. She had taken as her lover the handsome Wu San-ssu, a nephew of the late empress Wu Tse-t'ien. Chung-tsung was deceived and noticed nothing. A young prince of the blood, exasperated by this depravity, stabbed Wu San-ssu (707), but all to no avail, for the emperor repudiated his avenger. Finally this Chinese Messalina, who still found her phantom husband an embarrassment, poisoned him so as to be able to rule in his stead (July 3, 710). But she lacked the formidable authority of Wu Tse-t'ien, and no sooner was her crime discovered than it led to a revolt of members of the royal family led by the young prince Li Lung-chi. During the night of July 25 the conspirators re-enacted the drama of 705; they invaded the palace and killed the empress with a volley of arrows. Her head was impaled on a pike and hurled to the crowd. Li Lung-chi then had his father proclaimed emperor; this was the emperor Jui-tsung.

During this time the Turks of Mongolia, under their redoubtable khan Bekchor (Mo-chüeh), were continuing their ravages. In the year 706 Bekchor's nephew Kultegin (Ch'üeh-t'e-le) won a great victory against the Chinese at Ning-hsia. "We fought against the Chinese", Kultegin's epitaph relates; "first Kultegin mounted the grey horse Tadiking-chur and attacked, but his horse was killed. Then he mounted the grey horse Ishparar-yamatar and attacked, and this horse was killed likewise. Finally he mounted the bay horse Kedimlig, and for the third time led the charge. Upright in his armour, he shot down more than a hundred of the enemy with his arrows. His attack is remembered by many of you, O Turkish nobles. We annihilated the Chinese army there!"

The emperor Jui-tsung had great moral qualities, but he did not feel that he was endowed with the strength necessary to cope with the situation both at home and abroad. Being uncertain what action he should take, he asked the advice of a Taoist philosopher. The latter advised him to practise a cosmic inertia in accordance with the doctrine of Lao Tzu. "In what does the perfection of government consist? In inaction! Let events take their course and the world will govern itself." Jui-tsung preferred to hand over the power to his son Li Lung-chi, the same prince who had executed the empress Wei and whose outstanding energy and alertness augured a great reign. On September 8, 712, the emperor abdicated in favour of Li Lung-chi, now remembered as the emperor Hsüan-tsung, who was to have one of the most brilliant reigns in the whole of Chinese history.

CHAPTER XIX

A GREAT AGE

THE emperor Hsüan-tsung was only twenty-eight years old when he succeeded to the throne. He was active, courageous, and endowed with a lively sense of his duties, of the greatness of his house, and of China's imperial destiny in Asia. His reign (712–756) was one of the great reigns, and his age was from many points of view the *grand siècle* of Chinese history. Rarely have so many talents been found together. Himself a competent man of letters, a poet, and a musician, Hsüan-tsung was a patron of literature and surrounded himself with a constellation of poets. The two greatest Chinese lyric poets, Li Po (701–752) and Tu Fu (712–770), lived during his reign.

Although Chinese poetry, being largely dependent on literary allusions, too often escapes us, the T'ang lyric poets seem more directly accessible because the sentiments which they evoke are part of universal experience. Perhaps this characteristic is due to the multiple sources from which T'ang lyric poetry is drawn. If we analyse its elements, we find both the great cosmic reverie of ancient Taoism, caused by a wild surge towards the sublime, and Buddhist melancholy, evoked by the universal impermanence of earthly things. This twofold inspiration is very apparent in some of the more spacious lines in the poems of Li Po:

> The Yellow River flows towards the Eastern Ocean,
> The sun sinks into the Western Sea.
> Like time the water is gone forever,
> Neither ever stops its course.
>
> . . . .
>
> Would that I might ride a celestial dragon,
> To breathe in the essence of sun and moon
> And become an immortal.

Sometimes a line by Li Po seems by itself to convey the whole spirit of Buddhist teaching on universal impermanence:

The waves follow one after another in an eternal pursuit.

Sometimes the tone grows more bitter and more hopeless as in this poem which ends on a note of *vanitas vanitatum*:

The sun and the moon will go out,
The earth will return to ashes.
Why, because you will not live for a thousand years,
Do you complain that life is short?

And again:

Life is a journey,
Death is a return to the earth.
The universe is like an inn,
The passing years are like dust.
We complain when we think of the past,
We would complain more if we thought of the future!

And here is a familiar romantic theme: "To anchor one's boat for a single day":

The seaborne traveller seizes a favourable wind,
He raises anchor and sets sail for distant shores.
Like a bird flying through innumerable clouds,
The wake of his ship leaves no memories behind.

Other poems by Li Po are of purely Taoist inspiration:

I shall play on my *ch'in* the air of the restless pine-forest;
Raising my cup, I shall ask the moon to join me.
The moon and the wind will always be my friends;
My fellow creatures here below are but transitory companions.

Referring to the ancient myth of the roc, Li Po goes further even than Taoism in this extraordinary flight with its transparent symbolism:

The roc flies higher and higher;
Its wings shake the four corners of the earth.
Suddenly, high in the firmament,

Its flight comes to an end, its wings are weary and it falls.
But the wind caused by the beating of its wings
Will disturb many thousands of ages to come.

When they are not ascending to these heights, the T'ang poets may content themselves with a vision of land and water, mountain, and distance, which amounts to the creation of landscape. Here is a famous distich by Wang Po (648–675):

The low clouds fly with the solitary wild duck.
The autumnal waters merge with the limitless sky.

This line by Wang Wei, who was famous as a painter, is itself a painting:

In steady rain over lonely grove the hearth-smoke scarcely rises.

In the poetry of Li Po there are many of these visions of space, which are treated in a most penetrating impressionist manner. Here is a picture of Lake Tung-t'ing:

In the early morning I stray along the shores of Lake Tung-t'ing;
I let my gaze wander, nothing breaks the horizon.
Before me stretch the sleepy limpid waters of the lake.
It is a truly autumnal landscape
With an icy and sad appearance.
None the less the atmosphere is clear,
The blue mountains melt into the forests.
Little by little a sail appears over the distant horizon,
And, as dawn breaks, birds take flight.
Ashore a breeze springs up from towards Changsha,
And hoar frost whitens the fields.

In the mountains:

Birds cannot fly over the summit of the mountain,
Which the immense sky covers.
I climb to the summit to contemplate the glorious sight.
Down below the great river flows and does not return,
And the north wind chases the clouds for ten thousand li.

A twilight scene:

Coming down at dusk from the green mountain,
The mountain moon was following me home;

I stopped to look back up the path I came by,
A clear light lay across the verdant slopes. . . .

A nocturne:

Before my bed a patch of moonlight shone;
I thought there must be frost upon the ground,
And raised my head and stared at the moon so bright,
Sank back again and longed for my native land.

One could hardly fail to find Buddhist or Taoist inspiration in the classical theme, common both to poetry and painting, of the visit to the monastery:

The monk of Shu had brought his ancient zither
And come down to the west of Omei peak;
And when for us his fingers plucked the strings,
We heard the rustling pines of myriad chasms;
Our travellers' hearts were washed in running waters;
The dying notes like falling frost on bells.
I had not noticed dusk come on the mountains,
Nor seen how deep the autumn clouds were darkened.

Going to visit a Taoist recluse:

The barking of a dog through sound of water,
The petals of the peach flower thick with dew,
Deep in the woods from time to time a deer,
By the noonday stream no sound of bells at noon.
The wild bamboo stems part the bluish haze,
A flying cascade hangs from the verdant peak.
Nobody here can tell me where you've gone;
Disconsolate I rest against your pines.

When speaking of Li Po, it would be an injustice not to mention the other great T'ang poet, his friend and rival Tu Fu. He too was a landscape poet, as is shown by this vision of autumn:

In limpid autumn nothing obscures my view;
On the horizon a light mist is rising,
A distant river melts into the sky,
And a solitary city sinks in the milky mist.
A few last leaves are falling, blown by the breeze;
The sun sets behind the curving hill.
How late the solitary crane returns!
In the twilight the rooks are already flocking to the forest.

Li Po and Tu Fu were not only great lyric poets; the friendship of the emperor Hsüan-tsung gave them the position of court poets. They wrote of the inimitable life in the palace of Ch'ang-an, and of the charms of the imperial favourite, the beautiful Yang Kuei-fei. This woman, celebrated for her wit and beauty, was both the Pompadour and the Marie Antoinette of China. She was originally the mistress of one of the sons of Hsüan-tsung, but the latter became enamoured of her, took her away from his son, and made her his own favourite. It was she whom Li Po celebrated as the famous Han beauty "Flying Swallow":

> The prince is choosing the young ladies who will attend on him;
> Among the rivals who come eagerly from all the land
> Who is the most beautiful?
> It is the flying swallow who makes her nest in the palace. . . .

And further on, this delicate homage:

> When she ends her song and her dance,
> I fear she may turn into a rainbow cloud
> And float up to heaven.

Another of Li Po's poems, which was composed at the emperor's request, says of the favourite:

> The clouds are like her dress,
> The flowers her face.

Tu Fu also sang of

The goddesses whose lovely bodies are surrounded by clouds of fragrance.

Here is a courtly promenade sketched by Tu Fu:

> On the third day of the third moon, the weather fresh and clear,[1]
> Beside the waters of Ch'ang-an are many lovely women;
> With graceful step and distant air, so virtuous and demure,
> Their figures curving evenly, their skin so smooth and fine;
> Their garments of embroidered silk reflect the light of spring;
> The gold-brocaded peacock and the silver unicorn.
> What are the ladies wearing on their heads?
> Iridescent feather-flowers that hang before their ears.

[1] A large garden party was given in the royal park, and all the gentlefolk of Ch'ang-an would stroll by the Serpentine there.

What does one see when looking from behind?
Sashes sewn with pearls and fitting closely to the waist.
Beneath their cloud-worked awning are the sisters of the consort,[1]
Ennobled with the titles Lady Kuo and Lady Ch'in. . . .

Later, after these Chinese Trianons had been scattered and the favourite killed, Tu Fu recalled one of the court fêtes with its retinue of "amazons":

. . . The favourite palace lady from the Hall of Shining Light
Attended on her sovereign within the imperial car;
Before the car her sisters rode, with bows and arrows slung;
Their horses white were champing on the bits of solid gold.
One lady archer leaned in the saddle and aimed towards the clouds,
And smiled as her one arrow winged a pair of flying birds. . . .

In the next generation another famous poet, Po Chü-i (772–846), was to write of these gay parties in his *Song of Everlasting Remorse*:

The Lord of Han prized lovely women; he longed for a peerless beauty.[2]
He ruled the world for many years, but her he could not find.
In the House of Yang there was a girl who just had come of age,
Nurtured within the inmost courts, had never yet been seen;
By Nature graced with form so fair that none could pass her by;
One day was picked for the honour of a place at the sovereign's side.
From the glance of her eye and her lovely smile, a hundred charms sprang forth,
And all the palace ladies then looked very plain indeed.
It was wintry spring when they went to bathe in the Flower-Clear Palace pool.
In the Warm Spring's bubbling water she washed her cream-smooth skin;
Her serving-maids supported her, enticingly supple and languid,
And this was the first time she was graced to enjoy the Emperor's favour.
She had black-cloud temples, a flower-face, side-pendants worked in gold;
Within the perfumed curtains warm she passed that night of spring,
But in spring the night is, alas, too short, and the sun was high when she rose,
And from that day on the sovereign held no more early courts.[3]
She hung on his pleasure, was with him at wine, had never a moment to spare;

[1] Yang Kuei-fei.

[2] The song tells quite openly the best-known story about the T'ang emperor Hsüan-tsung. "Han" is simply a concession to form.

[3] At dawn. Imperial business should be conducted betimes.

In spring they went out to see the spring, and at night they took care of
 the night.
Of beauties, the inner palaces held at least three thousand women,
But the favour for three thousand was lavished all on one.
When she'd readied herself in her golden room, she'd enchant her lord
 through the night;
When the wine was done in his jewelled tower, she was heated as though
 by love. . . .

Apart from a few portraits of temple benefactors found among the banners and frescoes of Tun-huang, very few T'ang paintings of lay subjects have been preserved. However, the elegant pastimes of Hsüan-tsung's court are evoked in the development of the little people of the terracotta T'ang figurines—female musicians and dancers, noble ladies and their attendants, "amazons" and girl polo players. The delicate polychrome, which livens their complexions and accentuates their sashes, also adds to the grace of their attitudes. These little figures bring to life, as vividly as do the verses of Tu Fu and Li Po, the times of the inimitable court of Ch'ang-an. Likewise the T'ang cavalry with their horses saddled and pawing the ground, the barbarian auxiliaries of strongly defined racial type, and even the Buddhist guardian kings, all tell of the days of the Chinese epic in Asia, from T'ai-tsung to Hsüan-tsung.

The diversions of court life never prevented Hsüan-tsung from carrying on his great ancestor's policy of expansion in Asia. In the early days of his reign he had the good fortune to be rid of his principal adversary, Bekchor (Mo-chüeh), ruler of the Mongolian Turks, who was killed in a revolt and his head sent to the Chinese court (716). Bekchor's nephew and successor, Bilgä ("the wise") Kaghan (Mo-chi-lien), was sincere in his efforts to make peace with the empire (721–722). Friendly relations were established between the brilliant court of Ch'ang-an and the barbarian court on the upper Orkhon, and a marked deference was shown by the latter towards the former. In 743–744, however, the khanate of the Mongolian Turks was overthrown by a revolt of some related tribes. Its place was taken by one of these tribes, the Uigurs, who assumed control of Mongolia and established their headquarters on the upper Orkhon, where their capital occupied the present site of Karabalghasun—"the black city"—near the present-day Karakorum. The Uigurs were later to prove faithful allies of the T'ang dynasty.

In 714 the Chinese won a resounding victory near Tokmak, in the country of the Western Turks (present-day Soviet Turkestan), which brought a number of these tribes into the imperial camp. In the years 736 and 744 the Chinese generals won further victories against various rebellious Turkish khans of the Ili Valley, south of Lake Balkhash. In 748 a Chinese temple was built at Tokmak, to the west of the Issyk Kul—a visible proof of the extension of the T'ang empire into western Turkestan. In the Tarim Basin the little kingdoms of Karashar, Kucha, Khotan, and Kashgar, which had been disobedient for so long, had once more became faithful vassals. Indeed, these ancient Indo-European-speaking peoples were finding the Chinese protectorate an indispensable means of defence against their new invaders, the Tibetans and the Arabs. We have seen that in 670 the four towns were captured by the Tibetans, and that the Chinese were not able to deliver them until 692. There is no doubt that they preferred T'ang suzerainty to domination by the near-savage bands of Tibetans. As for the Arabs, after destroying the Sassanid Empire in 652 and overcoming Persia, they had extended their conquests into Transoxiana. In 709 they imposed their suzerainty on the kings of Bukhara and Samarkand. Between 712 and 714 they reached Tashkent and penetrated into Ferghana. The king of Ferghana took refuge in Kashgar, whence he appealed to the Chinese garrisons for help. His request was agreed to immediately, and in 715 a Chinese army entered Ferghana and restored him to his throne, driving away the Arabian outposts. The kings of Bukhara and Samarkand tried to obtain similar assistance from the Chinese, as too did the king of Tokharestan or Bactria (Balkh). From 718 to 731 all these princes kept sending declarations of vassalage to the Chinese court. The emperor Hsüan-tsung responded by conferring on them diplomas of investiture, and by having the Turkish tribes under his suzerainty go to their assistance against the Arabs, but he always hesitated to send a Chinese expeditionary force so far afield. Instead he intervened on the other side of the Pamirs.

Here his principal task was to arrest Tibetan expansion. China was now encountering Tibetans all over this area, and in particular was obliged to wage an exhausting frontier war against them in the wild region of Koko Nor. At the other end of Tibet, the Tibetans were threatening the little kingdoms which lay to the south of the Pamirs, on the Indian slope of the massif. Through these kingdoms of Wakhan, Gilgit, and Baltistan passed the most direct route between the Chinese protectorate of the Tarim Basin and India. T'ang China, joined to the Indian world by ties of trade and of Buddhist pilgrimage, attached the greatest importance to freedom of movement across these high valleys of the Pamirs. The Tibetans imposed their suzerainty on Gilgit, and in 747 the imperial general Kao Hsien-chih, a Korean in the service of China who was vice-governor of Kucha, crossed the Pamirs by the pass of Kilik, or by the pass of Baroghil, and established a Chinese protectorate over Gilgit. When in 749 the king of Tokharestan (Balkh, to the north of the Hindu Kush) asked help from the Chinese against a minor mountain chieftain, an ally of the Tibetans who was intercepting communications between Gilgit and Kashmir, Kao Hsien-chih again crossed the Pamirs and once more cleaned up the region (750). At this time both the rajah of Kashmir and the shah of Kabul were loyal allies of the Chinese court, which on several occasions sent them warrants of investiture.

Established on the T'ien Shan and the Pamirs, mistress of Tashkent, Ferghana, and Gilgit, protector of Kashmir, Balkh, and Kabul (the greater part of present-day Afghanistan), her aid sought against the Arabs by the peoples of Bukhara and Samarkand, China enjoyed an incomparable position in Asia. From his residency at Kucha, Kao Hsien-chih acted as Chinese viceroy of Central Asia.

Suddenly this whole fabric collapsed, and the same Kao Hsien-chih who had led the Chinese armies so far afield was largely responsible.

The Turkish king of Tashkent had always proved himself a loyal vassal of the Chinese, for whom Tashkent was an advanced outpost against the Arabs. But in 750 Kao Hsien-chih, hoping to appropriate the king's treasures for himself, invented an imaginary charge against him, arrived with an army, and cut off his head. This act of violence led to a revolt of the Western Turks. The victim's son appealed to the Arabs, who straightway sent their garrisons of Bukhara and Samarkand to his aid. In July, 751, Kao Hsien-chih's army was encircled and annihilated on the banks of the Talas, near present-day Aulie Ata, by the united Turkish and Arab forces. The Arabs led back thousands of Chinese prisoners to Samarkand. That historic day decided the fate of Central Asia, or at least of Turkestan; instead of becoming Chinese, as had seemed probable from the earlier course of events, it was to become Moslem.

Perhaps it might still have been possible to have retrieved the Chinese disaster of the Talas, had it not coincided with a general collapse of the military power of the T'ang dynasty. In the same year, 751, the Lolo kingdom of Nan-chao cut to pieces an imperial army near Lake Ta-li in Yünnan; and again in this disastrous year, the Mongol horde of the Kitan defeated the Chinese general An Lu-shan to the west of the Liao River, in present-day Jehol.

The truth was that China had become worn out by her military conquests. The people had grown weary of these far-flung expeditions in which they could see no benefit; above all they had grown weary of conscription. The court poets like Li Po did not conceal this state of mind:

The Great Wall, which separates China from the desert,
Winds on into infinity.
On all stretches of the frontier
No towns have been left standing.
Here and there a few scattered human bones
Seem to express their everlasting hatred.

Three hundred and sixty thousand men, dragged from their homes,
Weep as they bid their families farewell.
Since it is the order of the prince, they must obey,
But who is to cultivate the fields?

It is above all in the poems of Tu Fu that this war-weariness appears, even when he disguises his criticism by transposing it to the period of the Han dynasty. Here is his *Song of the War Chariots*, written in 752:

Waggon wheels rumbling, horses neighing shrill,
Every man with bow and arrows carried at the waist;
Fathers, mothers, wives and children follow with farewells;
Hsien-yang Bridge is hidden by the clouds of rising dust.
They cling to their men with dragging feet, weeping they block the road;
The sound of weeping rises up to pierce the cloudy sky.
A passer-by at the roadside asks a soldier where they go.
The soldier answers plainly: "They are calling up replacements.
Some at fifteen are sent to the north to hold the river line,
And then at forty are sent to the west to work in the army colonies.
Before they leave, the village chief binds on their black silk turbans;
When they return their hair is white, yet still they must go to the borders.
In the border districts blood has flowed, enough to fill an ocean,
But the Emperor's colonial aims are still unsatisfied.
Have you never heard
That though east of the passes two hundred counties are ruled by the House of Han,
Yet in every village among the fields are growing thorns and brambles?
Even where women are strong enough to handle the ploughs and hoes,
The crops spread over the boundary banks and nothing is done to rights.
And how much worse for us hardy soldiers born in the land of Ch'in,
Herded and driven from place to place as if we were dogs or fowls.
Although you, sir, may have some further question,
Pray let me as a conscript tell my troubles.
For instance, take what's happening this winter;
West of the frontier fighting never stops,
The district officers here demand their taxes;
But where do you think the taxes are to come from?
Truly it is not good to bear a son,
Better instead to bear a daughter now;
If you have a girl she can still be wed to one of the neighbouring houses,
If you have a boy he will disappear like grasses in winter time."
Have you never seen

By the Koko Nor,
From ages past the whitened bones no kinsman gathered home?
Vengeful, the new-dead spirits brood, the ancient spirits wail,
The sky is dark, the air is dank and filled with mournful sound.

In the following year Tu Fu's criticism became more direct:

Sad, sad, the soldiers leave their native land;
They are going beyond Turfan,
Where the net of misfortune awaits them.
The sovereign already possesses a vast empire;
Why should he wish to extend it still further?

Here is a description of the recruits arriving in Upper Asia:

Snow is falling, the army makes its way through the high mountains;
The track is dangerous; for fear of slipping they cling from rock to rock;
Their frozen fingers slip on ice several layers thick.
There they are far distant from the land of Han.
When will men be satisfied with building a wall against the barbarians?
When will the soldiers return to their native land?

Worse still, Tu Fu compares the wretched condition of the people with the luxury at the court, and in particular with the riches accumulated by the family of the favourite:

At court they are distributing rolls of silk,
Which the women of the poor have woven.
To extort it from them and offer it to the emperor their husbands have been beaten with rods.
Moreover I have heard it said that all the gold plates in the imperial palace
Have passed, one by one, into the hands of the family of the favourite.
In the palace there is such abundance that meat is allowed to go bad and wine to turn sour,
While in the streets people die from poverty and cold.

Conditions were ripe for revolt. It came from the quarter from which it was least expected, being led by a general at the court, An Lu-shan, who was a Tartar adventurer in the service of China. The emperor and the beautiful Yang Kuei-fei were so taken with him that they made him their favourite. But in 755 An Lu-shan, knowing of the general discontent directed against the sovereign, suddenly raised the standard of revolt in his military command of Liao-tung.

Within a few weeks he had crossed Hopei, descended on Loyang, and was marching against Ch'ang-an, the imperial capital. At his approach, the emperor fled during the night towards Szechwan, taking with him Yang Kuei-fei, her two sisters, and one of her cousins whom she had made a minister of state. During the journey, the soldiers of the imperial escort ran short of rations and mutinied. They killed Yang Kuei-fei's cousin the minister, impaled his head on the point of a lance, and brought it to the emperor. Then they proceeded to deal likewise with the two sisters of the favourite. Frightened by the soldiers' clamour, the emperor went out and tried to calm them with friendly words, but the mutineers now demanded the head of Yang Kuei-fei herself. Hsüan-tsung, hemmed in by rebels, allowed the unfortunate woman to be led away and strangled by the soldiers. Satisfied, the latter then reformed their ranks.

Tu Fu, who had sung the praises of Yang Kuei-fei in her days of magnificence, was to mourn her tragic end in a poignant poem:

> . . . Where are now those lustrous eyes and teeth of pearl?
> Blood has defiled her soul, which can never return;
> The sovereign and his favourite will never meet again.

A generation later, the poet Po Chü-i wrote of her dramatic death in his *Song of Everlasting Remorse*:

. . . When towards Yü-yang drums of war of a sudden shook the earth,
And alarms cut short the air of *Rainbow Skirts and Feather Jackets*.
Within the soaring palace walls, smoke and dust arose;
A thousand cars, ten thousand horse set out for the south-west;
The imperial standard fluttered as they moved and stopped again.
When west of the gates of the capital, just over a hundred li,
The imperial army refused to advance. There was nothing else to be done;
With a silken cord, before the troops, they strangled the Lady Yang:
Her flower-worked hair-clasp fell to the ground, and nobody picked it up;
Her kingfisher-pin, her sparrow-pin, and her comb of purest jade.
And then the sovereign covered his eyes; he could not save her life.
When he looked again, his tears flowed down and mingled with her blood.

. . . .

Heaven will last, and earth will endure, but some day both must end;
This remorse will go on and on through endless eternity.

Meanwhile An Lu-shan had occupied Ch'ang-an, the imperial capital (July 18, 756). The unhappy Hsüan-tsung continued his flight towards Szechwan, which was a virtual abdication. His son Li Heng took command of the loyalist forces in the region of Ningsia, where his soldiers proclaimed him emperor (August 12, 756).

This new emperor, Su-tsung, an active and well-meaning prince, devoted the whole of his reign (756–752) to winning back China from the rebels. In this task he was assisted by a great soldier, Kuo Tzu-i, a pattern of military loyalty and devotion to the dynasty, and it was to him more than anyone else that the T'ang dynasty owed its restoration. In order to obtain reinforcements, Su-tsung appealed to the Turks, among whom the T'ang dynasty had enjoyed considerable prestige since the time of T'ai-tsung. The most powerful of the Turkish nations, the Uigurs, at that time masters of Outer Mongolia, sent him some contingents, thanks to which the imperial forces were able to recapture Ch'ang-an and Loyang (757). But the revolt was far from being suppressed, and Su-tsung died with his task unfinished (May 762). The rebels even captured Loyang a second time. Their final expulsion and suppression required the intervention of the kaghan of the Uigurs himself, who came down from Mongolia with his cavalry (November 762).

In the course of this campaign the kaghan of the Uigurs made the acquaintance of a Manichaean priest. Manichaeism was a hybrid religion founded in Persia in the third century and derived partly from the indigenous Zoroastrianism and partly from Christianity. As a result of his meeting with the priest, the Uigur prince was converted to Manichaeism and made it the national religion of his people. This heretical doctrine, which had once almost made a convert of Saint Augustine, was now brought by a strange destiny to conquer Mongolia. It must be acknowledged that Manichaeism helped to humanize the manners and customs of the Uigurs; and, moreover, it spread among them an art which, like the doctrine itself, was largely borrowed from Persia. The Manichaean frescoes and miniatures found in the region of Turfan (dating from between 800 and 840) are in fact the earliest surviving examples of Persian painting.

The T'ang dynasty could refuse nothing to these Uigur kings by whom it had been saved and restored to the throne, and on several occasions they were given Chinese princesses in marriage. The Uigurs used their influence to protect Manichaeism in China, and at their request the court of Ch'ang-an authorized the establishment of Manichaean temples in several cities. This protection lasted as long as the Uigur domination continued. When in 840 the latter was broken by the attacks of the Kirghiz Turks, the Manichaean communities in China found the practice of their religion proscribed overnight.

On the other hand Nestorian Christianity enjoyed an almost unbroken protection under the T'ang dynasty. We have already mentioned the construction of the first Nestorian church at Ch'ang-an in 638. In the same year the emperor T'ai-tsung issued an edict favouring the Nestorians which is a praiseworthy example of the tolerant spirit of the dynasty: "The true law (of religion) has more than one name. The saints have no fixed residence. They travel all over the world, spreading religion, exhorting the people, and secretly succouring the multitudes. A-lo-pen, a man of great virtue, has come from the far distant kingdom of Ta-ch'in to offer us sacred books containing a new doctrine, the meaning of which he has explained to us. After looking through these books and examining this doctrine, it has been found to be profound, marvellous, and perfect, and especially beneficial to mankind". The now famous inscription about Nestorian Christianity in China was carved in Syriac and Chinese at Ch'ang-an in the year 781. It begins with a résumé of the doctrine of Christianity ("The Radiant Religion"), and continues with a list of the favours granted to the Nestorian community by the T'ang emperors since the time of T'ai-tsung, and especially by Hsüan-tsung, who presented the church at Ch'ang-an with a eulogistic inscription in his own writing. Nestorian Christianity was not to suffer until 845, when it was included in a persecution directed against Buddhism.

But Manichaeism and Nestorian Christianity were never widespread in China and were almost entirely restricted to Persian and Turkish residents. The main battle of ideas was still between the Confucianists, the Taoists, and the Buddhists. In 745, during the latter part of the reign of Hsüan-tsung (who towards the end of his life was greatly influenced by the Taoists), the Taoist books were first gathered into a single collection which formed the basis of the future Taoist canon. In 837, the texts of the nine works of the Confucian canon were engraved on stone; thus the scholars could take any number of rubbings of the texts. As for the Buddhist scriptures, we have seen how pilgrims such as Hsuan Tsang and Yi Ching returned from India with entire libraries of Sanskrit texts, which were quickly translated into Chinese.[1] The immense collection of the Chinese *Tripitaka* bears witness to the scale on which this work was carried out.

The literati protested energetically, in the name of ancient Confucian wisdom, against the advancing wave of Buddhist and Taoist mysticism. In 819 the emperor Hsien-tsung, himself attracted to both of the faiths, welcomed with great pomp a relic of the Buddha. For this he was censured by Han Yü, one of the most famous writers of the T'ang period, in a vehement memorial which is often quoted to this day: "This Buddha was a mere barbarian who was ignorant of our language and did not dress properly." Honest and courageous, if somewhat narrow-minded, Han Yü placed Buddhism and Taoism in the same class, and condemned both as anti-social and anarchic: "Now they say they would set their hearts in order, but detach themselves from the world, the state, and the family, and destroy the natural order. They are sons without fathers, subjects without rulers, men without work." The Confucian literati have always attacked the idleness and monasticism of the Buddhists and the passivity, alchemy and sorcery of the Taoists. Nevertheless, when

[1] Hsüan Tsang made the pilgrimage in 630–644, Yi Ching in 671–695.

the occasion arose, Confucianism and Taoism were capable of taking a common stand against "the foreign religion", Buddhism. In 845 the emperor Wu-tsung, himself an adherent of Taoism, issued an edict against Buddhism in which he repeated all the arguments of Han Yü. Large numbers of monks were forced to return to lay life, and four thousand six hundred Buddhist monasteries and temples were closed. But Yi-tsung (860–873), the next emperor but one, was a pious Buddhist, and during his reign the monks recovered all their influence.

Moreover, Buddhism was definitely taking root in China, for the reason that it was there becoming more Chinese.

The latter-day Buddhism which had been brought from northern India, by way of the Tarim Basin, during the early T'ang period, was a very much developed form of the ancient Indian faith, in fact almost a new religion. We have already seen that in India, from about the beginning of the Christian era onwards, an unlooked-for metaphysic and mythology had been superimposed upon the comparatively simple doctrine originally preached by the Buddha. This transformation was the work of sects known as the Mahayana or Greater Vehicle of Salvation. One section of them professed an absolute idealism, or more exactly an idealistic monism, which was somewhat analogous to the system of Fichte and which, eliminating both the self and the external world, finally admitted of nothing save the "nothing-but-thought" or "world of ideals". Such, as we have seen, was the system brought back from India by the pilgrim Hsüan Tsang. Somewhat similar conceptions formed the framework of another system founded in the last years of the sixth century by a Chinese Buddhist living on Mount T'ien-t'ai in Chekiang. The T'ien-t'ai sect discovered, amid the universal flux which according to Buddhism constitutes the world, a universal essence whose mastery would allow the faithful to attain Enlightenment. This doctrine led to a kind of mystical monism in which it is not difficult to reveal the infiltration of Taoism, for the universal essence shows a marked similarity to the *tao*. Another school of Buddhism, called the sect of Contemplation (*dhyana* in Sanskrit, *ch'an* in Chinese, *len* in Japanese), sought by intuition to discover the essence of perfection in the depths of the heart. This introspective immersion, this mystical cleansing, can doubtless be traced to the asceticism of the Indian yogis, both Brahmins and Buddhists. Yet here again one is conscious of the gradual penetration of Taoist concepts. Ch'an contemplation differs little from Taoist ecstasy. But if the ancient indigenous Taoism was thus influencing the evolution of Buddhism, the converse was equally true. In imitation of Buddhism, Taoism now endeavoured to organize itself into a church, and its sages gathered in communities on the model of Buddhist monasteries.

Buddhism's greatest appeal to the Chinese masses lay in its mythology, its numerous devotions, and above all the cult of the various bodhisattvas, the supernatural beings created to deputize for the historic, Buddha. Such a creation had been indispensable. A religion must be provided with celestial protectors to whom the prayers of the faithful can be addressed. Now, Buddhism did not include any idea of the absolute; and how could one pray to the historic Buddha, whose personality—and on this affirmation depended the whole Buddhist doctrine—had reached nirvana or final extinction? So it was that in India, from about the beginning of the present era, the Greater Vehicle (Mahayana) Buddhists had accorded a place of considerable importance to their Messiah, the bodhisattva Maitreya (Mi-lo-fo in Chinese), who was to become incarnate and, like Sakyamuni the Buddha, save the world again. During the first six centuries of our era, the piety of the masses was turned towards this Messiah, who in China—to judge from the images of Yün-kang and Lung-men—played a considerable role in the iconography of the Wei period. Then, as the saviour was slow in making his appearance, this cult of the Messiah gradually subsided. Popular devotion turned towards another bodhisattva, Avalokiteshvara, a sort of Buddhist Providence (his name means in Sanskrit: "The one who looks down from on high"). By a curious metamorphosis, on his arrival in China this bodhisattva seems to have assumed a feminine guise. Avalokiteshvara became the "goddess" Kuan-yin, a sort of Madonna, full of gentleness and compassion, who saved souls, rescued them from various hells, and caused them to be reborn, within the mystic lotus at her feet, into wonderful paradises. Kuan-yin shared this duty with another divinity, the *dhyani-buddha* (mystical Buddha) Amitabha (A-mi-t'o-fo), who was looked on as her spiritual father and whose image she carried in her hair. Devotion to Amitabha gave birth to a religion of the heart, a purely personal cult of true pietism, or more exactly, to a quietism based on a limitless confidence in the benevolence of the bodhisattva; a single look of compassion from Amitabha, or a single invocation addressed to him from the depths of the heart being sufficient to secure salvation.

This personal religion, so full of tenderness and confidence, was probably responsible for more converts to Buddhism among the masses of the Chinese people than were all the speculations of Buddhist philosophy. Neither Confucianism nor Taoism had anything comparable to offer. The goddess Kuan-yin was adopted by the people and took her place side by side with the Confucian sages and Taoist divinities in the popular pantheon. She was adopted by the Taoists themselves, and she still occupies a place of major importance in the general syncretism of all the different religious cults which constitutes the popular religion of China today.

The Tun-huang banners, dating from the T'ang period and the Five Dynasties, show the various Buddhist cults in the process of evolution; the Messianic faith of Maitreya is found side by side with the paradises of Avalokiteshvara, and the Indian Avalokiteshvara is transformed before one's eyes into the Chinese Kuan-yin. This is why the Buddhist grottos of Tun-huang are so particularly interesting; Tun-huang is not only the junction where one passes from the art of the Tarim Basin, still permeated with Indian influence, to a purely Chinese art; it also remains a unique testimony, after the conquest of China by Buddhism, to the counter-annexation of Buddhism by the Chinese.

CHAPTER XX

A SOCIAL CRISIS

T'ANG China never completely recovered from the shock caused by the revolt of An Lu-shan. The restoration of the imperial line, which seemed to have ended the drama of the rebellion, quite failed to bring back the country's former prosperity. During the revolt China had lost all her foreign possessions except Annam. The eight years of civil war (755–763), with their toll of plunder, destruction of wealth, and abandonment of farms, led to an enormous decrease in the population. On the eve of the civil war, after a period of a hundred and forty years of internal peace, the census of 754 showed a number of families equivalent to fifty-two million inhabitants. In 839, after the restored dynasty had already had three-quarters of a century to efface the scars of the civil war, the census showed a population of no more than thirty million.

This fall in the population was accompanied by an unprecedented economic and social crisis. In the T'ang period the state remained theoretically the sole owner of the land. In reality it was content to be the distributor. On attaining manhood, every peasant received an allotment of village land of from seven and a half to fifteen acres, which was his for life, and a "property" of up to three and a half acres, which he was entitled to leave to his descendants; the whole was inalienable. These grants made the peasant liable to the land tax, forced labour, and service in the militia. When he died, his allotment of land reverted to the community for redistribution. Only officials could acquire large estates and, which was even more important, preserve them through inheritance. The large landowners thus created had their lands cultivated by agricultural workers to whom they paid an annual wage. These large estates were either managed by stewards or let out to tenant-farmers.

The small peasant holding, which was based in each village on the life grant of a plot of land to the cultivator, suddenly disappeared in the middle of the eighth century. The revolt of An Lu-shan ruined the imperial finances, and its suppression necessitated ever increasing levies of militia. Henri Maspero writes that taxes, forced labour, and military service became so heavy, and the debts of the rural population so pressing, that most of the peasants, despite the laws which forbade such transactions, sold their lands to the large landowners and became tenants or agricultural labourers, that is to say little better than serfs. The small holdings thus disappeared and were swallowed up in the latifundia. At the end of the eighth century the landowning families represented no more than five per cent of the total population. Instead of a prosperous peasantry, China now had only a sort of agricultural proletariat.

Trade, too, had been ruined. In the years 781–783 the state confiscated a part of every merchant's goods in order to refill a treasury emptied by the civil war. After these measures had been carried out, Ch'ang-an, the imperial capital—which was the principal commercial centre, being the point of departure for the Silk Road and the destination of the caravans from India and Persia—was as devastated as if it had been sacked by the barbarians. The fiscal exactions were so harsh that they led to rioting. None the less the state continued to levy an extremely heavy tax on buying and selling, and on commercial operations and transactions of every kind. For example, in 793, tea coming from Szechwan was liable to a tax of ten per cent.

The stage was set for a revolution. It broke out at the end of the year 874. Its principal promoter was an embittered intellectual called Huang Ch'ao, a highly intelligent, unscrupulous and energetic man, the victim of a flagrant miscarriage of justice. The revolt broke out on the borders of southern Hopei and Shantung, a region which has been the starting-point for similar movements from the Yellow Turbans to the Boxers. As we have said earlier, it is an overpopulated area of impoverished villages set in a low-lying plain of alluvial soil and loess, where not an inch of ground is wasted, but where the land is exposed to periodic droughts and floods which destroy the crops and lead to appalling famines. The movement of 874 began as a peasants' revolt, a rising of desperate people who organized themselves into "big companies" intent on pillage. In order to combat this revolt, the government took a step which only served to aggravate the trouble and make it general. It ordered the peasants to arm themselves, and furnished them with the means to do so. As soon as they were armed, the peasants, whom excessive taxation had forced to sell their lands, and the shopkeepers, who had also been ruined by the tax-collectors, speedily joined forces with the rebels.

Huang Ch'ao amalgamated all these varied elements, and within a few months he had laid waste part of Shantung and the rich plain of Kaifeng in Honan. From there he led his bands to pillage the two great ports of South China; Foochow (878), and Canton (879). Canton was one of the greatest commercial centres of those times, "the port where the largest foreign ships put in, and the warehouse for the whole maritime trade". The Arab geographers, who knew it by the name of Khanfu, tell us that it contained a very important colony of Arab and Persian merchants of all faiths—Moslems, Nestorians, Manichaeans, and Jews—who were exporters of silk, porcelain, tea, camphor, aloes, and other products of "Sinistan". When Huang Ch'ao's bands arrived, the Cantonese shut the gates and prepared for a siege. Huang Ch'ao offered to make peace if the court appointed him governor of Canton. The ministers refused, "not wishing to hand over to a rebel the immense riches which were contained in that city". He took the town by assault, massacred the entire population, including the Arab colony, and plundered the warehouses from roof to cellar. "In addition, he cut down the mulberry trees throughout the region, so that for a long time there was no silk to send to the Arabian Empire" (autumn of 879). In the meantime the peasants of Huang Ch'ao's rebel armies, natives of the northern provinces, were suffering from the tropical climate of Canton; they were decimated by malaria. He led the survivors back to the north and captured the imperial capitals of Loyang and Ch'ang-an, sacking the two cities and massacring their inhabitants (December 20, 880, and January 15, 881) while the court fled—once more—to Szechwan.

In this extremity, the T'ang dynasty appealed to a Turkish horde called the horde of the Sand-hills—Tchöl in Turkish, Sha-t'o in Chinese. The Sha-t'o, who were originally from the Gobi, had been established in the Ordos Loop as allies of China. Taking advantage of the civil war, they had recently settled in the northern part of Shansi (878). Their chieftain, Li K'e-yung, who was then only twenty-eight years old, is one of the most sympathetic figures of his age.[1] The bravery and loyalty of this Turk contrast with the corrupt behaviour of the other protagonists in this drama of the fall of the T'ang dynasty. The court turned to him to save them from the rebels. He agreed, and afterwards never wavered in his loyalty to the T'ang cause. From Shansi his horsemen (known as "the crows of Li K'e-yung", because they were dressed in black) descended on Ch'ang-an. There the troops of Huang Ch'ao were visibly melting away; after pillaging the capital the peasant rebels thought only of carrying their booty to safety, and one group after another deserted in order to get back to their villages. At the beginning of 883, Li K'e-yung drove out the last remaining bands and summoned back the emperor. "Grass and bushes were growing in the deserted streets of the capital, which had become the home of foxes and hares." Huang Ch'ao fled to Shantung, where he was put to death. His principal lieutenant, Chou Wen, who had rallied in time to the imperial cause, obtained as his reward an important fief about Kaifeng (Pien-chou). The saviour of the dynasty, Li K'e-yung, was given the province of Shansi, to which he later added the north of Hopei.

These were in fact only the most outstanding examples of a general parcelling out of the empire. Taking advantage of the civil

[1] The T'ang imperial surname of Li had been conferred upon his father for services rendered to the dynasty.

war and the arming of local militias, governors of provinces and army commanders became more or less independent. A hereditary feudalism grew up throughout the country, as it did in France at about the same period (and under somewhat similar circumstances), at the time of the collapse of the Carolingian Empire. In this way the whole of South China was soon divided up between seven provincial dynasties, while in the north the contenders were the Turkish chieftain Li K'e-yung and the ex-bandit leader Chou Wen.

It was Chou Wen who finally carried the day. Li K'e-yung was impeded by his loyalist scruples; the chivalrous Turk refused to violate his oath of fidelity to the T'ang dynasty. No such considerations embarrassed Chou Wen. The former bandit chief attempted to do away with his rival by enticing him into a trap. He invited him to a banquet, made him drunk, and then had him attacked by a band of assassins. Li K'e-yung's companions roused him by pouring cold water over his face, and managed to secure his escape by letting him down on a rope from the top of the ramparts. Chou Wen treated his own soldiers as harshly as his enemies; he had the number of their regiment tattooed on their faces so that any deserter could be easily recognized and instantly decapitated. Having lured the imperial family into his fief in Honan, he had the emperor assassinated (September 22, 904); later he assembled the brothers of his victim at a banquet, at the end of which he massacred all eight of them (905). In the meantime he had put on the throne the last of the T'ang princes, a boy of thirteen. On May 12, 907, he deposed the child (who was executed nine months later) and proclaimed himself emperor.

For half a century the Chinese world relapsed into anarchy. South China, as we have seen, was divided up among seven provincial dynasties. In the imperial domain, which was reduced to the provinces of the north, centring on Honan, the house of Chou Wen remained in power for only sixteen years. They were expelled by Li K'e-yung's family, but the latter in turn reigned for only thirteen years (923–936), and was replaced by another family of Turkish stock. The Sha-t'o had by this time become completely Chinese in manners and customs; but now in the region of Peking appeared a horde which had remained entirely barbarian: these were the Ch'i-tan, who were to claim a share in the division of China.

The Ch'i-tan[1] were a people of Mongolian race who led a nomadic existence to the northeast of the Peking region, in the Sharamuren-Liao basin between Liao-yang and the Dalai Nor. Their opportunity to intervene in Chinese affairs was provided by the Chinese themselves. In 936 the Ch'i-tan were appealed to by a Chinese general, Shih Ching-t'ang, who was in revolt against the imperial court. Their khan Yeh-lü Te-kuang came down into Hopei with fifty thousand horsemen and helped Shih Ching-t'ang to establish himself as founder of a new imperial dynasty at Kaifeng. As the price of their intercession, the Ch'i-tan obtained the northernmost part of Hopei, including present-day Peking, and the northernmost part of Shansi, including Ta-t'ung (963). The barbarians were thus established inside the Great Wall, in the northern marches, whence they were able to control the politics of China. Shih Ching-t'ang's treason caused the first breach in the integrity of Chinese territory, a breach which was later widened and through which swept the hordes who conquered North China in the twelfth century and those who conquered all China in the thirteenth. After the Peking area had been occupied by Yeh-lü Te-kuang, it passed from the hands of the Mongol horde of the Ch'i-tan to those of the Tungus horde of the Ju-chen (Djurchet), and again from the Ju-chen to the Mongols of Genghis Khan; in this way it remained in Tartar hands from 936 to 1368.

The painful consequences of the Ch'i-tan occupation of Peking were soon felt by the very people who had brought it about. Shih Ching-t'ang's successor, who had desired to free himself from the onerous protection of the Ch'i-tan, only succeeded in provoking the

[1] In Mongolian, *Kitan* singular, *Kitat* plural. In Chinese, *Ch'i-tan*. In Turkish, Persian and Arabic, *Khitai*. This became the Turkish (and thence the Russian) name for China. Marco Polo also used this name (*Cathay*) for North China.

latter to a further invasion. On January 25, 947, the Ch'i-tan khan, Yeh-lü Te-kuang, made his entry into the imperial capital of Kaifeng. He did not return to Peking until he had conscientiously sacked the city, and he carried off the entire Chinese court as prisoners. After the departure of the Ch'i-tan, a fresh Chinese dynasty ascended the throne of Kaifeng, but they only retained it for four years (947–951). When in February, 960, the throne passed to a great imperial dynasty, that of Sung, China had been still further divided by the creation of another dissident Chinese kingdom, which had been established in Shansi with Taiyüan as its capital. As South China was already divided into seven independent kingdoms,[1] this made a total of eight provincial secessionist states, as opposed to an empire that was reduced, for all practical purposes, to Shensi, Honan, northern Anhui, Shantung, and southern Hopei.

[1] Not to mention Annam, which had taken advantage of the break-up of China to shake off Chinese domination in 939.

CHAPTER XXI

THE SUNG DYNASTY AND THE PROBLEM OF REFORMS

THE Sung dynasty has long been recalled with affection by the Chinese people. It did not repeat the Asiatic conquests of the Han and the T'ang; on the contrary, it did not even succeed in driving the Tartars from those portions of the national territory which they still held, and during the second half of the period was forced to abandon all North China. However, the Chinese literati have never considered military prowess to be on a level with cultural achievement. Their classical turn of mind, and probably also a certain class jealousy towards the military, caused them systematically to disparage all warlike policies on philosophical grounds; when their anti-militarist theories led to invasion, they would oppose the victorious armies with impotent protests and belated patriotism. The *T'ung-chien-kang-mu*, a general history of China edited by perhaps the best qualified representative of the Sung literati, is characteristic of this point of view. In addition, the Sung dynasty inevitably won the sympathy of the literati by its taste for classical culture, philosophical speculation, erudition, archaeology, and dilettantism.

It was no fault of its founders that the Sung dynasty did not follow in the glorious footsteps of the Han and the T'ang. The first Sung emperor, Chao K'uang-yin (Sung T'ai-tsu), is one of the most sympathetic figures in Chinese history. Before he became emperor he was a general in the service of the preceding dynasty. The emperor had just died, leaving as his heir a seven-year-old boy. Meanwhile a war was being waged against the formidable Ch'i-tan, a war which Chao K'uang-yin was directing with remarkable success. The army, which felt it necessary for a strong man to take power, forced the hand of its general. One morning at dawn the soldiers surrounded Chao K'uang-yin's tent. Waking up with a start, he saw around him his officers who, drawing their swords, declared that they proclaimed him emperor. Before he had had time to reply, they dressed him in the imperial yellow robe and, carrying him on their shoulders, lifted him on to his horse. They led him into the middle of his troops, who acclaimed him with a great shout, formed into column and set out in the direction of the capital. However, after some minutes he reined in his horse, ordered a halt, and addressed the soldiers: "Do you intend to obey me? Because if you are not willing to obey me, I do not wish to become your emperor!" Dismounting from their horses, all the officers cried that they would obey him. "In that case," said Chao K'uang-yin, "listen to me carefully. You will make no attempt on the lives of the empress dowager and the little emperor, who were my former masters. You are not to molest my old colleagues the ministers. You will neither pillage the treasury, nor the stores, nor the imperial arsenals. If you fail me in any of these respects, I shall not spare you." All swore to observe these commands, and the army resumed its march in perfect order. The following day they entered Kaifeng (Pien-chou), the capital, where Chao K'uang-yin took care to assure not only the safety, but also the well-being of the boy emperor and the dowager, after which he ascended the throne (February, 960).

His subsequent reign was in keeping with this beginning. He was a humane and able administrator with a well-balanced mind; he healed the wounds of three-quarters of a century of civil war, and reunited nearly all the Chinese. During the fifteen years of his reign, he subjugated one after another the various provincial kingdoms in South China (Canton fell in 971, and Nanking in 975). The most remarkable thing was that, despite the warfare involved, these conquests were accompanied by no violence towards the civil population. The imperial generals had orders that as soon as a town was captured they were to proclaim a general amnesty. As for the princes whose territory was thus brought back within the imperial domain, Chao K'uang-yin not only did not molest them; he gave them allowances and attached them to his court. In the case of the ex-ruler of Nanking, who had resisted longest, the emperor, not without humour, gave him the title of "The Recalcitrant Marquis".

Chao K'uang-yin ascended the throne by means of a military pronunciamento, as all the founders of dynasties had done since the fall of T'ang. But once in power, he determined to put an end to such practices. He gathered all the army chiefs, his former comrades in arms, at a friendly banquet and obtained from them, by persuasion alone and without threats, the assurance that for the sake of the state they would renounce their military commands; in exchange, he rewarded them with lands and riches. Thus ended the system of frequent military *coups d'état* which had exhausted China for more than half a century; the "civilian empire" was finally re-established.

Chao K'uang-yin showed the same wisdom to the end. Feeling that death was approaching, and considering that his son was too young to accept the responsibility of government, he summoned his brother, took down the battle axe which hung near the imperial bed, handed it to him as the emblem of authority, and exhorted him to be a good emperor. Then he died (November, 976).

The new emperor, T'ai-tsung (976–997), completed his brother's achievement by restoring to the empire the last provincial kingdom (in Shansi), whose capital of Taiyüan was captured after a long siege and despite the intervention of the Ch'i-tan (June, 979). He then attempted to seize back from the Ch'i-tan those territories which they held within the Great Wall, the regions of Ta-t'ung and Peking. In July, 979, he marched against Peking and besieged it, but was defeated by the Ch'i-tan to the northwest of the city and forced to beat a precipitate retreat. In 986 he launched another attack, and this time was not even able to reach Peking. Between Peking and Paoting his army was routed; and the pursuing Ch'i-tan advanced into southern Hopei. During the reign of his son Chen-tsung (998–1022), the Ch'i-tan continued their invasion of Chinese territory and reached the banks of the Yellow River opposite the imperial capital of Kaifeng. The courtiers panicked and advised Chen-tsung to retire below the Long River to Nanking, or even to Szechwan, but the emperor refused. To the north, across the Yellow River, the little Chinese town of Shen-chou (Shen-yüan) had managed to hold out against the enemy, and its resistance was holding up the Ch'i-tan advance on the capital. The emperor courageously went there himself; his firm attitude electrified the defenders and impressed the Ch'i-tan. At Shen-chou the Ch'i-tan signed a peace treaty, by which they agreed to withdraw from their recent conquests in southern Hopei and to content themselves, as in the past, with the possession of Peking and T'a-tung (1004). Meanwhile, in the course of the struggle with the Ch'i-tan, the difficulties of the empire had been turned to advantage by a Tibetan people, the Tangut (Tang-hsiang), who about the year 1000 made themselves masters of the Ordos, the Ala Shan and Kansu, where they founded the independent kingdom of Hsi-hsia.

The failure of the two attempts by the imperial forces to recover Peking from the Ch'i-tan, and the creation of this new barbarian kingdom of the Tangut in the northwestern marches, gave the Sung dynasty a distaste for warlike policies. Satisfied with having checked the counter-attack of the Ch'i-tan, they resigned themselves to leaving the latter in possession of the marches of Peking and Ta-t'ung, and to leaving the Ordos and Kansu to the Tangut. In the case of Peking, the sacrifice was far less important than it would seem to us today. Quite apart from its outlying position, it was at that time merely a provincial town of very secondary importance, a frontier place which so far had never played any great part in Chinese history; its importance dates from the time when the Ch'i-tan made it their capital. From the point of view of the Chinese of the eleventh century, to renounce Peking and Ta-t'ung on the one hand, and Kansu on the other, was no great sacrifice. With the exception of these three distant frontier marches, the Sung dynasty was retaining the whole of historical China. For over a hundred years they were free to indulge their taste for literature, art, and intellectual controversy; the Sung period was, above all, a time of great ideological discussions, the most important of these being the dispute between the "conservatives" and the "reformists".

This controversy, however, was not merely an intellectual pastime. The economic and social crisis which had led to the fall of the T'ang dynasty had resulted in the general enslavement of the rural population; the small landowners had been forced to sell their land and become tenant-farmers or labourers on the estates of the large landowners. Su Hsün (1009–1066), a famous writer of this period, describes the situation:

> "The fields are not the property of the men who till them, and those who own the fields do not work on them. The fields of the tillers belong to the rich. These rich men have extensive lands and vast properties; their estates join up one to the next, and they bring emigrants among whom they divide the work of cultivation. The lash and the rod are used to urge on the levies of forced labour; their master treats them no better than slaves. . . . He takes half of the produce: there is only one landowner to every ten cultivators, so that day by day the landowner accumulates his half and grows rich and powerful, while the cultivator lives from day to day on his half and grows poor and hungry, and there is no remedy." A text of 1308 says likewise that under the Sung dynasty "the landowner regarded the life and death of his tenants as no more important than a blade of grass."

A poem by Wang Yü-ch'eng (died 1001) paints a poignant picture of rural destitution in times of famine, with long lines of peasants, uprooted from their native soil and forced to emigrate as best they could:

There is a famine . . .
Everywhere food is lacking.
No smoke rises from the chimneys.
A group of beggars passes on the road:
They are a family: an old man with his old wife, who is ill;
Three children, led by a man, follow weeping.
Their food for the journey is only a quart of grain, and they have not so much as a hundred cash for expenses.
They left Ch'ang-an last year, driven by famine.

The mother of the children is dead and they have buried her in a foreign land.
Now they are trying to get back to the garden which once kept them alive.
Haggard and thin, without strength and without support,
I fear that on some day of rain or snow their dead bodies will be lying in a valley.

It must be admitted that these conditions were not confined to the Sung period; years of famine, with their train of suffering and misery, recur periodically throughout Chinese history. But it is certain that at this time, when no solution had been found for the agrarian problem, the misery of the peasants seemed irremediable. Besides this, the disappearance of small holdings completely upset the assessment of taxes and disorganized the finances of the state, which had in any case been ruined by a century of *coups d'état* and civil wars.[1]

The Sung dynasty, which after so much civil warfare seemed to promise a general restoration of traditional values, was from the first concerned with providing a definite intellectual basis for this restoration. From the time of his accession the founder of the dynasty, the wise Chao K'uang-yin, relied on the Confucian literati (*ju*), from whose ranks he and his successors recruited their administrative personnel. In order to provide a regular supply of recruits, they re-established and reorganized the system of civil service examinations, which then received its final form. The emperor Jen-tsung (1025–1063) completed these measures by creating academic schools in the principal cities and a higher imperial academy in the capital, and also by recasting the examination syllabus to include three principal subjects: documentary style, exposition, and poetry. Finally, he entrusted important public offices to two of the most eminent men of letters of his time, Ou-yang Hsiu (1007–1072) and Ssu-ma Kuang (1019–1086), both known as historians and the former equally famous as a poet.

[1] In 1065, on the eve of the reforms of Wang An-shih, the ordinary state expenditure—according to the *Sung History*—amounted to 120, 343, 174 cash, plus 11, 521, 278 cash extraordinary expenditure, while the revenue was only 110, 138, 400 cash.

It was not long before the literati became divided amongst themselves. While they all appealed to Confucian orthodoxy, they differed over its interpretation and over the proper solution for the economic and social crisis of their times. During the reign of the emperor Shen-tsung (1068–1085), the reformists came into power under the leadership of the famous Wang An-shih.

Actually, reforms were already in the air well before his time. Under the emperor Jen-tsung (1023–1063), "granaries of charity" (*kuang-hui*) were opened in 1057 for distributions of grain to old people, children, the poor and the sick. The emperor Ying-tsung (1064–1067), although a ruler of conservative tendencies, devoted a million cash to the endowment of "regulative granaries" (*chang-p'ing*). In years when the harvest was over-abundant and prices fell, these granaries bought grain at a rate higher than that of the market, and in years when the harvests were bad and speculation produced a rise in prices, they released grain at a lower rate. These state granaries thus served the double purpose of forming reserves of grain against times of scarcity and of controlling prices by frustrating speculation.

However, Wang An-shih soon surpassed these modest efforts.

Wang An-shih (1019–1086) is one of the most interesting figures in Chinese history. Few people have been so fiercely attacked during their lives. He was reproached because of his doctrinaire stubbornness, his careless garb and his unwashed face, all in such contrast to the other literati. Yet in recent times he has been lauded to the skies and regarded not only as a "state socialist", but as a democrat and a precursor of Sun Yat-sen. In reality his reforms seem to have been dictated above all by fiscal considerations. It was necessary to help the people to produce more, in order that the state might grow rich from the general prosperity. It was with this double object—to better the lot of the people while enriching the state—that in 1069 Wang An-shih instituted a permanent reform commission headed by himself. The remodelling of the economic system began immediately. Wang An-shih established a fixed budget of revenue and expenditure which was not to be exceeded under any pretext, and which reduced expenditure by forty per cent.

Agriculture was by far the greatest source of China's wealth. In order to increase the yield, Wang An-shih resolved to protect the peasants from destitution and from seizure by creditors. To this end the state granted loans to the peasants, on the security of the harvest.[1] These advances were made to them in the spring; in the autumn, after the harvest, the loans and the interest were repaid to the state. Another complaint of the countrymen was the arbitrary fashion in which local officials ordered them to do forced labour. Wang An-shih abolished forced labour, replacing it by a yearly tax which constituted a fund to pay for public works. This was a highly important innovation, for this tax was the first to be levied on individuals. At the same time he had the register of the land survey brought up to date, a reform which had been made indispensable by the agrarian changes of the ninth century. In ancient China the land tax had been levied on peasant lands which were often the property of the village. Since the ninth century, when these small holdings disappeared and became incorporated in the large estates, it had become necessary to find some other system. This is what Wang An-shih had in mind when he introduced a reorganization of the land register—not, as has been claimed by some, a redistribution of property. In 1073 he divided up the whole country into units of one li (about 630 yards) square, which were to be the basic units for the assessment of a new land tax. As Henri Maspero has pointed out, this was a purely fiscal reform, without any "social" character: "The ownership of the land remained unchanged and bore no relation to these new fiscal divisions. Where either the whole or portions of properties belonging to several landowners lay in the same square, each paid a part of the tax due on the whole square in proportion to the area belonging to him." The system of landed property remained that of the latifundia (even a reformer like Wang An-shih did not consider

[1] In Chinese *ch'ing-miao*. The institution dates from September, 1067 (*cf.* Tcheou Hoan, *Le prêt sur récolte*, Paris, 1930).

attacking it), but the empire was given an accurate and convenient cadastral survey.

Meanwhile state control was triumphant. After 1074 every landowner had to make a declaration of everything that he possessed, "including the pigs and the hens". Commerce was also regulated. All commodities were priced by the mandarins, who fixed the compulsory market rate. The state bought up stocks of all unsold goods. Taxes were paid in kind. The mandarins became, as it were, official warehousemen who stored these products and redistributed them as advances at sowing time or in periods of scarcity. "The object of these measures was to keep prices at a reasonable level and frustrate speculation by preventing any illicit rise or any excessive drop in commodity prices." But here again the ultimate object was a fiscal one. Merchandise in warehouses was liable to an annual tax of twenty per cent, which was guaranteed by the merchandise itself and by the buildings in which it was stored. If this tax was not paid in time, it was increased by a further two per cent. Along with the loans on the harvest, Wang An-shih in 1071–1072 had likewise created state loans on property so as to encourage commercial enterprise. More precisely, "a tribunal specially created for the organization of trade in the markets" (*shih-i wu*) was empowered to grant loans to merchants on the security of mortgages.

Wang An-shih was a man of letters, but he considered that the syllabus of the state examinations was more likely to produce pedants than administrators. In 1071 he cut out the literary compositions in which style was more important than ideas, as well as all literature in the sense of belles-lettres. Thenceforth the syllabus consisted of the interpretation of the Confucian classics in accordance with the new exegesis of the reformer, exposition, and administrative documents. Candidates were to be judged more by their personal ideas and practical knowledge than by the elegance of their style.

It was these literary reforms, rather than his economic innovations, that exposed Wang An-shih to the most violent opposition from the majority of the mandarinate. His new interpretation of the canonical books to accord with his own ideas appeared to conservative Confucianists as a form of sacrilege. All his reforms were treated with derision, and the subsequent accounts of the period read like a long pamphlet directed against him. Since the history was, in effect, written by his triumphant adversaries, it is difficult to form an unbiased opinion. It seems, however, that his agrarian reforms did lead to a reduction in the cost of living. According to his own testimony, as long as his reforms remained in force, "rice became as cheap as water". One of his poems (for like all the literati of his time he was also a poet) is movingly sincere, and shows what a deeply human feeling inspired his economic measures:

If anyone is in need of money for a wedding or a funeral,
I will lend it to him to dispel his anxiety.
If anyone has had a poor harvest,
I will give him all the grain that I possess so that he has something to live on.
If the crops are plentiful, I collect them;
If they are insufficient, I give out all that I possess so that work may go on.
In these days people bother little about them, but for my part I am resolved to put down the speculators.

It is nevertheless true that these reforms, which were perhaps applied too rigidly, gave rise to an opposition which was all the more formidable because it took the form of inertia. The storing of products by the officials demanded an incorruptible administration, and it appears that the actual administration was far from incorruptible. Even the loans made to the peasants at sowing time produced results contrary to the intentions of the legislator. All too often the peasants to whom these loans had been granted failed to pay them back, and as a result found themselves expropriated by the authorities. The leader of the conservative party, the historian Ssu-ma Kuang, had a good opportunity of criticizing the whole system on these grounds: "There is nothing more specious, nothing finer in theory, and nothing more prejudicial to the state in practice. You lend grain to the people and they begin by consuming part of it. You lend them grain and they sell it and their activity ceases; they become lazy." To this Wang An-shih replied: "The literati will only walk in the ways trodden by their ancestors; if they are offered safer, more useful and more convenient ways, they will not condescend to take a single step to test them."

The most serious criticism that could be levelled against Wang An-shih's reforms was that the state only granted the harvest loans at a rate of interest of twenty per cent. This was doubtless a comparatively moderate rate in comparison with the fifty per cent charged by private moneylenders. It is none the less true that the peasants thus got into debt under singularly onerous conditions. If the harvest were at all bad or if, as Ssu-ma Kuang predicted, they had unthinkingly squandered the amounts lent them, then, when repayment fell due, they had only the choice between expropriation and flight. The danger was all the greater because, while the poor were hardly able to resist the temptation of a sudden advance of funds, the local officials found it to their personal interest to make them succumb; for the interest on these twenty per cent harvest loans constituted one of the richest sources of provincial revenue. The administration was thus led to exert all available pressure to persuade the peasant to run into debt. Despite Wang An-shih's good intentions, the harvest loan was assuming the odious form of a supertax extorted from the simple-minded or destitute peasants, and the reformist state was acting the part of a large-scale usurer. Fundamentally, Wang-an Shih was suspended between his humane and generous desire to come to the aid of the people and the necessity of restoring the finances of the state. His adversaries the conservatives showed no lack of skill in contrasting his system of harvest loans with the more modest but more reliable scheme of "regulative granaries" (which we have already defined).

The death of the emperor Shen-tsung in 1085, and the accession of his fifteen-year-old son, under the regency of the dowager empress Kao, led to the disgrace of the reformists and the return to power of the conservatives led by Ssu-ma Kuang. Shortly after this Wang An-shih died, and his death was followed by that of Ssu-ma Kuang

(1086). The most prominent personality in the conservative party, after Ssu-ma Kuang, was the poet Su Shih, usually known as Su Tung-p'o (1036–1101), whose influence seems to have been a happy one. Having an intimate understanding of the people, and of the points of view and the true aspirations of humble folk, he sought to lower the barriers separating the throne from its subjects and to break down the dangerous isolation of the court. "In times of good government", he said, "the humblest subject should be free to let the emperor know of his grievances." However, Su Shih's frankness soon brought him into disgrace, and when the empress regent (who favoured the conservative party) died in 1093, the emperor Che-tsung reinstated the reformists. The next ruler, Hui-tsung (1100–1125), whose dramatic fate will be discussed presently, first recalled the conservatives in 1106, and then again placed his confidence in the reformists in 1112. But from now on it was probably less a question of the fate of the reform movement than a matter of personal conflicts between politicians of the two parties. At all events, despite political quarrels the peace which the Sung dynasty brought to China produced beneficial results. Whereas the census of 845 had indicated a population of some thirty million, the census of 1083 indicated nearly ninety million. This was probably not because of of any large increase in North China—the old China—which was already densely populated, but because the southern part of the empire—the new China—which had been systematically colonized since Han times, was beginning to acquire a considerable density of population.

Moreover, it was fortunate that this colonization of the south had now been completed. The policies of the emperor Hui-tsung, by bringing about a barbarian invasion of the northern provinces, were to make the south once more a refuge of Chinese independence.

CHAPTER XXII

A DREAMER ON THE THRONE—THE EMPEROR HUI-TSUNG

THE emperor Hui-tsung, who at nineteen ascended the throne at Kaifeng (in February or March, 1100) was one of the most cultured rulers that China has ever possessed. An aesthete and an archaeologist, a great collector and critic of art, he was himself a talented painter. He presided in person over the meetings of the T'u-hua-yüan, an academy of painting whose members, dressed in violet and carrying insignia of gold and jade, enjoyed the privilege of being admitted to the private apartments of the sovereign. Hui-tsung himself proposed the subjects for competitions and judged the candidates. Some of these themes are recorded, and they give a good idea of the emperor's taste: "An inn, surrounded by bamboos, near a bridge"; "A boat which remains idle all day because nobody wishes to cross the river"; "A pheasant walking in the palace park". The emperor himself specialized in painting birds and flowers, and it is possible that some of the works attributed to him in Japanese collections are really from his brush. In his palace at Kaifeng he gathered a unique collection of old masters, the catalogue of which has been preserved; it contains more than six thousand names.

Hui-tsung was equally interested in religious speculation. For the last hundred years a religious revival had been taking place in the various Chinese faiths. Among Buddhists it was found in the cult of the *dhyani-buddha* Amitabha. This was virtually a new religion within the bosom of the old; it brought the Chinese masses an equivalent of theism, or to be more exact, a pietism and a quietism accessible to all who were willing; it was a religion of the heart, something the like of which Eastern Asia had never seen before. The faithful soul had only to put his whole trust in the pity of Amitabha to be saved by the latter's grace and to be reborn among the blessed in an ineffable Beyond, a veritable paradise (*sukhavati*), "the Pure Land". The portraits of the *arhat* or Buddhist saints (*lo-han* in Chinese) by the painter Li Lung-mien (1040–1106), with their elongated ascetic faces, so strangely intellectual, show how deeply Buddhism had penetrated into the Chinese soul, for these essentially Indian subjects had by now become entirely Chinese.

At about the same period Taoism also evolved towards an analogous theism by creating the cult of a transcendent divinity, "the Pure August One", or literally "the Jade August One" (jade being in China a symbol of purity). It is true that this supreme god was born somewhat late; he appeared for the first time in 1012, when he revealed his existence to the emperor Chen-tsung. Hui-tsung, in his turn, showed great devotion to this deity. The monarch had long been seeking some direct contact with the genii and immortals of the Taoist pantheon when suddenly his prayers were granted. One winter's day, when he was walking in the country near Kaifeng—it was in December, 1113—he saw on the horizon a "celestial palace" whose fairy buildings floated in the air "above the clouds". It was beyond all doubt the home of the immortals, "and it gave him a longing to pass from the dust of this world to that island of the blessed". It was this beatific vision which, according to the evidence of contemporaries, Hui-tsung sought to reproduce in one of his paintings.

Hui-tsung seems to have envisaged a sort of Confucian-Taoist syncretism, in which Buddhism was also to be included. The supreme god of Neo-Taoism, the "Jade August One", was declared by him to be identical with the "Lord On High" and the "August Heaven" of the Confucianists, while into the pantheon presided over by this deity he incorporated the various Buddhist bodhisattvas from the skies of India.

Intellectuals should take care never to become involved in

politics, least of all in foreign policy. This imperial dreamer, Hui-tsung, could have led a happy life collecting works of art, painting quails and flowering plum trees, and amalgamating cults and divinities. Instead, to his own ruin and that of his country, he went in for world politics, in which he made an irreparable mistake: in the hope of recovering Peking from the Ch'i-tan, he allied himself with the Ju-chen (Djurchet), a Tungus people, ancestors of the Manchus, who inhabited the forests of what is today northeastern Manchuria and the Russian Primorsk.

This was an act of pure folly. For the last century the Ch'i-tan, largely assimilated to Chinese customs and thought, and satisfied with possessing the two marches of Peking and Ta-t'ung, as well as present-day Liaoning, Chahar and Jehol, had been enlightened and peaceful neighbours of the Sung empire. The Ju-chen, on the other hand, were still half-savage, and used to hold wild dances in their forest clearings, with their khan seated on a dozen tiger skins. China had everything to lose by putting the Ju-chen in the place of the Ch'i-tan; but Hui-tsung, fired by his desire to recover Peking and thus succeed where his ancestors had failed, persuaded himself that the victorious Ju-chen would be content with Inner Mongolia and Manchuria. He concluded a pact with their khan, Aguda, who in 1114 attacked the Ch'i-tan from the rear in Manchuria. At first all went according to the emperor's wishes; the Ch'i-tan were annihilated, and in 1122 Peking, their last outpost, fell into the hands of the Ju-chen. It was then that the troubles of the Chinese court began.

The former Ch'i-tan kingdom was now entirely controlled by the formidable Ju-chen, who had thus become the immediate neighbours of the Sung Empire. According to the terms of their former treaty, the emperor Hui-tsung asked them to hand over Peking. This they consented to do, though with reluctance. It would have been prudent to have been satisfied with this, but Hui-tsung also laid claim to a number of places between Peking and the Great Wall. When he failed to obtain these concessions, he secretly fomented revolts of the local Chinese population against the conquerors.

This meant war, and it was a war for which the court at Kaifeng was totally unprepared. The Ju-chen not only took possession of Peking, but within a few months their cavalry made a sudden thrust through southern Hopei, sweeping across the Great Plain to the banks of the Yellow River. At Kaifeng the court was stricken with terror. Instead of placing himself at the head of his troops, the incurably intellectual Hui-tsung proceeded to change his ministry. He turned out the reformists, recalled the conservatives and, in conformity with the wishes of the latter, re-established the former syllabus for the examinations, restoring literature to its place of honour. . . . In the meantime the Ju-chen had crossed the Yellow River and begun to blockade Kaifeng. Worried to distraction, Hui-tsung finally capitulated (towards the end of 1126). He was deported, with his eldest son, his attendants and his treasures, into the depths of the Ju-chen country in northern Manchuria (early in 1127).

The dilettante emperor, the refined collector of works of art, was to end his days in some clearing in the Manchurian forest, amidst the rough hunters dressed in animal skins; he never saw his own country again, and died at the early age of fifty-four after nine years of exile.

One of Hui-tsung's younger sons had escaped the catastrophe. This young man (he was twenty-one years old), who was to bear the dynastic title of Kao-tsung, was proclaimed emperor at Nanking (Chien-k'ang), a city protected from the invaders by the Long River (May or June, 1127). In the meantime the Ju-chen had completed their conquest of North China. They then crossed the Long River with two armies, one in Hopei, near to Lake Po-yang, and the other on the lower reaches of the river. The first pushed as far as southern Kiangsi, while the second took Nanking by surprise and then raced on to Ning-po, on the coast of Chekiang (1129–1130). However, their columns, which were composed entirely of cavalry, were delayed by the difficulty of finding remounts, and ran dangerous risks in a country cut up by hills, rivers and paddy fields. Soon they had to think of turning back. They had now to recross the Long River, which was as wide as an arm of the sea and blocked by Chinese junks. They finally succeeded in getting across east of Nanking, and made their way back into Honan. The south being now free from the invaders, the emperor Kao-tsung in 1132 took up residence at Hangchow (renamed Lin-an), the present-day capital of the province of Chekiang, a city which was to remain the capital of the Sung Empire until the time of the Mongol conquest.

The Chinese generals took advantage of the temporary exhaustion of the Ju-chen forces to recover several strategic positions. The most valiant among them was called Yüeh Fei; he had already won several battles, and in 1138 was preparing to march against Kaifeng. He would doubtless have restored the former capital to the empire, had not a minister who was jealous of his successes first compelled him to desist, then had him imprisoned on a trumped-up charge, and finally arranged for him to be killed in prison. The emperor Kao-tsung, a weak and indolent individual, was tired of war. In this same year, 1138, he made peace with the Ju-chen, giving up to them all the territory which they were occupying, that is to say the whole of North China down to the Huai River. The Sung dynasty retained South China, that is to say the Long River basin and the regions of Fukien and Canton; the Sung capital, as already stated, was at Hangchow, in Chekiang.

In North China, the Ju-chen were not long in adopting Chinese customs. Their kings assumed the dynastic name of Chin ("Gold"), the name by which they are known in the histories and by which we shall refer to them henceforth.[1] In 1153 the Chin dynasty, which until that time had kept its royal residence in Manchuria, transferred its capital to Peking—a clear sign that the state was becoming sinicized.

[1] This is a different word from the name of the Chin dynasty which followed the Three Kingdoms and which ruled at Nanking from 318 to 420.

CHAPTER XXIII

THE REFINEMENTS OF LIFE

THE Sung emperors, having given up hope of reconquering North China, now devoted all their attention to re-creating, in their southern domain, the atmosphere of poetry and art, the refinements of life, which had been enjoyed in the palace of Kaifeng. Two short wars against Chin, in 1161 and 1206, were only brief episodes of disturbance in the peace. The catastrophe of 1126, despite the immense territorial losses sustained by the empire, seems itself to have been a mere episode. In every field the refined civilization of the Sung dynasty, the flower of Chinese culture, continued. We must try to evoke its art and poetry, and we shall begin by going back to the Kaifeng period (960–1126), and then pass on to the Hangchow period (1132–1276).

There is a valuable document concerning the conception of landscape painting during the Kaifeng period, the treatise on "Mountains and Waters" (*Shan-shui*) of the painter Kuo Hsi (born about 1020). Here one sees what close observers of nature were these masters of the eleventh century:

> The clouds and the vapours of real landscapes are not the same at the four seasons. In spring they are light and diffused, in summer rich and dense, in autumn scattered and thin, in winter dark and solitary. When such effects can be seen in pictures, the clouds and vapours have an air of life. The mist around the mountains is not the same at the four seasons. The mountains in spring are light and seductive as if smiling; the mountains in summer have a blue-green colour which seems to be spread over them; the mountains in autumn are bright and tidy as if freshly painted; the mountains in winter are sad and tranquil as if sleeping.

And further on:

> The majestic big mountain rules over the lesser mountains which

surround it. The ridges and hillocks, the forests and ravines, far and near, large and small, acknowledge it as their master. Its appearance is that of an emperor enthroned amidst an assembly of princes.

The tall, straight pines are the leaders among trees. They support the climbing plants and creepers which trust to them as masters.

Kuo Hsi also points out that mountains change in appearance and, as it were, in personality, according to the distance from which one sees them.

Every distance causes a difference; the shapes of the mountains vary with every step. A single mountain may combine the shapes and aspects of several hundreds of mountains.

They also change in spirit according to the season: mountains in Spring are veiled in fleecy clouds, "and people are happy"; Summer mountains have shady trees, "and people are contented"; Autumn mountains are clear and pure, with falling leaves, "and people are composed"; Winter mountains are covered by dark clouds and swept by storms, "and people are silent and lonely".

It will be noticed that Kuo Hsi's treatise is purely and simply a commentary on the idea—discovered much later in the West—that landscape is a state of mind.

A topic on which the Sung master lays special stress is the importance of the interplay of light and shade on mountains, and above all the importance of the interposition of mists.

The shapes of a mountain depend on sunlight and shadow. The parts which are covered in mist and vapours must be hidden, and only the parts where the mists and vapours do not reach remain visible.

Mountains without mists and clouds are like spring without flowers.

We know from Chinese historians that Kuo Hsi himself followed these maxims and painted "ancient pines, winding streams, overhanging ledges of rock, deep gorges, high peaks and precipitous cliffs, partly hidden by clouds and layers of mist, or softened by haze". The paintings attributed to him in Japanese collections give at least an idea of his manner. A winter study: "Snow piles up in crevices, and ice blocks the river, where the ferry carries across its load of shivering travellers." Spring: "The waves lap against the boat, and the mountains are lost in a light haze." An autumn evening, his favourite subject: "The sky is clearing after rain, and wild geese cross the sky in long lines that seem to meet the distant mountain ranges." Mi Fei (1051–1107), the other great painter of Kaifeng, has left similar landscape paintings. He has never been excelled in rendering the characteristic features of the "Sinaean folds", which appear in his paintings just as they are described by modern geographers, as "breaking waves of wooded hills, and mountains with rounded summits which pierce through layers of fleecy mist".

Much of Sung poetry is a literary version of masterpieces of painting. For example the poet Ou-yang Hsiu (1007–1072), who lived during the Kaifeng period (and was one of the leaders of the conservative party), writes in his *Song of the Distant Mountains*:

> A single colour covers the mountains near and far.
> We have walked all day, but the mountain is still there in front
> of us.
> The appearance of the hills and peaks is for ever changing,
> But the traveller passes on without learning their name.

Or take this river scene:

> On the frozen river the ice, heaped up for several days, is melting;
> The banks are beginning to thaw.
> At dusk everyone returns to his home;
> Then the gulls come and settle on the fishermen's boats.

Or this, on the theme of the fisherman:

> The wind bows the line from the long fishing-rod.
> Wearing a straw hat and a grass rain-cloak, the fisherman hides
> among the reeds.
> He is lost from view in the fine spring rain,
> And the mist rising from the water hides the mountain opposite.

Ou-yang Hsiu has left an equally penetrating musical impression, this time in prose, on the subject of the sounds of autumn:[1]

[1] There are no exact equivalents to the words " poetry " and " prose " in Chinese. *The Sounds of Autumn* is a *fu*. The *fu* is said to have developed from early spells or invocations, and was the principal form used by the Han poets. The Sung *fu* have been called "prose" *fu*; they are in "loose style", that is, without rhyme or strictly antithetic phrases.

> One night I was reading when I heard a sound that came from the south-west. At first something seemed to fall, as drops of water fall, one by one, with a sound soft and sad. Then a gust of wind suddenly arose, burst forth, rushed on its way and started crashing like wild waves in the night, like a storm suddenly broken loose. It was like warriors marching silently towards the enemy: neither cries nor orders, only the muffled sound of the tramp of men and horses. I sent my young servant to find out what was happening outside. He came back and said to me: "The stars and the moon are bright and serene, the Milky Way is in the sky. There is no human sound in any direction. The noise is among the trees. It is the sound of autumn. . . ."

The other great Sung poet, Su Shih, usually known as Su Tung-p'o (1036–1101) (he too was one of the leaders of the traditionalist party during the Kaifeng period), has left writings worthy of the old T'ang masters. *The Red Cliff* (on the banks of the Long River in Hupei) is one of the most famous pieces in Chinese literature:

> . . . The breeze was almost imperceptible, the surface of the water was calm. . . . A little later the moon rose over the eastern hills and began her lingering journey among the constellations. Her light fell like dew upon the sparkling river, which seemed to become one with the sky. We let our boat drift as it would, sailing over the vast expanse, and felt that we were sailing in empty space and riding on the wind . . . we were light as if we had forsaken the world, and free of all support like one who has become an immortal and soars through space. . . . One of my guests played on his flute. The notes sighed as if with complaint and yearning, weeping and lamenting, and the echo, like a silken thread, wove endlessly in. . . . One of us said: "We are passengers of a day between earth and sky. Oh to be the Long River that flows on for ever! To join with an immortal and fly away with him, to grasp the bright moon and live for ever!" I replied: "But do you understand the water and the moon? This water that runs away is never gone, and that moon, though it waxes and wanes, is never augmented or diminished. For if we consider things from the point of view of that which changes, then earth and sky pass away in an instant; but if we consider them from the point of view of that which does not change, then all things, and we ourselves, are immortal. . . ."

Such was the heritage which the Sung Emperors brought with them to South China when they abandoned the northern provinces to the invader.

And it was not jeopardized by the migration. The new capital at Hangchow (which remained the chief city of Sung from 1132 until 1276) soon eclipsed the memory of Kaifeng, becoming a city of even finer art treasures. When he moved his official residence to Hangchow, the emperor Kao-tsung (1127–1162) gathered together the artists who had won fame at his father's court at Kaifeng, and he was soon able to reconstitute the academy of painting. Like Hui-tsung in former years, he personally conferred the decoration of the Golden Belt on the most celebrated artists, and lodged them in his palace. He liked to write out old poems in his own calligraphy and then entrust his artists with the illustrations. His grandson the emperor Ning-tsung (1195–1224) also became a great lover of painting and conferred the Golden Belt, not only on masters of the official school of the Confucian literati, but also on a number of artists of the independent, that is to say Buddhist, school. Texts of this period attest the loving care with which Kao-tsung and Ning-tsung supervised the decoration, by members of the imperial academy, of the palaces and pavilions which were being built all over Hangchow.

The town lent itself to this adornment. It was admirably situated, and well suited to captivate such born artists as the last Sung emperors. Washed by the waters of the Ch'ien-t'ang on its eastern side, close to the point where that river flows into Hangchow Bay, and skirted on the west by the shores of the "Western Lake" (Hsi-hu), it is, like Venice, a city of waters. Marco Polo, who loved it because it reminded him of his native land, marvelled at the innumerable boats, the stone bridges, and the lake whose wooded islands and verdant banks sheltered a multitude of pavilions, summer-houses, pagodas, and palaces. On the horizon, like a back-drop, were mountains with deep valleys and curiously shaped peaks, mountains sheltering many Buddhist monasteries and immortalized by painters and poets—for all the scenery in the region of Hangchow has long ago been treated by the old Sung masters.

The imperial court led the fashion. The emperor Kao-tsung had a large and magnificent pavilion built in the mountains above the

Western Lake, and the painter Hsiao Chao decorated it with a vast panorama of rivers and mountain peaks, "so well done that one did not know if one was looking at a painting or at the neighbouring landscape". It was not only the Hangchow scenery, but that of all Chekiang which caused a renewal of artistic inspiration. It is a province remarkable for the diversity of its scenery. In the north, from the mouth of the Long River to Hangchow, there is a coastal zone of polders, land reclaimed from the sea, reminiscent of Dutch landscapes, with a maritime plain rising only three to six feet above sea level, stretching as far as the eye can see, and broken up in every direction by innumerable canals. In the south, from Hangchow as far as Fukien and beyond runs a broken coastline, with complex bays which divide suddenly soaring granite mountains, with jagged cliffs, and with grass land bristling with rocks of porphyry. Geographers have long ago pointed out the similarity between these formations and those along the shores of the Inland Sea in Japan. Thus it is not surprising to find marked affinities between Japanese landscape painters (from the fifteenth century onwards) and the Hangchow masters. The former doubtless copied the latter, but they also copied the scenery of their own country.

The Japanese have recently published some highly interesting comparisons between the most famous paintings of the Sung period and photographs of the coastline and mountains of Fukien and Chekiang. They show in a striking fashion how faithful to nature were the Sung masters. As for the similarities between Chekiang and Japan, Sion describes how Richthofen, when he visited Chekiang, "filled page after page of his travel diaries noting this resemblance to Japan: few forests, but near each strangely shaped crag a pagoda surrounded by majestic cypresses; down in the valleys dense thickets of bamboos and lofty trees, innumerable water-mills, and massive white houses. Above all, an abundance of vegetation on these well-watered hills: here and there clumps of pines and oaks, tallow and varnish trees; immense thickets of shrubs with fleshy leaves, where creepers such as honeysuckle and wistaria intertwine; entire hillsides covered by myrtles, azaleas, rhododendrons, and wild roses. It is a country of flowers and green shrubs. In no other part of China does one find a countryside so picturesque, or such a variety of shapes and colours". There is undoubtedly an expression of a certain philosophy of nature, both in the Sung landscape paintings of the twelfth and thirteenth centuries and in the Japanese of the fifteenth and sixteenth; but there is also a realistic depiction of actual places, whether in Chekiang and Fukien or in Japan—and the former are very often akin to the latter. Thus the granite or porphyry mountains of Chekiang, with their abrupt slopes which are ascended by "stairways" cut in the rock, where waterfalls drop from heights of three hundred feet and more (like those in the "Snowy Valley" near Ningpo), appear to abound in "Japanese" landscapes—as is confirmed by Japanese series of comparative photographs.

Artists of the Sung and Ming period naturally took a special delight in reproducing the historic sites in the neighbourhood of Hangchow, above all the shores and islands of the Western Lake. The best description of this celebrated lake is that of Arnold Vissière:

> In the distance the mountains rise in tiers and bound the lake on the west. The nearest is surmounted by a lofty pagoda, built on a rocky base the sides of which are covered with inscriptions. Skirting this high place, you arrive at the bridge called Tuan-ch'iao, which is considered to be one of the "ten wonders" of the lake and is continued by a causeway. This paved embankment was constructed under the T'ang dynasty by the poet Po Chü-i, and leads to the Solitary Mountain island or Ku-shan. When you have traversed more than half this cool and pleasant path, you arrive at another stone bridge crossing a break in the embankment which allows the waters to flow from one lake to another. This is "The bridge which resembles an embroidered silken belt."

The most famous beauty spots are those found on the Solitary Mountain island:

> To the right is the mountain from which the island takes it name. It is of a fair height, wooded and verdant, and is dotted here and there with summerhouses and little white buildings sheltering stone inscriptions, witnesses to the past. To the left, on the water's edge, are pavilions, temples, landing places for pleasure boats, and farther on, an imperial

retreat surrounded by dark red painted walls which ascend the southern slopes of Ku-shan as far as its summit. The first pavilion, whose stone balconies, railings, and typically Chinese bridge extend over the waters of the lake, is also on the list of the beauty spots of Hsi-hu. It carries as its motto:

On the tranquil lake, the moon in autumn.

On all sides, on the shores and on the islands in the middle of the lake, are to be seen the elegant buildings of temples and private villas, surrounded by foliage. Taking a paved road you climb Ku-shan, which is covered with crowded vegetation, rockeries and stone inscriptions. Notice an elegant pavilion, known as "The pavilion from which the storks take flight", whose stone balustrades overhang the edge of the little lake. On the mainland, among the mountains to the west, there rises a peak so sheer that the Chinese have called it "The peak that was borne through the air", and there too is "The paved road which winds between gigantic trees, among streams falling in cascades, and leads upwards to an ancient Buddhist temple". The imperial palace itself, now ruined, stood on the southern slopes of the island "whence the eye could take in the gracious and imposing vistas of the lake, from the walls of Hangchow to the lofty peaks in the west".

Yet for the Hangchow masters these material elements served merely as a vehicle for transporting the thoughts to a purely spiritual plane. Despite their unsurpassed drawing, the world of forms was for them, to use the Buddhist idiom, only "a world of dew", a shawl of vapours through which the most precipitous mountain peaks rise up as mere apparitions. Their landscapes, drowned in mist and lost in distance, are poignant as a face. And it is indeed the face of the world that the Hangchow masters wanted to express in its most general aspect; or rather, they wanted to render its deeper significance, for the material attributes of forms are indicated only in order to suggest what lies hidden beyond. The more this outward face of land and waters, mountains and valleys, were softened by mist and simplified by distance, the better could the inward spirit be discerned. Hence the habitual use of wash. In the foreground, drawn intentionally in the barest outline, are a few trees with twisted trunks, a tumbledown hut, a boat on a shore which quickly becomes indistinct as the mist which floods the valley merges with the water. On the horizon, at distances which it is impossible to calculate—the intervening mists having made us lose all touch with reality—appear mountain ranges whose vaporous outline seems suspended in mid-air. These are landscapes where the enveloping watery vapours, by separating the various planes and half-veiling the concrete forms of near objects, finally leave nothing but pure space in an abstraction of distances.

Among the masters of this school, several names stand out as being among the greatest painters of all times: Ma Yüan, the first record of whose work is dated 1190 and who must have died before the middle of the thirteenth century, and his son Ma Lin; then Hsia Kuei, who like Ma Yüan worked during the reign of the emperor Ning-tsung (1195–1224); and finally Liang K'ai and Mu-Ch'i, who lived between 1200 and 1270.

Japanese and American collections possess several wash drawings which are believed to be the work of Ma Yüan. Sirèn describes a landscape of early spring, from the Boston Museum: "High hills in the background; at their foot a village veiled in mist. A sheet of water spanned by a bridge, and right in the foreground two willows with slender, quivering branches; one feels the morning breeze lightly touching the trees; the mist is just rising; otherwise no movement, no sound. The spring is still hesitating." In the Mitsui collection is a painting of a solitary fisherman, who is fishing with a line from his boat, on a lake in winter. The boat is lost in the immensity of the lake, whose shores cannot be seen; there is nothing but the still water and the man attentive to his task. In the Iwasaki collection there is a rainy landscape; in the foreground a moored boat, rocks, and tall trees, then there is mist and, in the background, hazy mountain peaks. In the Kuroda collection, a poet, under a pine tree which overhangs the mountainside, watches the moon rising in the sky. Ma Lin is represented by the famous *Evening Landscape* in the Nezu collection: "Only the high places of the shore emerge from the mist; a flight of swallows carries the imagination off into space." The Musée Guimet possesses a copy of a picture by Ma Lin, *Genii Meeting*

Above the Sea, a romantic evocation of a dreamlike dwelling which looms up amidst steep crags, while its lofty terrace dominates a misty scene of ocean and reefs, with birds flying across it.

There are probably original works by Hsia Kuei in the Iwasaki and Kawasaki collections and in the Palace Museum of Peking. The picture in the Kawasaki collection evokes a mountain squall in a few strokes of the brush: "In a mountain gorge a gust of wind beats down the trees above a thatched pavilion, leaves scatter, a countryman with an umbrella crosses a little bridge, battling against the blast, another has taken shelter in a pavilion. Beyond the rain showers that hide the landscape rises the crest of a hill, where some bushes are furiously shaken by the wind, the whole being indicated with hurricane force and speed." The painting attributed to Hsia Kuei in the Iwasaki collection is a view of a bay or river, with a boat moored behind a promontory; on the right are water plants and some trees, treated in the artist's usual manner with blobs and little brush strokes; in the background are glimpses of a mountainous horizon; an impression of space is created by the stretches of water and the soaring mountain chain in the distance; light and water melt into each other and contrast with the "pencilling" of the foreground. Lastly, there is the scroll in the Peking museum; a long panorama where everything tones into the atmosphere: "Rocky shores, mountains where pine trees grow thickly, bent and twisted trees, huts nestling in the thickets, bamboo bridges connecting the promontories, deep bays whose waters now flow through gorges, and now widen out into an arm of the sea where the opposite shore disappears from sight and distant junks are lost in the haze. All this is expressed by means of wash-drawing alone. . . ."

These various landscape painters belonged to the Confucian circles of the imperial academy at Hangchow. The artists inspired by Buddhism, such as Liang K'ai and Mu Ch'i, form a different group.

These men were followers of the contemplative Buddhism of the *Ch'an* school, and painted in the temples and monasteries of that sect which were scattered around the Western Lake and on the mountain slopes near Hangchow. Liang K'ai, although he enjoyed the personal favour of the emperor Ning-tsung, abandoned the imperial academy to go and live in one of these monasteries. His masterpiece, which is now in the Sakai collection in Japan, represents "Sakyamuni on his way to the Bodhi Tree". The founder of Buddhism is depicted with the features of an ascetic, standing in meditation near a torrent and leaning on his staff, amid a strange landscape of steep mountains; intensity of thought and force of meditation are expressed with piercing spirituality in the hairy, almost savage face; it is this inner force, as much as the wind blowing through the mountain gorge, which animates the bizarre folds of the thin garment and finds its counterpart in the knotted branches which, like monstrous beasts, crawl writhing at the feet of the ascetic. Of another Liang K'ai painting in the Sakai collection it may be said that it is composed of nothingness: in the foreground is a rock overhanging the water, and on it three bare and exhausted-looking trunks of trees; to the left, a snow-covered height which quickly disappears from sight; other snow-capped mountains are almost invisible in the background, while the space between is filled with mist; the real subject of the picture, and the spirit of the landscape, is *dhyani* meditation, communion with the universe.

Mu Ch'i, the greatest genius of this period, became a monk in the Buddhist monastery called Liu-t'ung-ssu, near Hangchow. He painted superhuman apparitions which belong to the realm of divinities or to that of fabulous animals. The Daitokuji possesses, among other works of this great visionary, a dragon of astonishing power: from the light and shade of a storm cloud looms this fabulous creature with its terrifying snout, its long crustacean tentacles, its demonic horns, and its flashing eyes whose look is like the flicker of lightning; all the indefinable menace of the unknown is suddenly present in this divine and bestial mask. Mu Ch'i seems here to have rediscovered the ancient pre-Confucian mythology which figures on the Shang bronzes of a period some twelve centuries before Christ.

Mu Ch'i's work is even greater when his genius is turned to the rendering of Buddhist ideas. Here the wild and almost savage power expressed in his dragon serves the cause of *Ch'an* mysticism, as in the painting in the Iwasaki collection which shows an ascetic in ecstasy. The hermit is seated on a mountain ledge. An enormous serpent encircles him with its coils and rests its menacing head on his knees. But the ascetic remains impassive and dominates the reptile by his power of concentration. This strange group appears to be borne upon clouds which rise from a chasm in the mountainside. Quite different in inspiration, but similar in composition, is the Kuan-yin in the Daitokuji; a pale apparition with a meditative expression, at once gentle and grave, seated beside the water at the foot of the mountains; the misty atmosphere blurs the peaks in the background. "Kuan-yin's robe is indicated in long lines with soft curves which suggest internal harmony and absolute calm, like the perfect stillness of the water which bathes the rock." As a painter of landscape Mu Ch'i could surpass the Confucian masters themselves, for example in the scroll in the Matsudaira collection which shows the boats returning to a fishing village on the shores of Lake Tung-t'ing. One can hardly make out the boats, because so much of the picture is filled with water, misty air, space and distance; the mountains disappear little by little into the mist; three-quarters of the picture is occupied by an expanse without foreground or background; the village itself is almost lost in the haze and shelters in its cluster of trees at the bottom corner of the scroll—to such an extent are the works of man overwhelmed by the vastness of nature. "Infinite space and silent harmony": it was the very face of the earth that the old Sung masters painted, and it has never been so well felt interpreted, or loved, as it was by them.

In such works Chinese painting approaches the realm of metaphysics, and we return to pure art with Sung ceramics, which flourished equally with painting. Just as the painters had chosen to adopt wash-drawing, that is, monochrome in Chinese ink, so too Sung ceramics shows a preference for monochrome, or at most one tone upon another. This is because both arts "were catering for the taste of a society of dilettanti who considered moderation as the height of luxury. The beauty of Sung ceramics lies in its muted richness, delicate shades and subtle harmonies; more than at any other period the material is valued for its own sake, for its texture, lustre, resonance and brilliance, and is made both to delight the eyes and to satisfy the delicate pleasures of touch". This is expressly set forth in an imperial rescript issued between 954 and 959, on the eve of the Sung period, which required that Ch'ai-yao ware be "blue as the sky, clear as a mirror, thin as paper, and resonant as a musical stone of jade".

The *Ju* ware, so called after the kilns of Ju-chou, in Honan, was being produced before the twelfth century, and it answers well to the above description. The glaze is generally a bluish lavender-grey or a pale lavender blue. Another pottery centre was Tz'u-chou, in Hopei, which had developed under the T'ang dynasty and which continued to produce throughout the Sung period. It is famous for elegant floral decoration in brown on a cream background. The *Ting* ware, which is called after the town of Ting-hsien, also in Hopei, usually has an ivory, cream or chamois-coloured glaze, sometimes crackled, sometimes with floral decoration, and often with a metal rim. "Because of the fineness of their material and decoration, and because of the elegance of their shapes", writes an enthusiastic collector, "these pieces may be considered the best pottery of all countries and of all times". After the removal of the Sung court from Kaifeng to Hangchow, the Ting-hsien potters retired to Ching-te-chen, in Kiangsi, where production continued throughout the Ming period and where the Ch'ing dynasty again established an imperial manufactory. A related group of wares, known as the "Honan group", includes a series of black or dark chestnut pieces with a metallic reflection in imitation of bronze. During the Kaifeng period there also appeared the celadon ware, characterized by its darkish olive green colour.

These "Northern celadons" are related to Korean ceramics, of which so few examples are to be found in Europe. The "Southern celadons" came from the kilns of Lung-ch'üan, in Chekiang; their brilliant light jade green distinguishes them at first sight from the earlier variety. The crackleware from the *Ke* pottery at Lung-ch'üan has infinitely delicate "spiders' webs" in a glaze which is generally sea green, grey-green, bluish grey or ash grey. It is often difficult to distinguish from another variety of crackleware, with a blue-grey or lavender glaze, which came from the *Kuan* ("Official") pottery—that is, from the imperial manufactory at Kaifeng. After 1127 the *Kuan* potters followed the court to Hangchow. But the makers of the famous "moonlight" ware—which has an opalescent lavender blue or mauve glaze streaked with purple "flame marks", with one tint shading into another—seem to have remained in the neighbourhood of Chün-chou, and their products are known as *Chün* ware. Chün-chou continued production up to the Mongol period. *Chien* ware, which originated in Chien-an, Fukien, is famous for bowls in dark maroon or burnt sienna glaze, flecked with lighter reflections, and known for this reason as "hare's fur" or "partridge feathers". Lastly, there are the several kinds of pieces with no written tradition. These have been collectively listed as the "pale group" by Michel Calmann; they are usually referred to as *ying-ch'ing* (clouded blue) and often do have a bluish glaze.

CHAPTER XXIV

THE CRYSTALLIZATION OF CHINESE THOUGHT

THE Sung period was distinguished, not only by an extraordinary blossoming in the realm of art, but also by a renascence of Confucian philosophy and, more generally, by the importance accorded to philosophic controversy. Now it so happened that just at this period the perfection of a most invaluable invention provided Chinese thought with a tool quite unknown elsewhere: this great event was the invention, or rather the popularization, of printing.

The discovery of printing in China was not the work of a single man, achieved in one stroke of genius, any more than it was in Europe—far less in fact. It was the work of centuries, proceeding by almost imperceptible transitions. Its origins lay in three much older inventions: paper, ink rubbings, and seals carved to print the right way round.

In ancient times the Chinese wrote on thin slips of bamboo, and later they also used a special kind of silk; but bamboo tablets were difficult to handle, while silk was expensive. According to tradition, a certain Ts'ai Lun, of the Later Han dynasty, who became a palace officer in A.D. 75 and died in 114, is credited with the invention of paper. He used the bark of trees, hempen thread, old cloth, and fishing nets; these ingredients he boiled for a long time, pounded, and reduced to a thick pulp which was "paper paste". In the T'ang period paper had become so common that Chinese prisoners captured by the Arabs at the battle of Talas in 751 are said to have introduced the technique into the Moslem world.

The technique of ink rubbings, as we have seen, goes back to the taking of copies from the Confucian classics, which were first engraved on stone in A.D. 175–183. However, since the writing was engraved on the stone it always came out white on a black background. Moreover the widespread use of rubbings is no older than the sixth century. The main technical improvements resulted from the use of seals. Like the stone inscriptions, seals had long been engraved, but at the beginning of the sixth century they began to be carved in relief and in reverse, so that the ink impression appeared right way round in black (or red) on a white background; this was an invention of the greatest importance, since it contained the fundamental principle of printing.

Under the Sui dynasty xylography (wood engraving) and the printing of characters by this means made fresh progress. An edict of 593 ordered that a large number of texts and drawings be engraved on wood. But it was the Buddhists and Taoists who were chiefly responsible for popularizing the process by printing magical charms consisting of a number of characters. Examples of Buddhist xylography of the eighth century were found at Tun-huang by the Pelliot and Aurel Stein missions, but it was on the lower Long River and in Szechwan that wood-block printing appears to have been most widespread during the T'ang period, for there it was used for making popular astrological calendars. The oldest Chinese printed book that exists today is a Buddhist text (the *Diamond Sutra*) of 868, a scroll composed of leaves of paper glued end to end. It is now in the British Museum.

With regard to printing, official Confucianism only followed the example of Taoism and Buddhism. In 904 an improvement was introduced in engraving the canonical texts on stone, when these too were engraved with the characters in reverse in order to have them appear right way round in the ink rubbings. However, this method came too late for it to be considered as the invention of printing; that had already been achieved by means of xylography, which process was soon being used to print the Confucian texts: in 932 an imperial edict ordered that the classics be engraved on wood. The final invention in printing is ascribed to a certain Pi Cheng, who was alive between 1023 and 1063, some four centuries before Gutenberg; he is said to have invented movable type moulded in terracotta.

The spread of printing was bound to have an influence on ideological developments in Sung China. The printing on paper of the Nine Classics, followed by a spate of canonical commentaries, multiplied the use of the intellectual tools and provided unforeseen facilities for the interchange of ideas.

This could not have occurred at a more opportune moment. Since the T'ang period Chinese thinkers had been endeavouring to draw up a spiritual balance sheet of the past, to discover wherein it was still deficient, and to add to it a definitive philosophy. This was a general tendency, as noticeable among the Taoists and Buddhists as among the "scholars", and it was producing a neo-Taoism, a neo-Buddhism, and a neo-Confucianism which were closer to each other than they were to the respective ancient schools which they claimed to represent. In fact, all three arrived at the same conclusion; monism, or the explanation of the universe and man by a single element. We have seen that since the sixth century the Ch'an and T'ien-t'ai sects of Buddhism had arrived at this conclusion by discovering the principle of Enlightenment, conceived as a universal essence, both in the depths of the human soul and in the heart of the universe. During the Sung period the Taoists built up a consistent cosmogony and metaphysics from the aphorisms of Lao Tzu. "The Void", one of their treatises explained, "is not really an absolute void (nothingness); it is *tao* (a term which here means the universal principle), though in a still imperceptible form. In order to manifest itself, *tao* becomes accessible to the senses. That which is sensible comprises all things that have shape and form; but shapes and forms contain *tao*, and it is this which operates within them. In all sensible beings there is a spirit which is identical with *tao*"—that is to say with the cosmic principle.

Ancient Confucianism was crowned with a similar monism by the scholastic philosophers of Sung. This great philosophical movement was initiated by Chou Tun-i (1017–1073), a writer of the Kaifeng period, when that city was still the capital. He was a soldier who had retired in order to meditate on destiny. The man himself, as he appears through the works of the philosopher, was a noble character, and he has depicted his ideal in a transparent allegory, the famous piece entitled *Love of the Lotus*:

> There are many flowers which give us pleasure. The poet T'ao Yüan-ming loved chrysanthemums alone, but since the days of the T'ang dynasty, men of the world have made a cult of the peony. I care only for the lotus, which rises up out of the mud without being soiled and bathes in the shining ripples without being enticed. Within, it is hollow (understanding); without, it is straight. It does not creep or branch, and its scent is purer at a distance; it grows clean and upright. You can view it from afar, but you cannot casually handle it. I should say that the chrysanthemum is the recluse among flowers, the red peony is the successful man, and the lotus is the gentleman. Alas! since the days of T'ao Yüan-ming few have been known for their love of the chrysanthemum; and who is with me in caring for the lotus? For most people it is natural to love the peony.

It was Chou Tun-i who introduced into Confucianism the idea of a first principle, for which he used the ancient term *t'ai-chi*, meaning literally "supreme ridge-pole" or "supreme limit" and conceived, like the ancient *tao* of Lao Tzü and Chuang Tzu, as the primordial unity. However, following the example of the neo-Taoism of his own times, he envisaged this primordial essence in an aspect that was purely cosmogonic and in no way metaphysical. It resembled the infinitely rarefied and diffused matter of what we call nebulae; a dust which, when subjected to the internal action of the laws of nature, becomes organized and through a process of evolution produces the whole universe.

Similar ideas were developed by Chou's contemporary Shao Yung (1011–1077). Chou Tun-i was a sort of mathematician of metaphysics, and has been called "a Chinese Spinoza". Shao Yung was an unconfined dreamer who has left verses worthy of Verlaine:

> I drink wine among the flowers, and get tipsy.
> Drunk, with a flowering branch in my hand, I go on singing.

> O enchanting flowers, do not laugh when you see my white head;
> For this white head has already seen fine flowers without number.

He lived on the outskirts of Kaifeng, in a wretched hut open to the wind and the rain, "with neither a fire in winter nor a fan to cool himself in summer". He gave this hovel the poetic name of "Nest of Tranquil Joy". He refused all official employment, and was content to receive at his cottage the most eminent men of his times, including the historian and minister Ssu-ma Kuang, who used to come to him, when wearied by the stormy life of the court, in search of a few moments of peace.

Shao Yung's doctrine was a pure monism:

> Man is one with heaven and earth, with all things of all times, for the law of the universe is unique. It is the law of heaven and earth, and all things partake of it. In each class of thing it reaches a degree of development which constitutes the specific nature of that class, and in each individual a degree of perfection which characterizes that individual. The primal being, from which came all that exists, is *tao*, the Supreme Limit (*t'ai-chi*), the August Limit (*huang-chi*); but these are only borrowed names; for this primordial being is indefinable, unnamable, and ineffable. Heaven and earth are not of a different nature from the rest of creation; they are the two intermediaries whereby the Supreme Limit produced everything else. Universal matter is one, and all things partake of it. Vital spirit is one, and all things partake of it. Beginnings and endings, births and deaths, are simply transformations of these two entities. All things are one with me. Then, taking the question from my side, are there really any external objects? Taking the question from the side of external objects, is there really any "I"?

It will be seen that this is not unlike the meditations of the ancient Taoist philosopher Chuang Tzu and is expressed in almost the same terms. But Shao Yung, like all the thinkers of his age, was not satisfied by these "poetic elevations". He co-ordinated these ancient ideas into a coherent system, a theory of evolution of surprising breadth: "The Supreme Limit is being in its first state of inaction. Itself a single entity, it produced by a first act another single entity, tenuous matter. Then in this matter it produced plurality through the double modality of *yin* and *yang*." It is strange to find here the most ancient notions of primitive Chinese society, in company, not only with the elaborations of later Taoism, but also with the Indian cosmogonies which Buddhism had brought to the Far East, and the whole covered, after a fashion, by the mantle of Confucian orthodoxy.

It was an ancient Hindu conception that the world passes by alternating phases of expansion and contraction through an eternal cycle of *kalpa* (ages). The same idea was expressed by the neo-Confucian philosopher Chang Tsai (1020–1076), and one may wonder if he did not in fact adapt some Sanskrit text:

> Everything began through the condensation of rarefied matter. Condensed to the point where matter becomes sensible, it was a gaseous, vaporous and flocculent mass (*ch'i*). Its quintessence, which is uncondensable, invisible and impalpable, is vital force or spirit (*shen*).
>
> Since the double motion of expansion and contraction began, all matter has been subject to it. Matter expands irresistibly into manifold shapes which return into its womb when it contracts. The double motion is continuous. It takes place in matter without causing it to change, and resembles the double phenomenon of the freezing and melting of water, in which the substance water remains unchanged in either state . . . Every birth is a condensation, every death a resolution of matter. Nothing comes at birth, nothing departs at death. In the individual, the celestial norm is vital spirit; after the individual, it becomes again the celestial norm. When condensed, matter has a form; when rarefied, it is the substratum of transformations.

This new philosophy of the literati was already formulated in all its essentials when Chu Hsi gave it its definitive form.

Chu Hsi was born in Fukien in the year 1130. He was more or less imbued with Buddhist ideas during his early life, but about 1154 he finally renounced them to return to official Confucianism. In 1163 he was summoned to the court of Hangchow by the emperor Hsiao-tsung, who appointed him imperial librarian. Later he held the position of governor in several important towns (1178–1196). In the year 1196 he finally fell into disgrace, a result of his participation in the party quarrels which divided the court, and he died in retirement in 1200. In addition to his treatises on philosophy, he compiled a general history of China, abridged from Ssu-ma Kuang's history, which still remains the most widely used work of its kind. His philosophical writings exercised so wide an influence and so completely eclipsed those of his predecessors that the entire system is generally called "Chuism".

At the beginning of things Chu Hsi puts the idea of *wu-chi*, a term which literally means "non-existence", "absolute non-existence", but which in this system really stands for potential existence, universal virtuality, or as this school describes it, the "Great Void" (*t'ai-hsü*). It is in fact from *wu-chi* that there emerges *t'ai-chi*, the principle of all things, which for Chu Hsi, as for his predecessors, is the keystone of the system. According to his definitions of it, this first principle is pure, infinite, eternal and absolute being, substance in its completeness, the principle of the world and the cause of all things. Therefore it is said to be "extremely lofty, extremely excellent, extremely subtle, and extremely spiritual". Although it can be regarded as spiritual, yet once located, it is located in matter. It is, if you like, spirit, but not spirit distinct from matter; it is one with matter, infused into the mass which it animates and organizes. Those who have seen in Chuism a metaphysical doctrine have taken *t'ai-chi* for a transcendent absolute. Others, for whom the doctrine is no more than a materialist monism, understand *t'ai-chi* to be a sort of cosmic ether. And it must be admitted that Chu Hsi's actual text lends itself to both interpretations. The following passage, for example, would seem to support the second meaning of the term: "*T'ai-chi* is like a root, which sprouts and grows, divides into several branches, then divides again and produces flowers and leaves, and so on unceasingly." One of his predecessors had likewise said: "When a plant has produced a seed, the seed, sown in the ground, produces another plant. This second plant is not the first plant, but its vital spirit is the same; for the universal vital spirit is one, and this is the law of all genesis." But in a later passage Chu Hsi, still speaking of the first principle, employs a different image which gives a quite different interpretation of his thought. Wishing to explain the omnipresence of *t'ai-chi* in the world, he writes: "It is like the moon which lights up the night. In the sky the moon is one, and yet when its soft light is spread on rivers and lakes one sees everywhere the reflection of its disc, but one cannot for this reason say that the moon is divided or loses its unity." In fact *t'ai-chi*, the reason behind the cosmic mass in general and each individual existence in particular, is at the same time transcendent and immanent, the intellectual principle of the moral world and the internal principle of the material world. Like the ancient *tao*, it gives forth the world, but the world, although consubstantial with it, is not identical with it, for the reason that the *t'ai-chi* is eternal, whereas the world which it periodically emits and reabsorbs is always ephemeral.

This emission, or organization, of the world is effected by *t'ai-chi* through the intermediary of the principle *li*, a term which can be translated as "reason" or "law," and which in fact represents the reason of things, the sum of the laws of nature. This unchanging and necessary law, valid for all orders of existence in all possible worlds, is the permanent mould in which ephemeral forms are shaped. Chu Hsi explains this in the following terms: "*Li* is like the master of the house who lives there and receives guests; he is always there, while the guests come and go." The laws of nature were pre-existent to creation: "*Li* existed before heaven and earth, and it was *li* that set energy (or matter) in motion and produced the world."

At this point there comes in another principle, *ch'i*, a term which possesses a wide range of meanings. It is originally a gaseous and aeriform mass, the essence and virtuality of the cosmos and the supporting medium for the laws of nature. The law or reason of things, *li* (and here it is clear that *li* refers to the laws of nature), awakens and sets in motion this mass, stirs up and liberates the energy dormant in it; this cosmic energy in turn, through the production and combination of opposites—*yin* and *yang*, the female and male principles—sets in motion the entire process of evolution. Thus universal reason, while infinitely transcending existence, is immanent in it. By realizing itself in matter, it animates, moulds, shapes and internally organizes things. It is the channel by which the first principle, *t'ai-chi*, is communicated to things. But this communication is only temporary: particular existences are only short-term loans from universal substance, and the destiny of each thing that exists is only an infinitesimal derivation from the laws of nature.

Chu Hsi lays particular stress on the relations between *li* and *ch'i*, the laws of nature and the gaseous mass which is the origin of all matter, and he does so in terms that Herbert Spencer would not have repudiated. The law of nature, he says, is not perceived by the senses; but its scope is limitless, and it is the principle of all unity. Matter, on the other hand, is perceptible to the senses, is limited, and is the source of all diversity. This is just the distinction which exists in European philosophies between the notion of natural laws and the notion of matter. However, like natural laws and matter, of which they are the Chinese equivalents, *li* and *ch'i* remain strictly complementary and cannot exist one without the other; it is merely for the sake of convenience that the philosopher isolates them. In reality they are two inseparable principles, although theoretically *li* is logically anterior to *ch'i*, as natural laws are to matter.

Once these philosophical principles have been laid down, Chu Hsi's cosmogony unfolds in a rigorously scientific manner. In the beginning was *t'ai-hsü*, literally the Great Void, which was space considered as the receptacle of ether, the infinitely rarefied and dispersed substance of the nebulae. In fact matter, however rarefied and diffuse it may have been in its primordial state, none the less existed with all its potentialities in the Great Void, as Chu Hsi himself points out when he says that the Great Void cannot exist without matter. Then through the action of the laws of nature, this matter agglomerates. This is the phase of primordial chaos (*hun-tun*), which corresponds to what we should call the condensation of the nebulae. Chaos in turn becomes organized, again by virtue of *li*, the laws of nature; and through gyration and the rhythmic alternation of *yin* and *yang* (again we find these ancient prehistoric Chinese conceptions) the whole of the visible cosmos is produced. "The force latent in all matter," says Chu Hsi, "produced the gyratory motion; heaven and earth were then a mass of evolving matter, turning like a millstone. As this rotary movement grew faster, the heavy parts became condensed in the centre and formed the earth, whereas the light parts, attracted towards the periphery, formed the heavens. Between earth and heaven, mankind made its appearance."

Chu Hsi explains, moreover, that this creation is only temporary. The organic cosmos is, like the individual, merely a momentary aspect of universal energy. After a hundred thousand years have passed, there will come a phase of dispersal of matter, followed by a new phase of condensation and creation. And so it will continue for ever, since this alternating rhythm is eternal and necessary, the mathematical consequence of the laws of nature. A rigorous determinism governs this evolution. Destruction and creation are linked together, as is shown by the example of the plant that dies in producing the seed which in turn will reproduce the plant: after a series of transformations the seed returns to its original form.

Chu Hsi's ethical teaching is derived from his fundamental philosophy. His ethical system is purely rationalist. The principle *li*, that is, the collective laws of nature, is the norm of the moral as well as of the physical world. Moral law is the human application of the laws of nature, as necessary and as binding as any other application of those laws.

This rationalism creates an appreciable division between Chu Hsi's philosophy and the incipient theism of certain moralists of Chinese antiquity. Chu Hsi expressly states: "Heaven is the azure which revolves above our heads. It contains no Sovereign of Heaven (whatever the ancient books may say); and matter evolves under the control of natural laws. Individual existences appear and disappear like the buckets of a chain pump,[1] some going down into the well empty and others rising again full, while the chain never stops. On the other hand, it cannot be said that the earth is without a master, since it is governed by *li* (the laws of nature)". But this

[1] The Chinese *shui-ch'e* for raising water into rice-fields is a portable device operated by treading.

motive power of the world, the principle *li*, is not to be thought of as a universal consciousness, an ineffable spirituality, the soul of souls and of worlds of Indian pantheism. "*Li*", the philosopher specifies, "acts without thought. Its action is necessary, inevitable and unconscious." Thus any idea of spiritualism is excluded.

> It is with the generations of men as with the waves of the sea; each wave is itself: the first is not the second, the second is not the third; but they are all modalities of the same water. Thus it is with man. I, who am today, am a modality of universal reason and of the matter of heaven and earth. My ancestor was also a modality of the same elements. He is no longer, but the elements remain. I am in communion with him, through community of constitution, of reason, and of matter. In the same way, heaven and earth and all things are one with me. I can call Heaven my father, Earth my mother, and all things my brothers; for they are all united with me: I am one being with the whole of the universe.

Lu Hsiang-shan (1139–1192), an opponent of Chu Hsi, expressed himself in a rather similar manner: "In fact, nothing is finite. Man, heaven, earth, and all things, exist in the infinite. . . . We are personally concerned in every affair of the universe, and the universe is concerned in all our personal affairs." It is noticeable, moreover, that in establishing, in a scientific spirit, this principle of the solidarity of man with the universe, Chu Hsi and Lu Hsiang-shan were only developing one of the most ancient conceptions of Chinese thought; a conception which dates from the dawn of history and on which all the ancient wisdom was based. Lu Hsiang-shan is still developing this train of thought when he writes:

> The universe is nothing else but my heart; my heart is the universe. Near the Eastern Sea a sage is born; his heart and his reason (literally, his *li*, or the laws which govern his thought) must resemble mine. Near the Western Sea another sage is born; and his heart and reason must also be similar to my own. In view of this principle, whether we go back to the earliest times or descend the course of future centuries indefinitely, the hearts and the reason of all sages, past, present, and future, must be identical.

If we were to translate this into Western phraseology, we might say that the sage of ancient Greece and the sage of medieval China must envisage the problem of the world in the same terms as a Leibnitz or a Kant, because the laws of thought are everywhere identical and operate everywhere on the same data. This is an affirmation of both the universal value of reason and the unity of human understanding. It is impossible to over-estimate the philosophical import of such an attitude, and any history of human thought which neglects these twelfth-century Chinese metaphysicians must be sadly incomplete; for what they have to show is nothing less than the philosophical foundation of a universal humanism.

There is a certain distinction between the system of Lu Hsiang-shan, which allows some scope for spirituality, and the purely mechanistic system of Chu Hsi. It was the latter which had a determinative influence on Chinese thought and which for seven centuries was accepted as authoritative. It is therefore important to judge it as a whole and to specify what effects it was to have.

The system is imposing. It is a coherent synthesis in which is elaborated most of the material furnished by the older doctrines, from the immemorial classifications of *yin* and *yang* to the metaphysical flights of the "Fathers" of Taoism and the ethical teachings of official Confucianism. It has even been possible to recognize in it some unacknowledged borrowing from Indian sources. The whole synthesis has been so well thought out by a powerful intellect that the completed chain unrolls with an impressive scientific rigour, as if a Spinoza were employing the material of a Herbert Spencer. The material, which in fact comes from such varied sources, has been so efficiently cemented together by Chu Hsi that the final edifice shows no sign of crack or fissure.

It was, however, something of a prison, from which the Chinese intellect was able only with difficulty to escape. For the strength of this system should not blind us to its dangers, and these were serious. By enclosing all speculation in a closed circle of mechanistic evolutionism bounded by a Nietzschean perspective of "eternal return", and by precluding any outlet for spiritualism, Chu Hsi stemmed the flow of Chinese thought and put a premature end to the great philosophical revival of the tenth, eleventh and twelfth centuries. His doctrine, which eventually became a sort of official positivism, barred the way to further speculation, plunged the mandarinate into materialism and routine, and was largely responsible for the ossification of Chinese philosophy between the thirteenth and the twentieth centuries. This was all the more serious because political events—first the Mongol conquest and then Ming conservatism—were to contribute to the same result.

CHAPTER XXV

THE CONQUEROR OF THE WORLD

WHILE the last emperors of the Sung dynasty, in their artistic city of Hangchow, were still indulging their enthusiasm for aesthetic and metaphysical problems, Genghis Khan had already begun the conquest of Asia.

He was born in the year 1167, in a felt yurt in Outer Mongolia, near the sources of the rivers Onon and Kerulen. The Mongol tribes were among the most backward of Asiatic peoples. Whatever their mode of life might be—whether they were hunters in the Siberian forest of the north, or nomadic herdsmen on the immense steppes stretching southward from the forest zone to the Gobi desert—they were still half-savage. Their entire wealth, like that of their ancestors the Huns, consisted in their flocks, with which they migrated seasonally in search of pasture and water holes. In a terrible climate of scorching heat and freezing cold they led a miserable existence, being in danger of death by starvation whenever drought withered the grass of the steppes and killed their herds. They were ignorant of writing, town life, and agriculture; and their only religion was a crude shamanism. Nestorian Christianity, which had spread among their neighbours the Kereits of central Mongolia, the Naiman Turks of western Mongolia and the Ongüt Turks of Inner Mongolia, had not filtered through to them. But these nomadic outcasts of fortune possessed a formidable military superiority over the ancient civilized empires whose riches they coveted. They were magnificent horsemen and infallible archers. The Mongol warriors of the thirteenth century were mounted archers who would appear unexpectedly, riddle the enemy with arrows, disappear, and then reappear farther on to shoot a fresh volley of arrows; this continued until the enemy was worn out and ready to break under a final assault. The mobility of this cavalry, in fact, gave it a deceptive appearance of being everywhere at the same time which in itself constituted a considerable strategic advantage over other armies of the period. Moreover, the virtuosity of these Mongol hunters and herdsmen in their use of the bow was an equally decisive factor in battles, being from a tactical point of view equivalent to a sort of "indirect fire".

The hardest campaigns fought by Genghis Khan were those against the other Turco-Mongolian hordes with whom he had to contend for the hegemony of Mongolia. By 1206 he had disposed of these rivals and made himself master of the whole region; then he turned his armies towards China.

The territory of China, as we have seen, was divided unequally between three different powers. The Ju-chen kingdom of Chin, with its capital at Peking (Yen-ching), held North China, that is to say the Yellow River basin. In the eighty years during which they had occupied these ancient Chinese provinces, the Ju-chen had become very much sinicized. The Chinese empire of Sung, with its capital at Hangchow, was in possession of South China, that is to say the Long River basin and the southern coastal provinces. Lastly, the Tangut, a people related to the Tibetans, had made themselves masters of Ordos, Alashan, and Kansu, that is to say the marches of the northwest, and had established the kingdom of Hsi-hsia. This people too was in process of becoming sinicized.

Genghis Khan began his conquest of China by attacking Hsi-hsia, and after several campaigns forced the Tangut to recognize his suzerainty (1209). He then turned his forces against Chin, and in 1211 attempted to break through the Great Wall where it defended the approaches to Peking from the directions of Jehol and Hsüan-hua. The Ju-chen, who despite their absorption of Chinese civilization had lost none of the military qualities inherited from their Tungus ancestors, put up a stubborn defence. The Mongol bard of the *Secret History* was the first to salute them as valiant and spirited adversaries. The fighting was of an unprecedented ferocity. Nine years afterwards, travellers along the road from Kalgan to Peking used to point out the battlefields, easily recognizable from the piles of human bones which were strewn about them. Some witnesses also tell of the heaps of corpses rotting on the ground, and of the epidemics which sprang from this putrefaction.

The Mongol army, composed entirely of cavalry and still ignorant of how to conduct a siege, was halted by the bastions of the Great Wall, and stayed for nearly two years in the regions of Hsüan-hua and Jehol before being able to descend into the plain of Peking (1211–1212). In 1213 Genghis Khan at last forced the passes and invaded Hopei and Shansi with three armies. He advanced into the heart of present-day Shantung, pillaging the countryside and plundering the smaller cities; but he was unable to take Peking and had to content himself with blockading it. During a truce in hostilities, the king of Chin—Marco Polo's "Golden King"—having abandoned hope of defending his capital any longer, moved his residence to Kaifeng, south of the Yellow River (June, 1214). Genghis Khan took advantage of this event to renew the war; and in May, 1215, his generals entered Peking (Chung-tu) and burned it to the ground after massacring the population. The destruction lasted for a whole month, and was so thorough that when, forty-five years later, Genghis Khan's grandson Kublai wished to make the city his capital, he had to have it re-planned and rebuilt.

This destruction shows how backward the Mongols were in comparison with the other barbarians who had preceded them. Both the Ch'i-tan, in 963, and the Ju-chen, in 1122, had made themselves masters of Peking; but far from destroying it, they had each before long made it their capital: after a minimum of bloodshed, they took over from the preceding dynasty. This was because the Ch'i-tan and the Ju-chen already had some acquaintance with Chinese civilization and were willing to be assimilated. The Mongols, on the other hand, were still a savage people, and their attitude towards their Chinese conquests was similar to that of a clan of Sioux Indians making inroads among the farms of North America.

Knowing only the nomadic way of life, they had no conception of what could be done with a great city or of the use they could make of it in consolidating their conquests. They did not at all realize the advantage of preserving what was thenceforward to be their property. Fortune had presented them with the rich agricultural lands of the Peking plain; and they destroyed everything there, not from depravity, but because they could think of no better plan.

There is a curious contrast between the personal character of Genghis Khan and the conduct of the Mongol armies. According to the most authentic available evidence, the Mongol conqueror appears to have been a wise prince; balanced in judgment, endowed with moderation and good sense, thoughtful of equity and morality; one who was able to mete out justice to a valiant enemy, but who abhorred a traitor. Yet he was not far removed from primitive savagery, and could not imagine the subjugation of conquered peoples by any means other than a general terror. To him, as to all his followers, the value of human life was negligible. Like all the nomads of the northern steppes, he was completely ignorant of the ways of sedentary peoples—customs such as living in towns, or ploughing the land—ignorant in fact of anything that lay beyond the horizon of his native steppes. Within these limitations, which were those of his age and environment, he was a natural organizer who was willing to listen to the advice of civilized people and who, by reason of his exceptional intelligence, had a natural aptitude for civilization.

Among the prisoners taken at the capture of Peking (Chung-tu), Genghis Khan singled out an illustrious figure named Yeh-lü Ch'u-ts'ai, a descendant of the royal family of the Ch'i-tan, the Tartars who had ruled in Peking a hundred years earlier and who had become almost completely sinicized. Like many of the Ch'i-tan, Yeh-lü Ch'u-ts'ai possessed a thorough knowledge of Chinese culture. He was also a statesman, and had held important positions in the Chin administration. Genghis Khan was impressed by his appearance: "by his tall stature, his long beard, and the commanding tone of his voice". He asked him why he had so long served Chin, whose founders had destroyed the former Ch'i-tan state, and said: "The Chin and Ch'i-tan rulers have always been enemies; I have avenged you!" "My father, my grandfather, and I myself, have all been subjects and servants of Chin," replied Yeh-eü Ch'u-ts'ai. "I would have been guilty if I had not served them loyally." The Mongol conqueror deeply appreciated dynastic loyalty, even among his enemies, and this reply particularly pleased him. He took this man into his service, and soon made him one of his most respected counsellors. Yeh-lü Ch'u-ts'ai made use of his influence for good ends: in the course of the ensuing campaigns, while the Mongol chieftains carried off goods and people, "he contented himself with rescuing Chinese books and medical stores; with the latter he saved the lives of many thousands of men when an epidemic broke out in the Mongol army".

The Chin kingdom, around its new capital of Kaifeng, was now reduced to Honan and several districts of Shensi. But to Genghis Khan Chinese affairs were no longer of more than secondary concern; from now on he looked towards the west. In 1219 he left for the conquest of Turkestan and eastern Persia, taking with him the main Mongol army, and did not return to Mongolia until the winter of 1224–1225. In the meantime the struggle against Chin continued at a slower pace; the generals whom Genghis Khan left in command had a greatly diminished force at their disposal. The war degenerated into a war of sieges; and strongholds changed hands frequently, because the Mongol cavalry was content to sack the cities and never set up any effective occupation.

Genghis Khan's last campaign once more had China as its theatre. It was directed not against Chin, but against Hsi-hsia, the Tangut kingdom in Kansu, which had given offence to the conqueror by refusing him auxiliaries. Genghis Khan began the campaign in the autumn of 1226 and pursued it tenaciously, despite attacks of severe internal pain caused by a fall from his horse. In order to end the resistance of the Tangut once and for all, the Mongol generals proposed a radical extermination of the population. "They represented to Genghis Khan that Chinese subjects were of no use to him, and that he would do better to kill them to the last man, so as at least to make use of the country, which would make good pasture land." It was Yeh-lü Ch'u-ts'ai who prevented this proposal from being adopted. "He demonstrated the benefit to be gained from fertile land and industrious inhabitants. He explained how, by levying a moderate tax on land, duties on merchandise, and taxes on alcohol, vinegar, salt, and produce of the waters and mountains, one could collect annually some five hundred thousand ounces of silver, eighty thousand pieces of silk, and four hundred thousand sacks of grain." He gained his point, and Genghis Khan entrusted him with drawing up a system of taxation on this basis.

While the Mongol army was laying siege to Ningsia, the Tangut capital, Genghis Khan, whose malady grew worse, moved to the Kansu mountains northwest of P'ing-liang in order to escape the summer heat. It was there that he died on August 18, 1227. Some days after his death the defenders of Ningsia capitulated. In conformity with his wishes, the entire population was massacred. The whole of the Tangut kingdom—Kansu, Alashan and Ordos—was annexed to the Mongol Empire.

Genghis Khan was succeeded as head of the Mongol Empire by his third son Ogotai (1229–1241). The latter was a true Mongol, brutish, simple, drunken, jovial, readily lenient, extremely generous to his entourage, yet at the same time by no means devoid of intelligence and even shrewdness. He continued to reside in Mongolia, where he built a permanent capital at Karakorum. His counsellor, the sinicized Ch'i-tan Yeh-lü Ch'u-ts'ai, encouraged him in this course. "The empire", he said to Ogotai, "has indeed been conquered on horseback, but it cannot be governed on horseback." Yeh-lü Ch'u-ts'ai strove to combine the military empire of the Mongols with an administrative empire on Chinese lines. He managed to establish a kind of regular budget, the Mongols having to pay a tenth part of their livestock, whereas their Chinese subjects paid a household tax in silver, silk, and grain. For this purpose the conquered areas of North China, which till then had been subject merely to arbitrary pillage, were in 1230 divided into ten regular districts, to be administered by Mongol officials and Chinese literati. Yeh-lü Ch'u-ts'ai arranged for schools to be opened in Peking and in Shansi to educate young Mongol nobles in Chinese, and at the same time he brought into the administration many Chinese who had come over to the Mongols.

The Mongol conquest, however, had by no means come to a halt. In China a fresh effort was becoming necessary as Chin gave evidence of an extraordinary vitality: not only did this state keep intact its stronghold of Honan; after the death of Genghis Khan it also counter-attacked in the neighbouring provinces. In order to put an end to this resistance, the Mongols devised an ambitious plan. The grand khan Ogotai left Shansi with the greater part of the army to attack Honan from the north. Meanwhile his younger brother Tulé, with a body of cavalry, made a great flanking movement to the west through southern Shensi and appeared suddenly in southern Honan, thus taking the Chin forces in the rear. In this final struggle the men of Chin fought to the end with a heroism which compelled the admiration of the Mongol generals—who were well qualified to judge of courage. Rather than go over to the conqueror, the Chin generals preferred to have their limbs cut off. But in the end they were encircled and annihilated. In May 1233 their capital, Kaifeng, was captured by the Mongol general Sabutai, the conqueror of Persia and Russia. Sabutai intended to destroy Kaifeng as Genghis Khan had destroyed Peking, but Yeh-lü Ch'u-ts'ai intervened. Ogotai was well aware of the meaning of these interventions: "Are you going to weep for the people again?" he said to him. But although the grand khan grumbled, he once more yielded to the advice of his counsellor and ordered that Kaifeng should be spared—an order which the Mongol soldiers, with their admirable discipline, carried out scrupulously. Meanwhile the last Chin sovereign had abandoned Kaifeng before its fall and taken refuge in a neighbouring fortress at Ju-ning; but when he saw the Mongols on the ramparts of this last redoubt, he committed suicide rather than fall into their hands alive. The whole campaign lasted from January 31, 1233 to March 2, 1234.

The whole of the former Chin kingdom and all North China was now in the hands of the Mongols, who had become the immediate neighbours of the Sung empire.

During the war between Chin and the Mongols, the Sung court at Hangchow had concluded an alliance with the latter in the hope of receiving a share in the spoils. After Chin had been defeated, the grand khan Ogotai did in fact hand over to the Chinese certain districts in southern Honan. The Chinese rulers should have considered themselves fortunate to have gained the good will of the formidable Mongols; but instead they declared that they had been poorly recompensed for their co-operation, and in their utter folly attempted to contend with the victors for the rest of Honan. The outcome was not long delayed; in 1236 three Mongol armies invaded the Sung empire and laid waste Szechwan and Hopei.

This, however, was no more than a reconnoitring expedition; and operations soon slowed down. In the immense human hive of Central and South China, divided up by so many rivers and mountains, and on a terrain cut up by lakes and paddy fields, with so many urban centres, the war could only be a war of sieges, in which the horsemen of the steppe still found themselves out of their element. The conquest of North China had been achieved, before the advent of Genghis Khan and his followers, by other Turco-Mongolian hordes, from the Huns and the T'o-pa in the fourth and the fifth centuries to the Ju-chen of Chin in 1126. None had succeeded in conquering South China. In order to conquer the south, it was necessary to wage war in Chinese style, with large contingents of Chinese foot-soldiers and an artillery of siege engines worked by Chinese or foreign engineers. Besides, the Mongol armies were absorbed in new European expeditions across Russia, Hungary and

Poland. In the year 1224 the death of the grand khan Ogotai interrupted the hostilities between Mongols and Chinese.

The war began again under the second successor to Ogotai, the grand khan Mangu, who ruled over the Mongol Empire from 1251 to 1259. Mangu was an energetic leader, a severe but just administrator, a hard but intelligent politician, and a first-class warrior. No longer interested in mere raids or pillage, but aiming at a complete conquest of the country, he decided to carry the war against Sung to its conclusion. One of his first moves, in 1251, was to appoint his younger brother Kublai as governor of Honan. It was a fortunate choice; for Kublai, who showed a keen interest in Chinese civilization, worked to restore the agriculture of the area, which had been ruined during the war, by distributing seed and tools to the peasants, and by setting his Chinese troops to work on the land. Decisive operations against the Sung Empire began in 1258. While Kublai launched an attack on the middle Long River line at Wuchang, Mangu struck into Szechwan in order to outflank South China to the southwest. But in the course of this campaign Mangu died, the victim of an epidemic, on August 11, 1259.

The death of the grand khan Mangu gave the leadership to his brother Kublai.

CHAPTER XXVI

KUBLAI KHAN

KUBLAI was forty-three years old when the death of his brother Mangu brought him to the throne. He was by far the most remarkable of the grandchildren of Genghis Khan. A born statesman—like his famous grandfather—a fine military leader, and a shrewd politician, he combined with the strong qualities of his race the advantages gained from a deliberate adoption of civilization in the form of Chinese culture. At the time of Mangu's death he was besieging the Chinese-held city of Wuchang, on the Long River. In order to have his hands free, he concluded an armistice with the Chinese and returned at once to Peking. He then continued his journey farther north, to his summer residence at Shang-tu, near the present-day Dolon Nor.[1] It was there that on May 6, 1260, he had himself proclaimed grand khan by his army.

Kublai's accession to the throne was not accepted by his family without opposition. His youngest brother, Arikbugha, proclaimed himself grand khan at Karakorum, in Mongolia; and in fact it was in order to combat his brother that Kublai had so suddenly made a truce with the Chinese. The war between the two brothers, which had Mongolia for its theatre and principal stake, lasted for four years. Finally in August, 1264, the defeated Arikbugha made his submission to Kublai.

As soon as he was rid of family competition, Kublai was able to resume the conquest of the Sung empire. The Sung emperor Tu-tsung (1265–1274) put his trust in ill-starred politicians, who

[1] Shang-tu has acquired literary fame as Xanadu, with an extra syllable, in Coleridge's *Kubla Khan*. Strictly speaking, Kublai's title was Kaghan or Ka'an (Grand Khan).

nullified the efforts of the often highly courageous generals. Nevertheless it took the Mongols more than eight years to end the Chinese resistance. The siege of the twin cities of Hsiang-yang and Fan-ch'eng, in Hopei, took over five years (1268–1273). The defenders showed extraordinary tenacity; when blockaded on the landward side, they managed for some time to get their provisions brought in by boat, thanks to two bold captains who succeeded in sailing up the Han River, and who lost their lives in this brilliant exploit. The Mongols then brought into action their artillery of *ballistae* and catapults, built and operated by Uigur and Arab engineers in their service. This bombardment finally overcame the heroic defenders, and the fall of the two cities enabled the Mongols to reach the middle Long River by way of the lower Han, and then to continue down the great valley from Wuchang to Nanking. Towards the end of 1275 all the Mongol armies were converging on Hangchow (Lin-an), the Sung capital.

There everything was in confusion. The emperor Tu-tsung, a highly cultured man but an inept sovereign, had entrusted the government to a worthless minister, Chia Ssu-tao, whose only policy was to bully the generals. Then Tu-tsung died; and Chia Ssu-tao, in order to stay in power, put a four-year-old child on the throne (1274). Meanwhile the positions on the lower Long River were one after another falling into the hands of the enemy. Finally the regent degraded Chia Ssu-tao, but it was already too late: Hangchow was besieged. Its defenders capitulated towards the end of February, 1276. The Mongol general Bayan made his entry into the great city, and sent the boy emperor to Kublai. The latter treated his young captive with remarkable humanity. After assigning him a pension, he did what was often done with dethroned Merovingian and Carolingian princes among the Franks—he had him brought up as a priest. The heir to the Sung dynasty was to die peacefully forty-seven years later in a Buddhist monastery. The dowager empress, according to Marco Polo, was accorded a courteous reception before she too retired from the world and entered a convent. This shows how far the

Mongols had advanced since the time of Genghis Khan. In two generations this half-savage people had reached the level of the older civilized nations.

It still remained to subdue the Cantonese region, where the remaining Chinese patriots had gathered round the brother of the dethroned boy emperor. Canton, the centre of this resistance, was unable to hold out for long and in 1277 fell to the conquerors. The last of the Sung pretenders, a boy of eight, was sheltered on board the ships of the loyalist hero Chang Shih-chieh, who for several seasons was able to hide in the remote harbours of the Cantonese coast. But the Mongols were persistent; they fitted out a superior fleet, and encircled the Chinese flotilla near the little island of Yaishan, to the southwest of Canton (April 13, 1279). It was a disastrous day for the loyalists. The faster of the Chinese junks succeeded in breaking through the enemy lines, but the imperial ship was too heavy to be able to follow the manoeuvre. One of the emperor's servants appeared before him: "The empire is doomed," he said gravely. "You should end your life with it. Your brother surrendered like a coward; do not repeat that disgrace!" Having spoken, he seized the child in his arms and threw himself into the waves. As for the valiant Chang Shih-chieh, it seemed that death had avoided him, when suddenly a typhoon blew up about his junk. "He refused to run the ship aground, but climbed to the maintop, and raising aloft a stick of incense called on Heaven: 'I, Chang Shih-chieh, have given my life to the service of the Sung dynasty. Now that the last of them is dead, if there is still some hope for their cause, if their imperial sacrifices are to be perpetuated, then let Heaven save me that I may continue to serve them. If not, I have lived long enough!' At this moment a whirlpool engulfed his junk, and he disappeared among the waves."

For the first time the whole of China had fallen into the hands of a foreign conqueror. Kublai had at last succeeded where the invaders of the early middle ages had failed; he had realized the vague dream of innumerable generations of nomads throughout the centuries, the dream of every yurt-dweller from the Kirghiz Steppes to the forests of Manchuria. Fortunately the conquest begun by Genghis Khan and completed by Kublai had been slow enough for its most dangerous results to be allayed. The conquest of China, from Genghis Khan's first incursion into the Tangut kingdom in Kansu to the destruction of the last Sung flotilla by Kublai's admirals, had taken the invincible Mongols no less than seventy-four years (1205–1279). When this gigantic task was finally achieved, instead of a Genghis Khan—a nomadic savage dressed in the skins of wild beasts and with no thought but to kill and to burn—the Chinese found themselves vanguished by a Mongol who was almost like one of themselves.

In fact Kublai Khan, grandson of Genghis, although he had conquered China, had first been himself conquered by Chinese civilization. His victory enabled him to realize his lasting ambition: to become a real Son of Heaven, and to turn the Mongol empire into a Chinese empire. At last the way was clear; with the disappearance of the Sung dynasty he became the legitimate master of the fifteen-centuries-old empire. The aim of his dynasty, which assumed the dynastic name of Yüan, was to carry on the tradition of its twenty-two predecessors. A visible sign of this sinicization was that Kublai, although master of Mongolia, ceased to live there. In 1260 he established his capital at Peking; and there in 1267, to the northeast of the old city of Chung-tu, he began to build the new city of Ta-tu, called by the Mongols Khanbalik, "City of the Khan", which Marco Polo spelled Cambaluc.

As grand khan of the Mongols, Kublai had to wage several wars in Asia. Having become ruler of China, he claimed homage from the other countries of the Far East. Korea, which had been more or less rebellious towards his predecessors, accepted his suzerainty; but the war vessels and expeditionary forces which he sent to Japan (in 1274 and again in 1281) and to Java (in 1293) were unsuccessful. The warriors of the steppe were strangers to the sea; and the Chinese and Korean sailors on whom they were forced to rely served them only under compulsion. A typhoon which dispersed the Mongol armada on September 15, 1281, put an end to Kublai's attempts to conquer Japan. He also failed in Indo-China; the forces which he sent against the kingdom of Annam (present-day Tonking and northern Annam) and the kingdom of Tchampa (southern Annam) in 1283, 1285, and 1287, all met with disaster because the warriors from the borders of Siberia were decimated by the Tonkinese climate. However, these setbacks did not afterwards prevent the sovereigns of Annam, Tchampa, and Burma, from recognizing the suzerainty of the Yüan dynasty. A far more serious conflict developed when Kublai was forced to dispute the title of grand khan and the possession of Mongolia itself with one of his cousins, Kaidu, who from near the Ebi Nor ruled over Tarbagatai and Sungaria.

Kublai, by becoming a Son of Heaven, adopting Chinese civilization, making the Mongol empire more and more Chinese, and moving his residence from Karakorum to Peking, had dissatisfied many of his Mongol subjects who remained faithful to the traditions of their race, to the life of the steppes and the nomadic spirit. These malcontents had first gathered round Kublai's younger brother Arikbugha, whose pretensions to the throne they championed without success. After Arikbugha had been defeated, they found a new pretender in the person of his cousin Kaidu, who was also a grandson of Genghis Khan and who in the remote west continued to live the rude life of his nomadic ancestors. This wolf of the steppes was the very opposite of Kublai the sinicized, sedentary Mongol. In 1267 he succeeded in wresting from Kublai the suzerainty of Turkestan (present-day Soviet and Chinese Turkestan), which was then called the Khanate of Jagatai because it had been the region allotted to Jagatai, son of Genghis. In 1275 Kublai failed in an attempt to recover Turkestan; and in 1277 Kaidu very nearly succeeded in taking Mongolia from him. Ten years later, Kaidu formed against him a new coalition of princes which extended from Turkestan to Manchuria. Kublai—then seventy-two years of age—shattered this coalition in 1278 in a difficult military campaign, which was fought in Manchuria and which is recounted by Marco Polo; but it was left to his successor, the grand khan Temur, finally to dispose of Kaidu (1301).

In short, as grand khan of the Mongols, Kublai was far from universally successful. Although he was able to retain possession of Mongolia proper, his cousins, who ruled in Turkestan and in southern Russia, refused to recognize his suzerainty; only the house of his brother Hulagu, who reigned in Persia, remained in loyal vassalage. All his difficulties with his own clan were due to the fact that he had abandoned his ancestral way of life to become a Chinese emperor.

It was as emperor of China (Yüan Shih-tsu) that Kublai was most completely successful, and it was in this capacity that he deserved to be called by Marco Polo, "The most puissant of men, in subjects, lands, and treasure, that there is on earth or ever was, from the time of our first father Adam to this day." No Son of Heaven ever took his duties more seriously than did this grandson of the terrible Genghis Khan. His healing administration cured the wounds of a a century of warfare. After the fall of Sung, he not only preserved the institutions and the administrative bodies of the fallen dynasty, but did all he could to obtain the personal support of the men in office. He conquered not only the land but also the hearts of the people, and his greatest claim to glory is perhaps not that he was the first to conquer the whole of China, but that he pacified it.

After so much devastation and destruction the country was in a pitiable state, and the census figures give some idea of what had happened. About 1125 China had 20,882,258 families, which according to the usual rate of calculation represented about a hundred million inhabitants. In 1290 the population had sunk to no more than 13,196,206 families, the equivalent of slightly under fifty-nine million people. In order to restore the prosperity of the country a great effort had to be made in all spheres.

Kublai was much concerned with the question of communications, a matter of the greatest importance to the administration and food supply of the vast empire. He repaired the imperial highways, planted most of them with trees for shade, and built caravanserais at intervals along them. He extended to China the Mongol postal system (*djam*) which was the admiration of Marco Polo and of Odoric de Pordenone. More than two hundred thousand horses, divided among the many posting stations, are said to have been assigned to this service. In order to supply food to Peking, and to bring rice from the lower Long River, Kublai undertook considerable canal-building between Yangchow and the capital. This imperial "Grand Canal" (*Yün-he*, "Canal") which was constructed under Kublai followed a course which is mostly still in use today. In order to combat famine, he brought back the measures of "national insurance", the Sung state-control legislation of the Kaifeng period —legislation associated with the name of the famous Wang An-shih. Like Wang An-shih, Kublai promulgated edicts of maximum prices. In good years the surplus from the harvests was bought by the state and stored in public granaries; in times of scarcity and rising prices these granaries were opened and the grain distributed free of charge.[1] In addition, public assistance was reorganized, and an edict of 1260 ordered the viceroys to provide for the needs of aged scholars, orphans, the sick and the infirm.[2] An edict of 1271 established charitable institutions. Distributions of rice and millet were made regularly to needy families; and Marco Polo says that Kublai himself fed some thirty thousand poor people every day.

The most defective side of the Mongol administration was its finance. Among the institutions of Sung, Kublai had found the use of paper money, or *ch'ao*, consisting of bonds or coupons which were given a value equivalent to an ingot of silver. Kublai extended this practice and made it the basis of his financial policy. Marco Polo remarks: "One may well say that the Great Kaan is a perfect alchemist!"—for the Mongols had discovered a true "philosopher's stone", the art of producing gold with notes made from mulberry

[1] This was the same system of "regulative granaries" (*chang-p'ing*) which was introduced under the Sung dynasty.

[2] This was a revival of the system of "granaries of charity" (*kuang-hui*), already existing under the Sung dynasty (see page 184).

bark. In 1264 an edict was promulgated fixing the value in paper money of all the principal commodities; this from the economic point of view was a law to control the market by establishing maximum prices, and from the financial point of view was a law to fix the rate of exchange for banknotes. Kublai's first financial minister, the Moslem Seyid Edjell (died 1279), who was a native of Bukhara, seems to have kept the issue of notes within reasonable limits; but unsound practices began under the ministers who succeeded him—first another Moslem from Transoxiana, Ahmed Benaketi, and then the Uigur Sangha. Both practised a policy of unrestrained inflation which rapidly depreciated the *ch'ao*. In order to find money they had recourse to repeated conversions and to heavily taxed monopolies. Ahmed, who was assassinated in 1282, was posthumously degraded by Kublai; and Sangha was condemned to death for embezzlement (1291). In 1309, under the second successor to Kublai, the grand khan Khaissan (Emperor Wu-tsung), attempts to check the fall in value of previous issues were abandoned, and new notes were made; but these in turn depreciated.

Finally the Yüan dynasty was obliged to return to the metal coinage used under former dynasties; but it is impossible that the permanent state of financial crisis which marked the reign of Kublai (1260–1294) and that of his grandson Temur (1295–1307) could have been without its repercussions on public feeling. This perpetual inflation, the successive devaluations which were its inevitable consequence, and the resulting unsettlement of the market, could not but make the Mongol regime unpopular in the most commercially developed part of China, in the large urban centres of the lower Long River and the ports of Fukien and the Cantonese region, places where most of the urban population—from the powerful guilds admired by Marco Polo to the little shopkeepers noted by Odoric de Pordenone—lived by commerce or banking. It was this region that in the middle of the fourteenth century was to begin the popular revolt against the Mongol regime.

We have just seen that two Moslems in succession were given

charge of the imperial finances. This was no isolated example, and the selection of Moslems was connected with the system of land tenure under the Mongols.

When they conquered Chin, the Mongols found in North China a system of land tenure which was very different from that of ancient China. The two Tartar powers which preceded the Mongols as rulers of North China, the Ch'i-tan (Liao dynasty, tenth and eleventh centuries) and the Ju-chen (Chin dynasty, twelfth century), had reduced a large number of Chinese landholders to the condition of serfs, in order to form large domains for presentation to their own nobility. In 1183, on the eve of the Mongol conquest, serfs formed more than a fifth of the total population of Chin: a reported 1,345,947 serfs or slaves out of 6,158,636 inhabitants.

The Mongols, when they replaced the Ju-chen in North China, took possession of all the appanages and fiefs that had been formed for the benefit of the Chin aristocracy. In South China, in the former Sung Empire, the Mongols expropriated land on a similar scale; the princes of the clan of Genghis and even members of the lesser Mongol nobility (*noyat, ba'atut*) were awarded a good part of China as their personal property. In order to get the Chinese economy going again once the period of sheer plundering had come to an end, they devised the scheme of granting cash loans, at high rates of interest, to the Chinese population—the same population which at the time of the conquest they had so often reduced to serfdom in the country, or whose businesses they had despoiled in the cities.[1] These loans were effected through the medium of banking guilds or companies, generally composed of Moslems and known by the Mongol name of *ortok*. These Moslems, who came from the region of Bukhara and Samarkand, played a role comparable at once to that of the Lombards in medieval Europe and that of the farmers-general in eighteenth-century France. "They were the great money merchants of the Far East during the Mongol period," says Pelliot. They

[1] These loans were similar in principle to the onerous "harvest loans" granted to (or imposed on) the peasants during the time of Wang An-shih (see p. 185).

must have been extremely avaricious; for in 1298 Kublai's successor, the grand khan Temur, felt constrained to protect the population of South China from their exactions, or rather from the exactions of the Mongol nobility who employed them. The population received guarantees against the usurious demands of the Moslem guilds and against the seizure of wives and children of debtors.

Apart from this particular question, the Mongol dynasty in its official legislation, the *Statutes of Yüan*, was also concerned with generally improving the position of the slaves, agricultural labourers and tenant-farmers working on the great estates. It attempted to protect these unfortunate people against oppression by their masters more effectively than the Sung legislation had done. An edict of 1295, the first year of Temur's reign, even forbade the Mongol lords to damage the crops by riding over planted fields. "The Yüan laws of the early fourteenth century," says Henri Maspero, "made it an offence punishable by a hundred and seven strokes for a proprietor to beat an agricultural labourer or tenant to death. The life of the tenant-farmers was so hard that on several occasions it was necessary to order a reduction in the excessive level of rents. In 1285 they were decreased in Kiangsu by one tenth, and in 1304 by two tenths; in 1354 this measure was extended to the whole empire."

The Mongol policy towards religion in China was particularly significant.

Marco Polo observed that Kublai showed the broadest tolerance, or rather a universal benevolence, towards the various religions. There was a twofold reason for this attitude. In the age of Genghis Khan, the basis of the Mongol religion was a form of shamanism which feared and respected every possible manifestation of the Powers which lay hidden in the sky, the mountains and the waters; which also, and from the same superstitious fear, revered the power of all miracle-workers. Hence all the established religions, and all the different priests who represented them, were equally entitled to this prudent deference. In addition, a first-class statesman like Kublai at once realized the value of conciliating these different priesthoods for his own political ends; in order to do so he concluded not one concordat, but as many concordats as there were established religions. When he took the place of the Sung emperor as head of the ancient imperial religion, Kublai performed the required ritual gestures of state Confucianism; but he did not wait for the Confucian literati to be won over before he sought the support of Buddhism and Taoism, because he realized that he could make use of this support against the stubborn Sung legitimism of the Confucianists. To this end he planned to organize the Buddhist and Taoist churches as state institutions, the head of each religion to be named by him and responsible to him. This was to be Napoleon's conception of the relations between church and state.

Apart from the old Mongol shamanism, which he never entirely abandoned, Kublai's personal preference was undoubtedly for Buddhism, and especially Tibetan Buddhism. When called on to act as arbitrator in certain ecclesiastical disputes between Buddhists and Taoists, his decision was emphatically in favour of the former and against the latter. According to Marco Polo, he had some relics of the Buddha brought from Ceylon. From Tibet he summoned to his court a young Buddhist holy man, the lama Phags-pa, who became his friend and protégé, and who was commissioned to devise an alphabet for the Mongols after the pattern of the Tibetan alphabet—an undertaking which came to nothing, the Mongols preferring in the end the Turco-Uigur alphabet derived from Syriac.

Kublai's successors continued and even increased the favour shown to Buddhist monks and especially to Tibetan lamas. Thanks to this imperial protection, there developed in China a lamaist clericalism which was not without its disadvantages. An administrative report of the period states: "These lamas are to be seen entering the cities where, instead of staying in hostelries, they establish themselves in private houses and turn out their hosts so as more easily to seduce their wives. Not content with indulging in debauchery, they take from the people the little money that they possess. They are public leeches and more cruel even than the tax collectors."

There is nothing new in these remarks: this is the old diatribe of the Confucian literati against Buddhist monasticism; but it is certain that the literati held the Mongol regime responsible for the excessive privileges which it granted to their clerical adversaries, and this was doubtless one of the causes of discontent which were to contribute to the unpopularity and final collapse of the dynasty.

In short, Buddhism enjoyed the same favour under the Mongol dynasty that it had known under so many of the Tartar dynasties of the past, for example the T'o-pa Wei of the fifth century. The great Indian religion, despite the personal protection accorded it by many Chinese emperors (as was the case during much of the T'ang dynasty, for example), had never been considered by the Chinese state as other than a foreign sect—the complaint was constantly reiterated—which the literati, the official counsellors to the throne, might temporarily have tolerated, but whose periods of favour they had never attempted to justify. On the other hand, the nomadic masters of China, whether Turks, Mongols or Tungus, accepted Buddhism without reserve. The Confucian administrators, who in each new Tartar conquest found themselves on the losing side, were quite left out of things—at least during the first stages of the occupation. Thus Buddhism in China never prospered so well as during periods of foreign domination.

It is necessary, however, to make certain reservations. What we have just stated is true of official Chinese Buddhism and of Tibetan Lamaism; but there also existed in China certain secret societies, such as the White Cloud and the White Lotus, which claimed to be Buddhist although they were really only heresies. It has been suggested that the sect of the White Cloud may have been contaminated by the Manichaean doctrine, which between 763 and 840 was spread, as we have seen, thanks to the support of the Uigur Turks. As to the sect of the White Lotus, which had its origins in Amitabha pietism, in 1133 it became a secret society with a grand master, nocturnal sessions and so forth. These secret societies, which had always been more or less opposed by the Sung government, seem to have collaborated in the establishment of the Mongol dynasty, which in return granted them freedom of worship and even an official existence. Before long, however, the White Lotus was once more forced to become conspiratorial, because it was prohibited by the Mongol administration (1308, 1322). Its nocturnal assemblies were soon in fact to serve as a meeting-place for the enemies of the Mongol regime.

Taoism had been favoured by the first Mongol conquerors, who quite naturally saw in its magicians the equivalent of their own shamans. Genghis Khan himself had this in mind when in 1222 he summoned to Afghanistan, where he was waging war, the Taoist monk Ch'ang Ch'un. Although the saint was unable to give him the secret of the elixir of life and was probably content to preach the doctrine of *tao*, the conqueror formed a high opinion of him, and granted warrants of immunity for the Taoist orders. Under Kublai the Taoists fell out of favour, and the Buddhists laid before him their old complaints against their rivals; for instance, that the Taoists pretended that the religion of Buddha was no more than a branch of Taoism. In an open discussion the Taoists were proved to have falsified texts and forged scriptures; as a result Kublai, whose sympathies lay unquestionably with the Buddhists, ordered a burning of works of doubtful authenticity, and returned to the Buddhists certain monasteries which had been usurped by their adversaries (1281).

These were quarrels between priests; the emperor was faced with a more delicate task in deciding what attitude he should adopt with regard to official Confucianism, since on this attitude would depend the sincerity with which the scholar class rallied to his cause, and Kublai was too shrewd a statesman to be unaware of this. As a symbolic demonstration, he summoned to his court the head of the K'ung family in Ch'ü-fu, Shantung (where the line of descent has continued unbroken from Confucius), and publicly honoured him. One of the first royal acts of Temur, the grandson and successor of Kublai, was to issue an edict commanding both Mongols and

Chinese to worship Confucius; this of course won him the sympathy of the literati (1295).

The at least temporary support of the Mongol regime by the literati is illuminated by the name of Chao Meng-fu (1254–1322). He was a peculiarly representative figure in that he was a member of the former Sung imperial family. After agreeing in 1286 to serve Kublai, he was appointed to various administrative posts (in 1316 he was given an important position in the Han-lin College) and served his master faithfully. Chao Meng-fu was also one of the greatest painters of his age, and was especially famous as a painter of horses. There exist so many paintings of horses attributed to Chao Meng-fu that one is obliged to conclude that the greater number are copies; yet even these copies, when they show the shaggy Mongolian ponies and their Tartar riders, form extremely interesting documents recalling the Mongol period.

Somewhat apart from Buddhism, Taoism, and Confucianism, whose beliefs were firmly anchored in China, stood the Nestorian form of Christianity.

Nestorian Christianity, it will be remembered, was introduced into T'ang China by missionaries from Persia; and in 635 a Nestorian church was built at Ch'ang-an. Under the T'ang dynasty the religion prospered, if not among the Chinese population, at least among the Persian and Syrian residents who were drawn to China by the commerce of the Silk Road, and also among the Turks who lived along the frontiers in alliance with China. It is again along these frontiers that we find Christianity in the thirteenth century, among the Ongüt Turks, then masters of the region around present-day Kuei-Sui (Kuei-hua-ch'eng and Sui-yüan-ch'eng) and to the north of the Great Wall where it bounds Shansi. The Ongüt held a position of considerable importance at the Mongol court, because from the first they had been faithful vassals of Genghis Khan. As a reward, the conqueror had given his daughter in marriage to their king; and since then there had continued to be marriages between the families of Mongol grand khans and Ongüt princes. Thus it came about that the Ongüt prince George (Körguz in Turkish)—a true Christian even to his name—married a granddaughter of Kublai. Through the Ongüt, Christianity was maintained for several generations on the very steps of the throne, within the imperial family; and since they continued to be loyal supporters of the empire (Prince George died heroically in 1298 in the service of the grand khan Temur), they won untold credit for their faith.

Moreover the Ongüt Turks were not the only inhabitants of the Gobi to profess Nestorian Christianity. As we have seen, there were also the Kereit, a people who dwelt near the Tula in Outer Mongolia and whom Genghis Khan had in 1203 included in his empire. Kublai's own mother, the Princess Sorghaktani, who was a woman of remarkable intelligence and ability, came of the former Kereit royal family and was a practising Nestorian. There can be no doubt that by protecting Nestorian Christianity Kublai wished to show himself faithful, not only to his friendship and family connections with the Ongüt princes, but also to the memory of his mother. This protection was clearly shown in 1287, when the Nestorian church was placed in a delicate position. A Mongol prince called Nayan, who was a Nestorian, started a revolt against Kublai in Manchuria, and when marching against him put the cross on his standards. As soon as the rebels had been defeated, adversaries of the Christian faith were not slow to seize this opportunity to discredit it. But Kublai "angrily rebuked those who mocked the Cross in his presence. Then, calling many Christians who were there, he comforted them, saying, 'If the Cross of your God has not aided Naian there was good reason for it; . . . Naian was a disloyal traitor, who fought against his liege . . . the Cross of your God has done very well in not helping him. . . .' " Moreover, and again according to Marco Polo, at the Easter following Nayan's defeat, Kublai had the Gospel brought to him and publicly burnt incense to it and kissed it.

It would probably be wrong, from the theological point of view, to consider this as anything more than a general manifestation of respect towards the principal religions known to the Mongols, an insurance policy with regard to the various manifestations of divinity. The emperor naïvely admitted as much: "These are four prophets who are adored and worshipped by all the world," he said (according to Marco Polo). "The Christians say their God was Jesus Christ, the Saracens Mahomet, the Jews Moses, and the Idolaters Sagamoni Borcan [Sakyamuni], the first man of whom an idol was made. I honour and revere all four, and thereby also the one who is the most powerful in Heaven and the most true, and I pray him to aid me." From the political point of view, however, Kublai showed his sympathy towards Nestorian Christianity, not only in words, but by more concrete measures. In 1275 the Nestorian patriarch of Baghdad was able to create an archbishopric in Peking. Nestorian churches were built in Yangchow and Hangchow; and in 1289 Kublai instituted a special office to deal with Christian affairs. In 1291 he appointed as commissioner for Christian affairs a Syrian Nestorian named Isa (Arabic for Jesus), who shortly afterwards became one of his ministers.

The life of the Nestorian communities in China under Kublai is well known through the story of the patriarch Mar Yabalaha and Rabban Sauma. Rabban Sauma (1225–1294) and Rabban Marcos were two Nestorian monks, the former born near Peking, the latter in the Ongüt country (in Suiyüan), who in 1275 or 1276 left China to make a pilgrimage to Jerusalem. The Ongüt princes tried in vain to dissuade them from this project: "Why do you leave for the West," they said, "when we are taking so much trouble to attract bishops and monks from those parts?" But, seeing that the resolution of the pilgrims remained unshakeable, they furnished them with the necessary equipment for the journey across Central Asia. Thus Sauma and Marcos crossed Kashgaria and Turkestan, and in 1278 arrived at last in Mesopotamia, in the Mongol khanate of Persia. The khan of Persia at that time was Abaga, a nephew of Kublai. He was delighted by the arrival of two of his compatriots, and in 1281 caused Marcos to be elected to the Nestorian patriarchal throne of Seleucia-Baghdad. Marcos, who thus became the patriarch Mar Yabalaha III, played an important part in the history of the Mongol khanate of Persia. As for Sauma, in 1287 Arghun, who had succeeded his father Abaga as khan of Persia, sent him on a mission to the West with a view to forming an alliance between the Crusaders and the Mongols against the Mamelukes of Egypt. In September, 1287, he arrived in Paris, where Philip the Fair in person did him the honours of the Sainte Chapelle. In Rome he was received by Pope Nicholas IV, who gave him communion with his own hand on Easter Sunday, 1288, and who discussed with him the organization of a new crusade. It was a strange destiny that led this Mongol subject, born near Peking, to become Persian ambassador to the Pope and the King of France.

CHAPTER XXVII

MARCO POLO

THE story of the two Mongol Christians who left Peking and crossed Central Asia to make a pilgrimage to Jerusalem shows to what extent the Mongol conquest, by unifying Asia, had opened up the old transcontinental roads. The route of the ancient silk trade and of the Buddhist pilgrimages, which had been closed since the eleventh century by the expansion of Islam, was once more travelled by caravans of merchants and pilgrims. This was an undeniable benefit of the Mongol conquest; the campaigns of Genghis Khan had made possible the travels of Marco Polo.

Marco Polo's father and uncle—Niccolò and Matteo—were two Venetian merchants who in 1260 left Constantinople to make a journey through the Mongol khanate of southern Russia. From there, by way of Bukhara and Chinese Turkestan, they made their way to China, where Kublai offered them a friendly welcome. When they were leaving, the grand khan charged them with a mission to the Holy See: to request that the Pope should send him a hundred doctors "well schooled in the seven arts." The Polos left China in 1266, recrossed Central Asia, and reached Rome by way of Syria. The Holy See unfortunately underestimated the importance of Kublai's request, the fulfilment of which—the dispatch of a hundred Latin scholars—might well have altered the course of history. At the close of 1271 the Polos again set out for China, taking with them nobody but Niccolò's son Marco, who is the immortal author of a narrative which we shall endeavour to recapitulate.[1]

The three travellers this time traversed the Mongol khanate of

[1] *The Travels of Marco Polo*, edited by L. F. Benedetto and translated by Aldo Ricci, London, Routledge, 1931.

Persia and the north of Afghanistan, crossed the Pamirs, and making their way across southern Kashgaria followed the old Silk Road via Kashgar, Yarkand, Khotan, and Lob Nor until they reached the Chinese province of Kansu. Here they stayed at Kan-chou, which Marco Polo calls *Canpchu*, a city in which they remarked the presence of a Nestorian community. They then resumed their journey towards the east, visiting the former Tangut capital of Ningsia (*Egrigaia*), where again they noticed the existence of a Christian community in a country where the majority of the population were Idolaters (Buddhists). From there they entered the Ongüt country (in present-day Suiyüan; Marco Polo refers to it as *Tenduc*); this Marco Polo took to be the kingdom of Prester John, and he mentions the family of the famous "Prince George", champions of the Christian faith. Leaving the Ongüt country, the Polos entered North China, which Marco Polo, like the Turks of those times (and the Russians today), calls *Cathay*, a word derived from the name of the Khitai or Kitat (Chinese, Ch'i-tan) who had ruled over the country in the eleventh century. At last the travellers arrived at Shang-tu (*Chandu*), the summer residence of Kublai, in the neighbourhood of present-day Dolon Nor. The Polos there presented a letter from Pope Gregory X to the emperor; and afterwards Marco Polo followed the court to Peking, then called Ta-tu or Khanbalik (*Cambaluc*). Kublai, who seems to have singled him out, entrusted him with a post in the salt-tax administration at Yangchow (*Yanju*).

Marco Polo's book describes two itineraries in China; one in the west, from Peking to Yünnan by way of Shansi, Shensi, and Szechwan; the other in the east, from Peking to Fukien by way of Shantung, the lower Long River and Chekiang. In the course of this account he presents a brief economic survey of North China (*Cathay*) and South China (*Manji*, the former Sung empire). Among other things he mentions the coal mines of North China: "There is a kind of black stone, which is dug out of the mountains like any other kind of stone, and burns like wood . . . these stones are burnt all over the province of Cathay." He was equally impressed by the use made of navigable waterways, and remarks above all the importance of the Long River (*Kian*), the main artery of Chinese economy: "There are more boats on it laden with more precious and costly wares, than sail on all the rivers and seas of the Christians put together." Marco Polo adds that each year two hundred thousand boats sail up the river, to say nothing of those that sail back. He also notes the economic importance of the Grand Canal, repaired and completed by Kublai, which made it possible to transport rice from the lower Long River to Peking.

In order to direct this immense internal commerce, as well as the trade with India and the East Indies, there had been formed, in the ports of the lower Long River, Chekiang and the Cantonese region, powerful merchant guilds which rivalled the Flemish *métiers* or the Florentine *arti maggiori*. Speaking of the guilds of Hangchow (which he refers to as *Kinsai*), Marco Polo writes: "The merchants are so many and wealthy, that no one could tell the whole truth, so extraordinary it is. And I will add that the great men and their wives . . . do nothing with their own hands: they live with as much delicacy and cleanliness as if they were kings." The general use of paper money, which Marco Polo humorously compares to the philosopher's stone, facilitated transactions: "I assure you that all his subjects, of all countries and peoples, readily accept that paper in payment, for wherever they go, they can pay for anything with it—wares of all kinds, pearls, precious stones, gold and silver." The marvellous commercial aptitude of the Chinese evoked the admiration of this Venetian, and he is constantly recalling the spectacle of all those riches—ships returning from India laden with spices; pepper, ginger, and cinnamon bark: junks sailing down the Long River or up the Grand Canal with their cargoes of rice: the shops of Hangchow and Ch'üan-chou overflowing with precious goods; cloth of gold, sendals, "and silk of many kinds". In short, his account provides an economic geography of China in the thirteenth century.

Marco Polo gives information about the principal markets of China. First of all Peking (*Cambaluc*), the silk centre of the north, where "a thousand cart-loads of silk enter Cambaluc daily. For they make much gold and silk cloth; indeed almost all the cloth they make is of silk." Then Chengtu (*Sindufu*), the chief city of Szechwan, which manufactured sendals and exported silks to Central Asia; Yangchow (*Yanju*), the great rice market of the lower Long River; and Hangchow (*Kinsai*), the former Sung capital, to which Marco Polo devotes a special chapter and which he describes as a sort of Chinese Venice.[1] Hangchow was the principal sugar market, as well as being a port visited by innumerable ships which brought cargoes of spices from India and the East Indies and left laden with silks destined for India and the Moslem world; the city contained a large colony of Arab, Persian and Christian merchants. Finally there were the two great ports of Fukien: Foochow (*Fuju*) and Ch'üan-chou (*Zaitun*). The merchants of Foochow possessed vast stocks of ginger and galingale; moreover, "In this province, sugar is produced in such quantities as to be beyond all belief. There is much trade in pearls and precious stones. This is due to the fact that many ships come there from India, with crowds of merchants, who traffic in the Indian islands." But the greatest emporium in all China was Ch'üan-chou: "Here is the harbour whither all the ships of India come. . . . It is also the port whither go the merchants of Manji, which is the region stretching all around. In a word, in this port there is such traffic of merchandise, precious stones, and pearls, that it is truly a wondrous sight. From the harbour of this city all this is distributed over the whole of the province of Manji. And I assure you that for one shipload of pepper that goes to Alexandria or elsewhere to be taken to Christian lands, there come a hundred to this port of Zaitun."

Early in 1292 Marco Polo, his father, and his uncle, embarked on a ship and set out for Europe, having been charged by Kublai with the escort of a young princess who was being sent as a bride to the Mongol khan of Persia. They broke their journey in

[1] Kinsai in Chinese meant "The capital", modern Peking pronunciation *Ching-shih.*

Sumatra, left the ship at Hormuz, and reached their native Venice in 1295.

Meanwhile, contemporary with the bold merchants of whom Marco Polo is the prototype, Catholic missionaries were beginning to arrive in Mongol China. In 1289 Pope Nicholas IV, who had recently learned from Rabban Sauma of the existence of numerous native Christians in the Mongol Empire, dispatched to the Far East the Franciscan friar John de Montecorvino. Montecorvino, after staying for a time in the Mongol khanate of Persia and then in India, embarked for China where the grand khan Temur (1294–1307), grandson and successor to Kublai, made him welcome. Montecorvino built two churches in Cambaluc (Peking), for which he was partially indebted to the liberality of an Italian merchant, Petrus de Lucalongo, who had accompanied him on his journey. Within a few years he baptized "more than ten thousand Tartars", and began to translate the psalms into one of their dialects. The Ongüt prince, George, until then a Nestorian, was converted by him to Catholicism; George's young son was baptized John, in honour of Montecorvino.

In 1307 the Pope appointed Montecorvino Archbishop of Cambaluc (Ta-tu, modern Peking). In 1313 there arrived in Cambaluc three Franciscans who were to be his suffragans; one of them, Gerard, became Bishop of Zaitun (Ch'üan-chou), where a church was built by a rich Armenian. The third bishop of Zaitun, the Franciscan Andrew of Perugia, in a letter dated January, 1326, wrote that the Grand Khan had bestowed on him a pension of a hundred gold florins; also that he himself had built a monastery for twenty-two monks in the neighbourhood of Zaitun, and that he divided his time between his church and his mountain cloister.

After Montecorvino and Andrew of Perugia, the most celebrated Catholic missionary to Mongol China was the Franciscan friar Odoric de Pordenone. Odoric embarked from Venice between 1314 and 1318, traversed the Mongol khanate of Persia, broke his journey in India, and about 1324 or 1325 disembarked at Canton, which he called *Sincalan*. In his account of his journey he remarks on the density of population in this city, on the wealth of the region, the abundance and cheapness of foodstuffs, the industrious character of the inhabitants, who were born merchants and skilled craftsmen, and on the great number of gods worshipped by the people. He was equally interested by Ch'üan-chou (*Zaitun*), a city "twice as big as Rome", where he was received by his Franciscan brethren and was able to admire the cathedral and the mountain monastery. Hangchow (*Kinsai*) filled him with an even greater admiration. According to him it was "the greatest city in the world, situated between two lakes, with canals and lagoons like our Venice". Speaking of the many diverse elements—Chinese, Mongols, Buddhists, Nestorians, and the rest—who all lived together in this enormous city, Odoric pays tribute to the Mongol administration: "The fact that so many different races can live peaceably side by side and be governed by the same power seems to me to be one of the greatest wonders of the world". Through the good offices of a Mongol dignitary who had been converted to Catholicism, Odoric was enabled to visit a Buddhist monastery and discuss metempsychosis with the priests.

Odoric was impressed by the importance of the fisheries of the lower Long River and especially by the method of fishing with the aid of cormorants (which is still carried on today). Finally he arrived in Cambaluc (Peking), where, he says, "the Grand Khan resides in a palace so vast that the walls have a circuit of more than four miles and enclose several secondary palaces. The imperial city is thus made up of several concentric enclosures and it is in the second of these that the Grand Khan lives with his court. In the centre rises an artificial hill on which the principal palace has been built. It is planted with very fine trees, and for this reason has been called the Green Hill. It is surrounded by a lake and a pool. The lake is spanned by a marvellous bridge, the finest that I have ever seen, both for the quality of the marble and for the delicacy of its architecture. On the lake you may see a multitude of water birds: ducks, swans and wild geese. The surrounding wall also encloses a large park stocked with wild animals. Thus the Grand Khan is able to enjoy the pleasures of the chase without having to leave his palace.

"And I, Brother Odoric," the missionary continues, "lived for three and a half years (1325–1328) in this city with our Franciscan brethren, who possess a monastery there and even hold rank at the court of the Grand Khan. Indeed one of our brothers (Montecorvino) is archbishop of the court, and gives his blessing to the Grand Khan each time the sovereign departs on his travels." And Odoric describes one of these audiences; the Franciscans, with the bishop at their head, approached in procession the sovereign who was seated in his carriage: "We bore before us a Cross fixed to a staff, and we sang the *Veni, sancte Spiritus*. When we had come near to the imperial carriage, the Grand Khan, who had recognized our voices, bade us come up to him. As we approached, holding up the Cross, he removed his headdress, whose value is incalculable, and did reverence to the Cross. The bishop pronounced his blessing, and the Grand Khan kissed the Cross in the most devout manner. I then placed the incense in the thurible, and the bishop incensed the sovereign."

Odoric remarks, like Marco Polo before him, on the excellent organization and extraordinary rapidity of the posting service which the Mongols had created: "The couriers gallop at full speed on horses of extraordinary swiftness, or on racing camels. When they come within sight of the posting-houses they sound a horn to announce their approach. On being warned in this fashion, the keepers make ready another horseman or camel-rider with a fresh mount. This rider seizes the dispatches and gallops to the next station, where the same relief takes place. In this manner the Grand Khan receives news in twenty-four hours from countries at a distance of at least three days' ordinary riding."

Odoric de Pordenone appears to have left Peking in 1328. He first crossed the Ongüt country where, like others before him, he noticed the Nestorian Christians. He then passed through Kansu, remarking that the towns and villages along the great caravan route were so close to each other that on leaving one you were already in sight of the walls of the next. He passed through Central Asia, and arrived at his own monastery in Padua in May, 1330.

Chinese Christianity was by this time well known in Europe. In 1340 Pope Benedict XII sent to the Far East the Franciscan friar John of Marignolli, who, after passing through the Mongol khanates of South Russia and Turkestan, arrived at Peking in 1342. On August 19 Marignolli was granted an audience by the grand khan Toghan Temur, tenth successor to Kublai, and presented the Grand Khan with a large Western horse, a gift which was greatly appreciated. He took ship from Ch'üan-chou on December 26, 1347, stayed for some time in India, and returned to Avignon in 1353. In 1370 Pope Urban V appointed a new archbishop to the see of Peking; but this prelate was never able to take up his post, because the Mongol Yüan dynasty had just been overthrown by the Chinese national revolt which established the Ming dynasty, and the victorious Chinese included Christianity in their general proscription of all the "foreign doctrines" favoured by the Mongols.

Before concluding this chapter, let us endeavour to summarize briefly the benefits and injuries resulting from the period of Mongol domination.

First, the benefits derived from the regime.

The unification of almost all Asia by the Mongols reopened the great transcontinental roads which had been closed since the tenth century. The Silk Road, whose stages we have followed in the times of the Antonines and the Han emperors and whose importance we have seen during the reign of T'ang Hsüan-tsung in the seventh century, when it was the route of Buddhist pilgrims—this long caravan track which crossed the Pamirs and connected Persia with the Far East, was now traversed by Marco Polo. China once again came into contact with Persia and, beyond Persia, with the Western world. Distances were diminished, the continents brought closer together. Two monks born near Peking became, the one patriarch of Baghdad, and the other ambassador to the Pope and the King of

France; disciples of Saint Francis were appointed archbishops of Peking, or went to build cathedrals on the coast of Fukien; and a Venetian merchant entered the Chinese salt-tax administration. The Mongol storm, which blew down the garden walls and uprooted the trees, carried from one garden to another the seeds of flowers. In this respect the *Orbis Mongolicus* brought the same kind of benefits that once had sprung from the *Orbis Romanus*; and not until the discovery of the Cape of Good Hope and of America was the world to see an age comparable to the age of Marco Polo.

Against these advantages must be set the evil consequences of Mongol rule. These were not so much in the material field; for we have seen that Genghis Khan's grandson, the great Kublai, who was one of the best rulers to appear in Chinese history for many centuries, restored during his reign all that his terrible grandfather had destroyed. But from the spiritual point of view, it was as if during the Mongol domination a spring had been broken in the Chinese soul; this was an injury that was slow to mend. To be sure, after the expulsion of the Mongols the new Chinese dynasty of Ming did its best in every sphere of activity to restore the past—to cancel the period of foreign occupation with one stroke of the pen and to resume history from the point it had reached, not indeed in 1260, but in 907. But by its very faithfulness to tradition, and because it wanted to copy the past in everything, the new dynasty was committed to a lifeless task. Here is the root of the evil wrought in China by the Mongol invasion. The Chinese organism had suffered such an intense shock, had been so fatigued, that as soon as the storm was over it recoiled tightly and timorously within itself. China, which for centuries had tirelessly poured out the most prodigious literary, artistic, and philosophical creations, now dared do nothing but reproduce the stereotyped forms and make copies of copies; in her attempt to remain faithful to the past, she betrayed her greatest tradition. For China's past greatness had consisted above all in her unlimited power of resurgence and renewal, in the creative spontaneity which had produced in turn the splendour of the Shang bronzes, the metaphysical flights of Chuang Tzu, and the superhuman visions of Mu Ch'i. In the subsequent history of China we find little trace of this vitality, but instead a lack of self-confidence and a general distrust of the outside world; a faint-heartedness far removed indeed from the great ages that had gone before.

CHAPTER XXVIII

A NATIONAL RESTORATION: THE MING DYNASTY

IN the course of her long history China can number few sovereigns as remarkable as Kublai. By his strong personality, his statesmanlike qualities, his profound wisdom, and the firmness and humanity of his government, this Mongol ranked with the greatest Chinese emperors of former times. His grandson Temur (Ch'eng-tsung, 1294–1307) was also an energetic and conscientious ruler; but after these two emperors the Yüan dynasty rapidly degenerated. Its princes, sunk in debauchery and lacking in will-power, atoned for their vices only by a Lamaist religious bigotry which gave the Confucian literati a fresh grievance against them. Worst of all, they never ceased quarrelling among themselves, and in a few years destroyed the imposing administrative façade which under Kublai had aroused the admiration of Marco Polo. The last emperor of this line, Toghan Temur (Shun-ti, 1333–1368), who took pleasure only in the company of catamites or of Tibetan Lamas, allowed disorder to degenerate into anarchy.

The decadence of the imperial family encouraged Chinese patriots to revolt against foreign domination. The insurrection was organized by secret societies, especially by the White Lotus, a sect which now prophesied the millennium and preached the advent of Maitreya, the Buddhist Messiah. Like the revolution of 1912 (which also appealed to the people to overthrow a foreign dynasty), the movement started on the lower Long River and in the Cantonese region. It began in the year 1352, and from 1355 onwards the revolt spread across the entire south of China—across the former Sung empire. It was accompanied by appalling anarchy, since it was led by numerous chieftains who were half patriots and half bandits, and who fought among themselves at the same time as they waged war against the Mongols.

The rest of these various adventurers were to be eclipsed by the cleverest among them, Chu Yüan-chang, the founder of the Ming dynasty. The son of a poor farm labourer in the province of Anhui, he was seventeen when an epidemic carried off his entire family. In order to live, he entered a monastery; but his Buddhist vocation was evidently very superficial, for when the popular revolt against the Mongols broke out in the south—he was then twenty-five—he discarded his habit and took up arms, leading a revolt on the lower Long River. Although at first he was no more than the simple chieftain of a band like the other rebels, he stood out among them by reason of his political sense and his prudent humanity towards the populace; wisely, he won the people over instead of oppressing them. Whenever he captured a town, he forbade his soldiers to pillage it, with the result that the inhabitants hailed him as a liberator who freed them, not only from the Mongols, but from the other insurgent chieftains. In 1356 he captured Nanking and made it his capital, the seat of a government which established order and put down the anarchy elsewhere prevalent. His principal rival, the son of a simple fisherman, had for his part become master of Hupei, Hunan and Kiangsi. In 1363 Chu Yüan-chang defeated his opponent, killed him, and took possession of his territory. In 1367 and 1368 he occupied the Cantonese region, and so gained possession of the whole of South China. Then he marched against Peking.

It was a triumphal march; for the imbecility of the last Mongols had made the task of the liberator an easy one. Instead of uniting against the insurrection, they continued to quarrel among themselves and thus to divide their forces. On the night of September 10, 1368, the cowardly Toghan Temur, the unworthy descendant of the great Kublai Khan, fled from Peking to take refuge in Mongolia, and Chu Yüan-chang made his entry into the capital.

In a Peking delivered from the Mongols, Chu Yüan-chang was proclaimed emperor by his army and became the founder of the

Ming dynasty. At the age of forty, after a struggle that had lasted thirteen years, this unfrocked monk, who had started life as a pauper, became the liberator of his country and successor to the heritage of Han and T'ang. This fortunate adventurer was already far better off than the founders of Sung, who had never succeeded in expelling the barbarians from this city of Peking that he himself had captured so easily. Thus he looked back for his examples beyond Sung, to T'ang, the last native dynasty to rule over the entire territory of China; in 1373 he promulgated an administrative code based on that of T'ang. However, he did not move his capital to the north, but continued to live at Nanking.[1] Being himself a native of the lower Long River region, and having expelled the foreign rulers of China with an army composed of southerners, to begin with he employed a government of southerners. Moreover, it must be remembered that the whole of North China had been in Tartar hands for two hundred and forty-two years, while Peking itself had been in their power for four hundred and thirty-two years; during these long centuries the northern provinces had been pervaded by barbarian elements. It was South China that from 1126 to 1279 had served as a refuge for Chinese independence; and it was from there that the new movement of national liberation had started. Thus the south represented the true China, and it was the south that triumphed with the establishment of the Ming dynasty. All the same, the new emperor was too shrewd a politician to accept the preponderance of southerners for very long. In order to bridge the gulf between north and south, a gulf which two and a half centuries of political separation had been steadily widening, and with a view to the spiritual as well as political reunification of China, he decided in 1380 not only to have the north administered by officials from the south, but also to staff the south with men from the north. For the same cause, he did not hesitate in 1370 to proscribe the secret societies of the White Lotus and the

[1] Nanking was the new name (*Nan-ching*, "Southern capital"). The Yüan capital of Ta-tu was renamed Pei-p'ing, later changed to Peking (*Pei-ching*, "Northern capital") when the Ming administration moved north (but retained Nanking as a secondary capital).

White Cloud, even though they had largely contributed to the overthrow of the Mongol domination; times had changed, and moreover the secret societies had previously backed the wrong horse by declaring their support for rivals of the new emperor.

The founder of the Ming dynasty sought in all fields to bring about a restoration of values, to bridge the hiatus of the Mongol and Ju-chen dominations and link the new China with the far-distant past; doubtless he applied himself to this eminently traditionalist enterprise with a zeal which was all the greater for the fact that he himself had been a nobody. In 1370 he remodelled the system of examinations for recruiting the mandarinate and re-established the titles of nobility. The worship of Confucius was solemnly celebrated, and the emperor enlisted the support of the literary academies, which under the Mongol regime had been centres of opposition to Buddhist clericalism. Meanwhile this former monk had not forgotten his co-religionists. He even continued to surround himself with Buddhist monks, and he soundly castigated any of the literati who attempted to remonstrate with him on these grounds; on one occasion he went so far as to execute a certain Grand Judge for this offence. This incident is symptomatic; for as the emperor grew older (he lived to the age of seventy) he became increasingly intolerant of remonstrance and lost the popular good-nature which had so largely contributed to his success. He became habitually suspicious, and once had eighteen dignitaries and all their families executed. As the result of a plot, real or imaginary, fifteen thousand people were put to death in Nanking. The former adventurer who had become Son of Heaven wished to re-establish absolutism before he died.

Chu Yüan-chang's real successor was the next emperor but one, his second son, whose reign-title was Yung-le (1403–1424) and whom we shall refer to as Yung-le-ti.[1] This warrior sovereign had

[1] When referring to the various Ming and Ch'ing (Manchu) sovereigns we shall use their "reign-title" rather than their "temple-name". See note, page 62. Ming Chuang-lieh-ti, who lost the throne to the Manchus, of course received no "temple-name" from the latter; but some hundred years later he was granted the epithet Chuang-lieh ("Bold and resolute").

an expansive conception of his role. Whereas Kublai had set out to build a Chinese empire for the Mongols, Yung-le-ti now attempted to win for China the Mongol heritage of Kublai's descendants. The grand khan Kublai, by his advance from the Yellow River to Tonkin, had obtained the submission of the whole territory of China and had become an authentic Son of Heaven. The third Ming emperor set out to conquer Mongolia and play the part of Grand Khan.

It was with this aim in view that in 1409 the emperor transferred his capital from Nanking to Peking. It was he who drew up the imposing plan of the Imperial City which forms the centre of modern Peking, as well as more detailed plans for the "Violet-purple Forbidden City"; [1] it was he who conceived that succession of palaces, marble terraces, throne rooms, gardens and perspectives worthy of the greatest Chinese traditions; he who enlarged the lakes, built the artificial hills, and planted the gardens with the flowers and shrubs of his native Long River Valley. All this was restored and perfected by the Ch'ing emperors in the eighteenth century, but everywhere it still bears the mark of the Ming emperor Yung-le-ti. And it was Yung-le-ti who first built the Temple of Heaven (1420) and the Temple of Agriculture (1422) near the south wall of Peking.

The transfer of the capital to Peking was in itself a declaration of policy. No other purely Chinese dynasty had ever thought of choosing this residence; the historic role of Peking had begun only with the Tartars. In the tenth century the Ch'i-tan established one of their capitals there; they were followed by the Ju-chen in the twelfth century, and by Kublai in 1260. Such a choice by conquerors from the north is easily understood, since Peking lay on the outer fringe of medieval China, being the principal town of one of the frontier marches. Just over the threshold of Shan-hai-kuan lay Manchuria, then untilled; just through the pass of Nan-k'ou lay, then as now, the steppes of Mongolia. Geographically and historically, Peking is a Sino-tartar compromise; the Chinese is still at home there and the

[1] In Chinese, Tzu-chin-ch'eng. There was a violet-purple palace in the sky—a constellation containing the pole star—and one on the earth; the latter was the abode of the emperor.

Tartar is not yet out of his element. Yung-le-ti, by moving his court from Nanking to the threshold of Mongolia, to Kublai's former capital, was staking a claim to the heritage of Kublai's descendants.

His father, it is true, had set him an example in this direction. Chu Yüan-chang, after expelling the Mongols from Chinese territory, had pursued them into their homeland. In 1372 a column of Chinese troops advanced to the River Tola in Outer Mongolia, and in 1388 a hundred thousand Chinese again crossed the eastern Gobi and fought the tribes to the east of the Buir Nor, between the Khalkha Gol and the Kerulen. However, these incursions were no more than the following up of a victory, expeditions of reprisal intended to inspire the nomads with a salutary fear. The emperor Yung-le-ti, on the other hand, practised a consistent policy in Mongolia, where the authority of the clan of Genghiz had been seriously weakened by the ignominy of their expulsion from China. The emperor sought to incite the chieftains of other tribes, particularly the Eleuths, or Western Mongols, to revolt against them. He intervened on several occasions in the ensuing civil wars in Outer Mongolia, notably in 1410 and 1411, when he led his troops as far as the Upper Onon and the native prairies of Genghis Khan. In this way he helped to transfer the hegemony of Outer Mongolia from the descendants of Genghis to the Eleuth khans; but it was not long before the Chinese had reason to regret the substitution of fresh clans in place of the decadent power whose lack of authority had paralysed the nomadic hordes.

In Indo-China, too, Yung-le-ti sought to resume the great imperial policy of Han and T'ang. In the kingdom of Annam, the legitimate dynasty had been overthrown by a usurper. The emperor made this an excuse to occupy the country, which he divided up into Chinese provinces (1407). But before ten years had passed, the Annamese were beginning a long and exhausting guerilla war against the occupation forces. Four years after the death of Yung-le-ti the leader of the insurgents, Lê Lo'i, captured Hanoi and expelled the Chinese (1428).

Yung-le-ti was not satisfied with laying claim to a protectorate over Mongolia and annexing Annam. He meant to establish Chinese naval hegemony over the Sunda Seas and the Indian Ocean. His fleets proclaimed the supremacy of the Chinese flag off the coasts of Tchampa, Cambodia, Siam, the Malaccan peninsula, Java, Sumatra, Ceylon (where the Chinese admiral chastised the local rajah for showing hostile intentions), Bengal and southern India. They sailed as far as Hormuz, on the Persian Gulf, Aden, and Jeddah, the port of Mecca. These voyages took place between 1405 and 1424, at the beginning of a century whose last years were to see the arrival of the Portuguese in the Indies (1498). What might have been the fate of Asia if, when they reached the Indies, the European navigators had found them ruled by Chinese sea power? But here again Yung-le-ti had a breadth of vision which was out of keeping with the temperament of his people, or rather, which went against the ideology of the mandarinate. The China which he was creating was on too large a scale for its own strength: the Chinese had no vocation for the sea; the climate of Tonkin was too hot and that of Mongolia too cold for their soldiers. The world of the literati remained consistently hostile to what it considered costly and useless foreign conquests. The *Weltpolitik* of the emperor Yung-le-ti had no future. China withdrew within herself and allowed the hour of destiny, on land and on the sea, to pass her by.

This same attitude of withdrawal was found in the world of ideas. Yung-le-ti, though himself a Buddhist, ordered the compilation of the Neo-Confucian texts, and in 1416 decreed that these works should have equal standing with the ancient Confucian canon as the basis of official instruction; this meant that "Chuism" was made the state doctrine of the Ming dynasty. A century later, however, there appeared a certain reaction against Chuist materialism, or at least against state positivism, in the doctrine of Wang Yang-ming (1472–1528). This philosopher did not openly attack the mechanist positivism of Chu Hsi. He taught that our share in the cosmic order, in the universal law (*li*), lies in the heart rather than in the faculty of reason; that in order to attain communion with the essence of the world one should have recourse to intuitive knowledge (*liang chih*), the supreme innate *dictamen* in the depths of the heart, rather than to what we might call discursive intelligence. "Throughout time and space", writes Wang Yang-ming, "the intuitive knowledge in the human heart never varies." In default of the metaphysical absolute, which Chuism refused to accept, one finds at least the absolute of moral law, the pure inner light which illumines every man who comes into the world: "In the heart of each and every man there lives a Confucius." The personality of Wang Yang-ming and his nobility of character make him a sympathetic figure; but his work, which in any case was limited to ethics, represents a tendency rather than a system. That the doctrine of Chu Hsi retained all its authority is shown by the fact that Wang Yang-ming had to claim to support it in order to get his own teachings accepted.

The emperor Yung-le-ti, who died in 1424, was the last great figure of the Ming dynasty. After his death, his descendants continued in power for more than two centuries without producing a single remarkable personality. Once again, as at the end of the Han and T'ang dynasties (although comparatively far sooner), a camarilla of eunuchs assumed control over a series of mediocre sovereigns and governed in their name. Meanwhile in Mongolia the Eleuths, or Western Mongols, who with assistance from Yung-le-ti had replaced the descendants of Genghis Khan in the hegemony of the hordes, had become a formidable power. Their khan, Essen, asked for the hand of a Chinese princess in marriage and, when this request was refused, came at the head of his troops to ravage the frontiers of northern Shansi and Hopei. The emperor Ying-tsung marched against them in company with his favourite, a eunuch who assumed command over the generals. The Chinese army, which had advanced without rations, was cut off and annihilated near Hsüan-hua, in the mountainous region between Peking and Kalgan. A hundred thousand Chinese corpses lay strewn in the passes, and the emperor Ying-tsung was taken prisoner (1449). The Eleuths, whose victory exceeded their wildest hopes, marched on to camp beneath the walls of Peking. But they were not equipped to carry out a siege, and after a few months their khan, Essen, decided to release the emperor; in 1453 Essen made his peace with the empire.

A century later came a new alarm; this time the danger came, not from the Western Mongols, but from the descendants of Genghis Khan. During the last quarter of the fifteenth century, a restoration of Genghis Khan's line had taken place in Mongolia. One of the khans of this line, Altan, who pastured his herds in Inner Mongolia to the north of Shansi, came on several occasions between 1529 and 1570 to pillage the northern districts of Shansi and Hopei. In the year 1550 he advanced as far as the gates of Peking, and the fires kindled by his army lit up the suburbs of the capital. Finally he acknowledged Ming suzerainty, and his main encampment was given the name Kuei-hua ("Turning to civilization").

The Mongols were traditional enemies of China; but now, along the coasts, there appeared new adversaries, the remoteness of whose island home rendered them unconquerable—the bold and elusive Japanese. A swarm of adventurers and corsairs from every creek in the archipelago began to infest the ports of Chekiang, Fukien and the Cantonese region. In 1555 they sailed up the Long River as far as Nanking, pillaging open villages and towns as they went. These pirates were only the young bloods of that Japanese expansion whose full force was to be experienced in the affairs of Korea.

The conflict finally broke out during the reign of the thirteenth emperor of the Ming dynasty, Wan-li-ti (1573–1620). At this time Japan was governed by the celebrated Hideyoshi (1585–1598), one of the greatest statesmen in Japanese history, who conceived the audacious plan of conquering the Ming empire. The corsairs who periodically raided the ports of Central China had doubtless told him of the decrepitude of the Ming dynasty. At all events, the ease with which the Manchus were able to conquer Peking fifty years later proves that Hideyoshi's idea was realizable. In order to achieve this project, it was necessary for his troops to obtain passage across Korea; this the Koreans, who looked on the Japanese as their hereditary enemies, refused to grant. Hideyoshi then sent an army of two hundred thousand men to Korea. They entered Seoul, the Korean capital, on June 12, 1592, and advanced as far as Pyongyang, in the direction of Manchuria. The plan of the Japanese general staff was the same as that employed during the Sino-Japanese war of 1894. Their intention was to reach the Yalu, cross the Liao-tung peninsula, and through the pass of Shan-hai-kuan to bear down on Peking. However, the resistance of the Koreans gave the Chinese time to intervene with superior forces. The Japanese were forced to evacuate Seoul (May 1593) and beat a retreat towards the south coast. In 1597 Hideyoshi sent another expeditionary force to Korea; but this time the Japanese failed even to reach Seoul. They were once again thrown back to the south coast, and the struggle degenerated into a war of sieges (1597–1598). The death of Hideyoshi on September 16, 1598, led to the repatriation of the Japanese troops and the cessation of hostilities. Japan had to wait three centuries before recommencing this struggle against China, a struggle carried on over the corpse of Korea.

The lesson that the Ming dynasty should have learned from this war they had won was that the naval isolation of their country had come to an end. In fact, even at the time when this isolation was first being menaced by the raids of the Japanese corsairs in Central China, the Portuguese navigators were already making their appearance on the Cantonese coast.

Since 1498, when the Portuguese explorer Vasco da Gama reached India after sailing round the coast of Africa, the sea route to China had been open to Europeans. In 1511 the Portuguese admiral Albuquerque captured Malacca, whose commercial and strategic importance in those days was similar to that of Singapore today; and in 1514 the first Portuguese trading ships reached the China ports. Some time between 1549 and 1557 the Portuguese received permission from the local mandarins to found an establishment of an essentially commercial character at Macao, at the entry to the Canton River. In the year 1582 the Portuguese authorities of Macao paid a tribute of five hundred taels to the viceroy of Canton for this privilege.

With the arrival of the Portuguese, Christianity, which had been banished from China after the fall of the Mongols, again entered the country. This new evangelization was the work of the Society of Jesus and more particularly of two of its members, Matteo Ricci and Adam Schall.

The Italian Jesuit Matteo Ricci (1552–1610) arrived in Macao in 1582, and for thirteen years carried on his mission in the Cantonese region. In order to get themselves accepted, the missionaries were obliged to identify themselves with one of the existing social categories. Ricci, who used the Chinese name of Li Ma-tou, at first adopted the dress of a Buddhist priest; then, with remarkable discernment, he abandoned this and assumed the costume of the literati, thereby managing very cleverly to associate Christianity with the Confucian state doctrine. The whole policy of the Jesuits was based on this happy understanding of the Chinese mentality. In 1595 Ricci, who had managed to gain favour with important officials in Canton, was able to leave for the north. He first settled in Nanking, where he succeeded in carrying on his mission without being interfered with. On January 4, 1601, he was permitted to go on to Peking, and at once sought to make contact with the imperial court, presenting the emperor with a harpsichord, a map of the world and two chiming clocks. He petitioned Wan-li-ti, and wrote: "Your humble subject is perfectly acquainted with the celestial sphere, geography, geometry, and calculations. With the aid of instruments he observes the stars, and he understands the use of the gnomon." Ricci received a monthly pension and was permitted to reside in the imperial city. He attained the highest favour when he was commissioned to give lessons in science to one of the emperor's sons. When he died in Peking on May 11, 1610, at the age of fifty-eight, there were more than three hundred Catholic churches in China. His works include a great "world map" (*Wan-kuo-yü-t'u*) and a Chinese translation of Euclid's *Elements*.

His real successor was the German Jesuit, Adam Schall, who was known to the Chinese by the name of T'ang Jo-wang (1591–1666). He reached China in 1620, and at first preached in Sian. A mathematician, an astronomer and a remarkable linguist, he was entrusted by the imperial court with the reform of the calendar. The last Ming emperor, Chuang-lieh-ti, whose reign-title was Ch'ung-chen (1628–1644), showed a particular regard for Schall, and in 1636 had him establish a cannon foundry near the palace. We shall see that after the Manchu conquest Adam Schall enjoyed no less favour with the new masters of the empire.

The interest aroused at the Ming court by the scientific knowledge of the Jesuits shows that the last sovereigns of the dynasty were vaguely aware of the necessity of modernizing their country; but this realization came too late. At the beginning of the Ming dynasty (1368) China and the West had been on more or less the same level of development as regards technical and mechanical skill. At the end of the dynasty, in 1644, Europe was already in possession of modern science and equipment, whereas China was still in the Middle Ages.

The literary production of the Ming dynasty confirms this judgment. The liveliest works are the novels and plays; Ming is considered the great age of the novel. One of the five "classic" novels (four of which were written during the Ming period) has as its theme the travels of the Buddhist monk Hsüan-tsang, who set out for India by way of Central Asia in 629. Unfortunately, if one has read the vivid account of this journey written by the famous pilgrim himself, it is difficult to find much interest in the incredible tale which the Ming novelist has spun from it.[1] In place of the precise and picturesque descriptions of the medieval text—sandstorms in the Gobi, the snow-covered peaks of the T'ien Shan and the Pamirs, the great palm trees of India—there is nothing but fantastic adventures,

[1] The novel is extremely popular, but the "original" is little read. There is an excellent English translation of the novel, made by Arthur Waley and entitled *Monkey* (London, Allen & Unwin).

magic, and sorcery, such as one finds in Tibetan tales. The other Ming novels usually deal with sentimental intrigue and romantic adventures, often, it is true, giving interesting glimpses of the manners and customs of the times.

Ming painting can be defined in one word—academic. Treatises such as the *Mustard Seed Garden* (*Chieh-tzu-yüan*) studied the picturesque qualities in Sung landscape painting and gave a list of carefully itemized recipes. The result was all too often a forced and artificial picturesqueness, such as unnaturally overhanging rocks in paintings of mountains; another result was the pictorial equivalent of the abuse of literary allusions in poetry. All the same, one must not exaggerate these criticisms. Ming painting has the misfortune to be compared with the overwhelmingly superior works of the great creative period of the Sung dynasty; but there is much charm in the Ming portraits of young girls and the scenes in the women's apartments, a remarkable virtuosity in the paintings of birds and flowers; and in their wash-drawing the Ming landscape painters still show considerable power. The Ming tombstone portraits—a *genre* in which there was a considerable revival—are remarkable for their sober realism, their sharpness of expression, and the boldness and precision of their craftsmanship; there is occasionally something very close to the drawings of Dürer, Holbein or Clouet.

The greatest art of the Ming dynasty was ceramics. Here again, in order to be fair one must avoid comparisons with the Sung period and judge the Ming pieces on their individual merits. They are worthy of it, especially since much was done for the art by the Ming emperors. In 1369 the founder of the dynasty rebuilt the imperial manufactory at Ching-te-chen, in Kiangsi, where the greater part of the trade became established; kaolin takes its name from the white clay found at nearby Kao-ling.

Sung ceramics had produced chiefly monochromes or gradations of one tone into another, and one still finds this use of monochrome in Ming ceramics. There are varieties of celadons which, if less luminous and more milky than those of the Sung period, are none the less very beautiful; they were exported to places as distant as Ispahan, Cairo, and Stamboul. There is also the white ware manufactured at Te-hua, in Fukien—this is usually in the form of statuettes of Buddhist divinities—as well as other pottery in aubergine-violets and rich dark blues. But it was above all in the use of polychrome, and more particularly in illustrative decoration, that the Ming potters were triumphantly successful. The quality of kaolin employed at Ching-te-chen was able to resist the highest temperatures and thus made possible the coexistence of the most varied glazes. Outstanding among the high-temperature glazes is the blue-and-white, where the cobalt blue is deeper or lighter according to the proportion in which indigenous blue has been mixed with "Mohammedan blue". The fashion for blue-and-white was gradually eclipsed by the "three-colours" or *san-ts'ai* (green, yellow and aubergine-violet), and the "five-colours", *wu-ts'ai* (the same three colours plus blue and red). This preference for "colours in bold juxtaposition, glowing tones, and painted decorations" is characteristic of the period. Ceramics tended more and more to become a branch of painting, and pottery competed with the silk scroll in drawing from the brush of the Ming painter his customary themes of delicate feminine forms, butterflies, birds, and flowers.

This style was to reach its peak during the Ch'ing dynasty.

CHAPTER XXIX

THE DRAMA OF 1644

DURING the period Wan-li (1573–1620) China had successfully resisted the Japanese menace; but hardly had this danger passed when the Chinese were faced by the Manchu peril.

The Manchus were a Tungus people related to the Ju-chen who had conquered North China in the twelfth century. They lived in the forest clearings of northern Manchuria, in the basin of the Sungari, near what is today the Russian Primorsk region. These forest hunters, who lived in a cold and damp climate amidst immense forests of pine, fir, and larch, were originally divided into rival clans; but at the beginning of the seventeenth century a forceful chieftain, Nurhaci, united them and founded the historical Manchu kingdom. At that period the Chinese held the southern part of Manchuria, that is, the region of Mukden and the Liaotung peninsula. Nurhaci made war against China, and in 1621 and 1622 captured the whole of this region; in 1625 he established his capital at Mukden, where his tomb can still be seen. He even attempted to force the Great Wall, but failed when he came against the cannons which the Jesuits had made for the Ming emperors.

Nurhaci's son Abahai (ruled 1627–1643) was one of those barbarians of genius, so often found in the history of the Far East, who combine the military qualities of their own peoples with an intuitive understanding of the ways of civilized life. Realizing how decadent and unstable the Ming dynasty had become, he made it his avowed ambition one day to become emperor of China. In order to make his people worthy of the high destiny he dreamed for them, he endeavoured to give them a polish of Chinese culture, just as another

Tartar conqueror, the great Kublai, had done three and a half centuries earlier; it was Abahai's intention to repeat, with his Manchus, the achievement of Kublai and his Mongols. During the winter of 1629–1630 he advanced to the gates of Peking; but the Manchus were not yet equipped to conduct a siege. Before retiring, however, Abahai paid a visit to the tombs of the old Ju-chen Chin sovereigns, the "Golden Kings" of the twelfth century with whom he was connected by a blood relationship, and offered solemn sacrifices; this significant ceremony renewed traditional links of kinship and proclaimed the legitimacy of Manchu claims to the imperial throne of Peking. In Mukden, where his court had many Chinese advisers, Abahai was in 1636 declared emperor of China, first ruler of the Ch'ing dynasty.

Yet whatever the damage periodical Manchu raids might cause to the countryside and the open towns of northern Hopei, there was as yet no serious threat to the country as a whole. The eastern bastions of the Great Wall, from Shan-hai-kuan to Hsüan-hua, held firm. It needed an internal revolution followed by a civil war to deliver China into the hands of her enemies.

The Ming emperor in Peking, Chuang-lieh-ti (1628–1644), was gentle, well-meaning, and educated, but a weak ruler. As often happened in China when the central government became weak, revolts broke out everywhere. Soldiers discontented with their pay, and peasants suffering from famine, organized large bands which, under the leadership of rebel generals or bold adventurers, set about pillaging the countryside. The most intelligent of these adventurers was Li Tzu-ch'eng, an educated peasant who had become a brigand chieftain; in 1640 he gained effective control of Honan and Shensi, and in 1644 he marched against Peking. His approach found the imperial court completely unprepared. The best of the imperial armies, under the command of the general Wu San-kuei, was stationed at the pass of Shan-hai-kuan, far from the capital, where it was holding back the Manchus. Li Tzu-ch'eng, without encountering any serious resistance, marched on to Peking, where traitors opened the gates to him. On the same day, the unfortunate emperor Chuang-lieh-ti hanged himself so as not to fall into the hands of the rebels alive (April 3, 1644).

So far everything had gone in favour of Li Tzu-ch'eng; but this bold adventurer had reckoned without the imperial army at Shan-hai-kuan and its commander Wu San-kuei. As soon as he heard the news of the fall of Peking and the suicide of the emperor, Wu San-kuei hastened to conclude an armistice with the Manchus. The latter not only agreed to stop fighting, but even placed a strong force of troops at his disposal for the task of punishing the rebels. When Li Tzu-ch'eng heard that the army on the frontier was coming to an agreement with the Manchus against him, he took fright and offered to share his power with Wu San-kuei. The latter refused this offer, and routed Li Tzu-ch'eng's army in their first encounter (at Yung-p'ing). The usurper, out of spite, ordered the execution of Wu San-kuei's parents; and from that time there raged a bitter hatred between the two men. The sacred sentiment of filial piety and the thirst for vengeance blinded Wu San-kuei to the most elementary prudence. He trusted the Manchus completely, and in company with them he marched against Peking. At his approach Li Tzu-ch'eng, after rifling the imperial treasury, set fire to the palace and retreated into Shansi.

Wu San-kuei entered Peking with his Manchu allies. He then thanked them for their co-operation and sought to dismiss them. The Manchus soon made him realize his mistake; they had an army of a hundred thousand men in Peking, and it was constantly being reinforced by fresh contingents from Mukden. Disregarding the remonstrances of Wu San-kuei, they took possession of the gates of the city. Their king, Abahai, had died several months before, leaving as heir his seven-year-old nephew. The Manchu leaders now proclaimed this child emperor of China under the reign-title Shun Chih. The Ming dynasty was declared to have forfeited the Mandate of Heaven.

Wu San-kuei, the dupe of the Manchus who through force of

circumstances had become their accomplice, was obliged to accept the situation. They appointed him to the wealthy viceroyalty of Shensi, conditionally upon his expelling Li Tzu-ch'eng from that province. The rage which he must have felt on account of recent events he now turned on his father's murderer. He pursued Li Tzu-ch'eng implacably, forced him back far beyond Shensi, and finally organized a veritable man-hunt across the provinces of Honan and Hopei which ended in the death of this former bandit (1644).

Meanwhile the regents in Peking, uncles of the young emperor Shun-chih-ti, were organizing the Manchu regime. They had the good sense not to alter the form of government; they retained the various government posts and also their occupants, being content to appoint a Manchu official alongside the Chinese official in the more important positions. The custom of shaving the top of the head, imposed on the Chinese by the conquerors, was the only sign that marked the accession of a Tartar dynasty.

The authority of the Peking Ch'ing government was still only recognized in North China. A Ming prince had been proclaimed emperor in Nanking, and the whole of the south supported him. The first concern of the Manchus after the conquest of Peking was to wipe out this centre of resistance. In the spring of 1645 their armies converged on Nanking, and the Ming pretender—who all too late had thought of asking help from the Portuguese at Macao—was drowned in the course of his flight. Nanking was occupied by the Manchus on May 9, 1645.

The last defenders of Chinese independence and the Ming dynasty took refuge in Chekiang and the Cantonese region; three Ming princes, who had escaped the disaster which had overtaken their family, sought to organize the resistance. Unfortunately they were unable to agree among themselves, and used up their last forces in internecine conflicts; hence the Manchus had no difficulty in subjugating Chekiang and Fukien (1646).

The hinterland of the Cantonese region held out longer. A last

Ming prince, whose name was Chu Yu-lang, was proclaimed emperor, with the reign-title Yung-li and a "capital" at Kweilin, in the mountains of Kwangsi. The Manchus marched against Kweilin, but were repulsed by the legitimists, the latter being reinforced by three hundred Portuguese armed with cannon, who had come from Macao under the command of Nicholas Fereira. Indeed it was the Portuguese intervention that saved the Ming forces. This intervention is easily explained; for one of the pretender's most respected counsellors was a Jesuit, Father Koffler. Chu Yu-lang's wife was a Christian, baptized as Anne; his son was baptized as Constantine, and the dowager empress as Helen. Their most faithful champion, the heroic Ch'ü Shih-ssu, also became converted to Catholicism and took the name of Thomas; this Christian soldier brought a ray of glory to the last days of the dynasty. In 1650 the Jesuit father Boym left Kweilin for Europe to solicit the aid of Christendom on behalf of the Ming dynasty. But in the same year a large Manchu army was sent from the north with the mission of subjugating Kwangsi and Kwangtung at any cost. At its approach, the weak Chu Yu-lang grew frightened and, despite the entreaties of Ch'ü Shih-ssu, fled from Kweilin. Abandoned by his master and by half his troops, Ch'ü Shih-ssu nevertheless defended Kweilin with his last remaining followers. The town was finally captured, and he himself, sword in hand, was taken prisoner. Following their usual policy, the Manchus sought to obtain his support, even offering him a viceroyalty. As he stubbornly refused to betray his master, he was decapitated, but on account of his heroism the conquerors accorded him a magnificent funeral (1650). The Manchus later captured Canton, while Chu Yu-lang took refuge in Burma (1651).

The last defender of the Ming cause was the corsair Cheng Ch'eng-kung, who was known to the Dutch and Portuguese as Koxinga (from a popular Chinese name for him).

Cheng Ch'eng-kung is one of the most curious figures in the history of the Far East. He is the first representative of that overseas China, then being born, whose expansion on every shore of the

Pacific and Indian Oceans represents one of the most important happenings of the nineteenth century. Cheng Ch'eng-kung's father, Cheng Chih-lung, was a simple fisherman who became a pirate captain. He spent his youth in Macao, where he was baptized by the Portuguese; next he lived in Spanish Manila, and from there went to Japan, where he took a wife: Ch'eng-kung was the son of this marriage. After his return to China, Cheng Chih-lung became a corsair in the service of the Ming dynasty and fought the Manchus along the coasts of Chekiang, Fukien, and Kwangtung (1645). Betrayed to the Manchus and taken captive, he was sent to Peking, whence he never returned (1646). His son Ch'eng-kung, swearing to avenge him, put to sea again: at the head of his elusive flotillas, for sixteen years he carried on a relentless campaign of privateering against the Manchu governors of the southern coastal provinces.

Koxinga began by securing reliable bases on the coast. In 1653 he established a naval base on the island of Amoy, in Fukien, and in 1656 occupied the island of Ch'ung-ming which commands the estuary of the Long River. In 1657 he sailed up the Long River and boldly laid siege to Nanking. After being repulsed, he turned his attention to the island of Formosa, where the Dutch had been established since 1625. He assembled a powerful fleet in his lair at Amoy, and landed in Formosa on April 30, 1661. On February 1, 1662, after a long siege, he captured the Dutch stronghold of Zelandia. He gallantly accorded the governor all the honours of war, but compelled the Dutch to leave the island. He was planning to capture Manila from the Spaniards in the same way when on July 2, 1662, he died prematurely at the age of thirty-nine.

Cheng Ch'eng-kung's destiny was not of the common run. The son of a Chinese Christian father and a Japanese mother, a pupil of the Spanish conquistadors who was forced by a foreign invasion to live on the outer edge of his country, his horizon was obviously wider than that of his Chinese compatriots. It was doubtless in imitation of the Spanish, Portuguese and Dutch navigators that he conceived the bold idea of building himself a maritime empire in the China seas.

His attempt to do so is of great interest to the historian, being the earliest revelation of something which is by no means apparent in previous history: the maritime and colonial vocation of the Chinese people. Indeed Cheng Ch'eng-kung's venture may be said to have started the era of the great emigration of the Chinese, who today are to be found on all the shores of the southern seas, from Cholon to Singapore, and from Batavia to Manila and Hawaii; it is a movement of immense importance, the ultimate consequence of which cannot yet be estimated.

The Formosan kingdom established by Cheng Ch'eng-kung passed to his son Cheng Ching, who ruled there undisturbed from 1662 to 1681. After his death it was annexed in 1683 by the Ch'ing emperor K'ang-hsi-ti.

CHAPTER XXX

THE GREAT MANCHU EMPERORS

THE manner in which the Manchus captured the imperial throne had every appearance of a sleight-of-hand trick. With a cleverness that was most surprising for barbarians, the Manchu regents made use of the struggle between a bandit usurper and a legitimist general to edge themselves into Peking; by aiding the general to punish the usurper, they obtained the full approval of the loyalists and the mandarinate; then, there being no active central power to challenge them, they succeeded without bloodshed in making themselves masters of the ancient empire. There was a great difference between this peaceful taking over and the twenty years of massacre and devastation that had marked the Mongol conquest in the thirteenth century. In South China, it is true, the Manchus had to fight for seven years more before they got rid of the last Ming pretenders; but these campaigns were limited to the southern frontier provinces, and were negligible in comparison with the forty-two years of fierce struggles that it had taken the Mongols to conquer the same region. Moreover the regent who was adroitly directing the government on behalf of his nephew the child-emperor took care to employ mainly the Chinese themselves in this task, and Ming notables who came over and supported Ch'ing were rewarded with titles and perquisites. In order to make the best use of these Chinese supporters, he created three great principalities in the south and appointed three Chinese dignitaries to rule them; one of these rulers was Wu San-kuei. After the death of the regent, the emperor Shun-chih-ti, in spite of his youth—he was only fifteen—declared, like Louis XIV, that he wished to be his own prime minister, and assumed direct control of the government (February 1, 1651).

The young sovereign soon gave proof of his wisdom and capability. He showed a marked regard for the Jesuit father Adam Schall, who in 1645 had already been appointed to supervise the Board of Astronomy, and in 1653 he conferred on him the title of "The religious teacher who comprehends the mysteries." In 1654 Schall presented a treatise on European astronomy which was officially adopted by the court in the following year. Moreover, it appears that Schall had occasion to play a more intimate part in the service of his sovereign.

The emperor was only seventeen or eighteen when one day, at a palace celebration, he noticed the beautiful Tung Hsiao-wan, the young wife of one of his chief officials, and immediately fell passionately in love with her. Her husband, on learning of the emperor's feelings, committed suicide. Shun-chih-ti had the young woman brought to the palace and, since he was already married, conferred on her the title of Second Consort. "For several years he was happy, his love becoming ever greater. The Second Consort gave birth to a son, and the Emperor's happiness was complete. Then, without anyone's knowing from what illness they were suffering, the mother and child both died, perhaps poisoned." The emperor's grief was terrifying to behold. "He had thirty members of the young woman's suite put to death and buried at the foot of her coffin. It is not known if he did this with the intention of avenging the deceased or, in the old Tartar manner, in order to provide her with companions in the other world." [1] Shun-chih-ti even attempted suicide; he was stopped

[1] Soulié de Morant, *L'épopée des jésuites en Chine.*

Translator's Note: M. Grousset gives the long-accepted story of Tung Hsiao-wan and the Emperor which the investigations of Yü P'ing-po and others have shown to be an historical legend.

In fact the Consort and Tung Hsiao-wan were two different ladies. Tung Hsiao-wan was a beautiful and talented singing-girl, who became the concubine of a Chinese scholar and died young. As it happens, she died before the Emperor was old enough to have appreciated her charms. The Second Consort was the daughter of a Manchu general. Her clan name was Tung-e, spelt with the same "Tung" character as Tung Hsiao-wan, and evidently this was sufficient to convince some writer that the romantic singing-girl was in fact the romantic empress.

The attendants are not recorded to have been slaughtered, but to have committed suicide, and there are later instances of such actions.

in time, but fell into a decline. Father Schall, with whom he became more and more friendly, did his best to encourage him to regain control of himself—but in vain; for the emperor, who had ceased to care about his health, died soon afterwards of smallpox (or so it was said). A popular rumour was current that he had secretly abdicated and become a monk in the sacred mountains of Wu-t'ai-shan. Some people have claimed to find an echo of this drama in the great Ch'ing novel *Hung-lou-meng*, by Ts'ao Hsüeh-ch'in (died 1763); but the allusion, if there is one, is very heavily veiled.[1]

On the death of Shun-chih-ti, the Manchu princes placed on the throne a seven-year old boy; the new reign-title was K'ang-hsi (1662-1722).

K'ang-hsi-ti, who was to have a reign almost as long as that of his contemporary Louis XIV, was one of the greatest sovereigns in Chinese history. As was the case with Louis XIV, his contemporaries were unanimous in praising his beauty, his natural majesty, and his presence of mind.[2] "His figure was taller than the average and well proportioned, his features well formed and full, his eyes lively and more open than is common among the Chinese, his forehead large, his nose slightly aquiline, and his mouth generous; his manner was mild and gracious, yet so grand and majestic that he

[1] The *Hung-lou-meng* (usually translated *Dream of the Red Chamber*, though the title means something more like *A Dream of Splendour*) has for its principal themes the blighting of a passionate love and the decay of a noble house. It was long felt to represent some real events, and acquired a number of long and exhaustive commentaries. It was rescued from this morass by Hu Shih, who by diligent investigation confirmed a plain implication in the first chapter that the story was autobiographical. This disposed of most of the "reflections" of historical personalities which the commentators had been at such pains to discover.

[2] Father Gerbillon and other Jesuits have left us some amusing anecdotes about him. The following is an example: One day, when riding in his park, he espied a mandarin of his entourage whom he knew to have extorted twenty thousand silver taels from a petitioner. "Take the reins," the emperor said to the mandarin, "and lead me round the park." As soon as they returned the emperor dismounted. "This is for your trouble," he said, and gave him a tael. "And now," he added, "it's your turn. Mount!" The other had to do as he was told; the emperor took the bridle, and after leading him on the same round, said: "Now it is your turn to pay. How much greater am I than you?" "Infinitely," stuttered the mandarin. "Let us put it at twenty thousand times," curtly replied the emperor. "You owe me twenty thousand taels!" And the dishonest official was obliged to pay.

might readily be distinguished among his numerous court."—Such is the portrait drawn by the Jesuit missionaries, who knew him well. "His prepossessing appearance", they added, "betokened a noble heart which rendered him the absolute ruler of his passions, a sharp and discerning mind, a sound and reliable judgment, and an excellent memory which allowed nothing to escape." His natural intelligence was combined with a taste for study that made this Tartar prince an emperor after the heart of the Confucian literati. Nevertheless we shall see that in his dealings with Christianity he remained—however sinicized he may have been—sufficiently independent of Confucian routine. Questions of foreign policy brought out the Manchu chieftain in this Son of Heaven—or rather, the two aspects of his powerful personality were in these matters complementary. It was doubtless to his Manchu heritage that he owed his great vision when in Upper Asia he resumed the work, not only of the Han and T'ang dynasties, but also of the Mongol grand khans.

During the minority of K'ang-hsi-ti, the power was exercised by four regents who on certain points reversed the policy of Shun-chih-ti. For example, on January 4, 1665, they promulgated an edict proscribing Christianity.[1] Father Schall, who had been a personal friend of the late emperor, was arrested and condemned to death; but the dowager empress was indignant, and had him set free. The old man, whose spirit had been broken by this catastrophe, died not long afterwards (August 15, 1666). By a decree of 1662, the regents ordained that thenceforth candidates for government service examinations would be judged chiefly by their literary compositions, which should expound the official teaching of the school of Chu Hsi. This system remained in force until 1905.

Meanwhile K'ang-hsi-ti, in spite of his youth, was impatient to end the tutelage of the regents. On August 25, 1667, when only thirteen years of age, he took the reins of government into his own hands. Two years later he instituted a rigorous inquiry into the

[1] The Jesuits were accused by their enemies of organizing a secret society and laying spells on the emperor.

administration of the regents; one of them was arrested on June 14, 1669, and sentenced to death by decapitation (later commuted to life imprisonment), and another was degraded. As a gift to the Chinese population on the happy occasion of his accession to the throne, he ordered that all lands unjustly seized by the Manchus be restored to their former owners. Despite these liberal measures, it was not long before a revolt broke out against the Ch'ing government.

We have seen that the Manchu conquerors, in order to subjugate the southern provinces as cheaply as possible and to ensure popular support, had entrusted the government of South China to three important Chinese dignitaries, who enjoyed the rank of prince and whose fiefs were practically autonomous. One of these princes governed in Fukien, another ruled the Cantonese region, and the third—who was none other than the famous Wu San-kuei—had control over Szechwan and Yunnan. We have seen the decisive role of Wu San-kuei in the tragi-comedy of 1644, how this loyalist general, after taking up arms to avenge the legitimate dynasty, found himself unwittingly playing into the hands of the Manchu invaders. The dupe of the Manchus, he had by force of circumstances become their accomplice, and had been royally rewarded by them, first with the viceroyalty of Shensi, and later with the principality of the southwest. Here he was not only independent, but practically invulnerable, since the Alpine ranges of Szechwan and Yunnan protected these two outlying provinces and seemed ready to defy all attacks. The Manchus, who had not forgotten how much they owed to Wu San-kuei (for without his collaboration in 1644 they would never have occupied Peking), humoured him and treated him almost as an equal; they even gave a sister of the emperor Shun-chih-ti in marriage to his son.

The new emperor K'ang-hsi-ti disliked these regional autonomies and, disturbed to see Wu San-kuei setting himself up as a sovereign ruler, he summoned him to appear at court. At first Wu San-kuei excused himself on grounds of old age; but later, on receiving a further and more pressing invitation, the old man came out in open rebellion, calling on the Chinese people to join him in a national revolt against the Manchus (1674). His example was followed by the two other autonomous princes of the south, the rulers of Canton and Fukien. Meanwhile in Inner Mongolia the most important of the Mongol tribes, the Chahars, who pastured their herds north of the province of Hopei, also rose in revolt. The khan of the Chahars, Burni, who was a direct descendant of Genghis and Kublai, appealed to the Eastern Mongols to join in this revolt against Manchu suzerainty; but the other tribes failed to support him, and he was defeated and killed. In the south, Fukien and the Cantonese area were soon subjugated (1676–1677). Wu San-kuei retreated from Szechwan into Yunnan, whither the Ch'ing forces deemed it inadvisable to pursue him; and there, soon afterwards, he died of old age (October, 1678). The Ch'ing armies did not occupy Yunnan until late in 1681, when all the family of Wu San-kuei was put to death; the remains of the rebel himself were ground into powder and scattered to the winds. K'ang-hsi-ti completed his victory by annexing the independent Chinese kingdom in Formosa. Southern China, which till then had enjoyed an exceptionally lenient government, now learned to know the rigours of a military annexation.

The defeat of the Chahars had securely established K'ang-hsi-ti's suzerainty over Inner Mongolia (the Mongols of Chahar and Ordos); he was now free to devote his attention to Outer Mongolia.

Outer Mongolia was divided between two groups of clans: the Eastern Mongols or Khalkas, and the Western Mongols or Eleuths. The Khalkas were divided under five different khans, all of whom were descended from Genghis Khan; they occupied Mongolia proper, from the lower Kerulen to the lakes of Kobdo. The Eleuths pastured their herds farther to the west and southwest, between Kobdo and the T'ien-Shan. The most important of the Eleuths were the Choros, who lived around the Tarbagataï mountains, between Kobdo and the River Ili, and the Choros included a tribe called the Sungars. From 1676 to 1697 the Sungars had as their chief an extraordinary character called Galdan, a sort of unsuccessful Genghis Khan, who dreamed of re-establishing the old Mongol empire under the domination of his own Western Mongols. In his youth Galdan had lived as a novice in Tibet, under the Dalai Lama of Lhasa, the pope of Lamaist Buddhism. He had remained on cordial terms with the Lamaist "Holy See", whose enormous political influence over the Lamaists of Upper Asia (nearly all the Mongols were now Lamaists) was at his service. While he was the protector of Lamaism in Tibet, Galdan contrived at the same time to be the defender of Islam in Kashgaria, where he overthrew the khan descended from Genghis, and replaced him by the Moslem theocracy of the Hodjas. He then undertook the conquest of the Khalkas in Mongolia proper, and after two years of warfare (1688–1690) succeeded in subduing this region, which extended from Kobdo to the River Kerulen.

The dispossessed Khalka princes took refuge in the neighbourhood of the Great Wall and sought the aid of K'ang-hsi-ti. The emperor could not afford to allow a new Mongol empire to grow up at the very gates of China. Moreover Galdan, having set out in pursuit of the Khalkas, now dared to advance into Inner Mongolia along the road from Urga to Kalgan. K'ang-hsi-ti sent against him an army equipped with artillery—cannon which had been made in Peking by the Jesuits. In the battle which took place on September 2, the Sungars, who had taken up their position behind a marsh, were able to hold their own against the imperial forces; but the gunfire seems to have intimidated them, and late in 1690 Galdan evacuated the whole of the Khalka territory in Outer Mongolia. As a result of this check to the Sungars, the empire was assured of a protectorate in Outer Mongolia; and the Khalka princes, who had been saved from Sungar domination by the intervention of K'ang-hsi-ti, came to pay solemn homage to the emperor at a diet held at Dolon Nor in May, 1691.

The status of Outer Mongolia that was then established was to last until 1912. The Khalka princes paid tribute to the Ch'ing Empire and in return received titles and gifts from the emperor. A link of personal fidelity was thus formed between these descendants of Genghis Khan and the Manchu emperor, and it was strengthened on various occasions by intermarriage between the families. The Ming emperor Yung-le-ti had envisaged a similar system, but as a Chinese he could never get the Mongols to accept it. K'ang-hsi-ti, on the other hand, succeeded without difficulty, because he was himself a Tartar. Indeed the new status of Mongolia was based on the nomad-to-nomad relationship between the Mongol khans and the Manchu grand khan. As soon as the Manchu dynasty fell and was supplanted by the Chinese Republic, the Mongol princes considered themselves released from their oath of fidelity and declared themselves independent.

The war between Galdan and the empire broke out anew in 1695, when the Sungar chieftain again invaded Outer Mongolia—the Khalka country—and advanced to the River Kerulen. In order to dispose of this menace once and for all, K'ang-hsi-ti assembled a great expeditionary force under his personal command. On February 16, 1696, he summoned all his generals to the palace and with his own hand offered them a stirrup-cup. On April 13 he set out, accompanied by the Jesuit father Gerbillon, who has left an eyewitness's account of the expedition. In it he noted "the perfect order that was maintained, the frugal existence of the sovereign and his entourage, and his solicitude for his troops; for he always insisted on seeing his men encamped before going to his own tent". "The march across a country which had always been poor, and which at that time was devastated by war, imposed terrible hardships on the army. The emperor took his share of these and scornfully rejected the entreaties of the mandarins who besought him to expose himself no longer. His vigorous attitude gave new courage to the troops." The army corps under the emperor's personal command advanced to the Kerulen, while his lieutenant Fei Yang-ku marched to the Tola in order to cut off Galdan's retreat. On June 12, 1696, Fei Yang-ku came in contact with the enemy on the southern bank of the Tola, at Jao

Modo, to the south of Urga, and thanks to his musketry and artillery inflicted a crushing defeat on them. Galdan's wife was killed, and all his baggage and animals fell into the hands of the imperial army. After losing half his troops, the Sungar chieftain fled in the direction of Kobdo, while K'ang-hsi-ti returned in triumph to Peking. The Khalkas, once again saved by his intervention, took permanent possession of their country, whose protection by the Court of Peking was thenceforth unchallenged.

For this great achievement—the rescue, rallying and pacification of the Khalkas—K'ang-hsi-ti was personally responsible. He devoted himself wholeheartedly to this task, endeavouring to establish relations of lasting confidence and friendship between himself and the Mongol princes. Moreover he took the keenest pleasure in everything Mongol, and when he was among the Khalka or Ordos chieftains, this Son of Heaven became a true leader of the horde. He spoke to them in a language they understood, appealing to the honour of the "banner" and to military fidelity, sentiments which lay very close to their hearts. Contact with these men seemed to reawaken the hereditary nomad in him, and he was never so happy as when, far from the pomp of the Forbidden City, he was able to hunt the hare or the antelope in the company of his Mongol vassals. "The hares of Ordos have an exquisite flavour," he wrote to his son during one of his campaigns. "Everything here has more savour than the best that Peking can provide."

K'ang-hsi-ti, satisfied to have expelled the Sungars from Mongolia proper, did not seek to pursue them into their homeland (Sungaria), which comprised the regions of Kobdo, Tarbagataï and Ili. Their chief, Galdan, died shortly after his defeat in 1696; but his nephew and successor, Tsewang Araptan, soon resumed his uncle's ambitious projects, turning this time towards Tibet. On December 2, 1717, a Sungar army entered Lhasa, massacred all the lamas who were partisans of the Chinese, and installed itself permanently in the Holy City. K'ang-hsi-ti immediately sent an expeditionary force to Tibet, but it was driven back (1718). The emperor bided his time, and in the autumn of 1720 a larger imperial army entered Lhasa and expelled the Sungars. A Dalai Lama of the imperial party was enthroned, and two Chinese high commissioners were appointed with the task of directing the foreign policy of the Lamaist church.

In northern Manchuria K'ang-hsi-ti came into collision with Russian expansion. The Russians had been masters of western Siberia since the late sixteenth century, and in their advance towards the Pacific they had now reached the banks of the river Amur, where in 1651 they built the fort of Albazin. This region, which was inhabited by Tungus tribes closely related to the Manchus and under Ch'ing suzerainty, was rich in sables. The Russians had no sooner became established than they came into serious competition with the indigenous trappers and Chinese furriers. When in 1682 a Russian governor was appointed to Albazin, the Peking government finally took umbrage. K'ang-hsi-ti, who thanks to the Jesuits had efficient artillery, acted with decision. In June, 1685, fifteen thousand Ch'ing troops with a hundred and fifty guns and fifty mortars were sent to Albazin, and the Russians capitulated. They were required to leave, and their fortifications were demolished. However, after the Chinese left, the Cossacks returned to Albazin and built a new fort, which was very soon besieged by the Chinese. Eventually negotiations were opened at Nerchinsk, where the Chinese delegation included two Jesuit fathers, one of whom was Father Gerbillon. It was largely thanks to the efforts of Gerbillon that a compromise was reached, and on September 7, 1689, the Treaty of Nerchinsk was concluded; it was drawn up in Latin, Manchu, Chinese, Mongolian, and Russian. The Russians abandoned the territory of Albazin, where their fort was razed to the ground, but kept Nerchinsk. The rivers Shilka and Argun marked the frontier between the two empires. The entire basin of the Amur, including its northern tributaries, was assigned to China. In short, the Russians were enjoined to remain far from the banks of the Amur, beyond the Stanovoi Mountains; and Manchuria, the homeland of the Ch'ing dynasty, was freed from a danger that had been hanging over it.[1] K'ang-hsi-ti showed his gratitude to Father Gerbillon, to whom principally he owed this diplomatic success.

At the time when K'ang-hsi-ti took the government into his own hands, there was still in force the edict of the council of regents of January 4, 1655, the edict proscribing Christianity. However, the Jesuits were becoming indispensable on account of their scientific knowledge. Among the former companions of Father Ricci was a Belgian Jesuit, Father Verbiest—with the Chinese name of Nan Huai-jen (1623–1688)—who had arrived in China in 1659 and was outstanding for his knowledge of mathematics and astronomy. In 1669 K'ang-hsi-ti, disregarding the advice of the Confucian literati, deferred to Verbiest on scientific grounds and adopted his reform of the calendar; at the same time he appointed him associate director of the Astronomical Board. Christianity could not fail to benefit from the imperial favour enjoyed by Verbiest and the other Jesuits. Apparently K'ang-hsi-ti, while respecting the Jesuits for their knowledge and permitting them, contrary to the edict of 1665, to practise their religion in private, nevertheless upheld prohibitions of 1669 and 1671 against proselytism among the Chinese people. But the viceroys, learning what favour the Jesuits enjoyed at court, showed the greatest tolerance towards the preaching of Christianity. Father Verbiest's reputation was greatly enhanced when in 1674, during the revolt of Wu San-kuei, he founded a number of cannons which contributed largely to the success of the imperial forces.

Father Verbiest died in Peking on January 29, 1688, at the height of his favour, and on February 7 there arrived the man who was to continue his work, the French Jesuit Gerbillon. Presented at court on March 21, Gerbillon made a favourable impression on K'ang-hsi-ti, who arranged for him to be given lessons in Manchu so as to be able to talk more freely with him. When they were able to talk together, the emperor held frequent conversations with the mission-

[1] The greatest danger would have been an alliance between the Russians and the Western Mongols.

ary on scientific subjects, and had him write an explanation of Euclid's geometry in Manchu. The services which Gerbillon rendered to China as negotiator of the Treaty of Nerchinsk have been mentioned above; out of gratitude for this, K'ang-hsi-ti promulgated two edicts of toleration in favour of Christianity (March 17 and March 19, 1692). The first declared: "The men of the West have rectified the calculation of the calendar. In times of war they have repaired old cannon and constructed new ones. They have devoted their energies to the good of the empire and have taken much trouble to this end. Moreover, since the Catholic religion contains nothing evil or irregular, its adherents should be able to continue to practise it freely. We order that the former memorials and resolutions against the said religion be withdrawn."

China was thus opened to Christianity. But the unfortunate "Rites Controversy", which aroused such excitement in the West and which was completely misunderstood there, was to ruin all the results so far obtained. The Jesuits had admitted that in principle the Confucian notion of *T'ien* (Heaven, the God of Heaven) could correspond to the Christian conception of God, and that moreover both the ceremonies performed in honour of Confucius and the respects paid to ancestors could be regarded as purely secular rites, as simple homage to the Sage or simple acts of filial piety. Thus, without sacrificing any part of Christian dogma or admitting any act of paganism, they avoided a direct conflict with the Confucian literati, that is to say the entire mandarinate. Pope Alexander VII had been in agreement with this; and in modern times Pope Pius XI and Pope Pius XII have taken the same attitude. The campaign against the "Rites" was prosecuted by Christians who, while undoubtedly zealous for their religion, knew far less about China than did the Jesuits, and were thus less capable of appreciating the metaphysical and theological significance of Chinese concepts. In 1715 the "Rites" were condemned by the Catholic Church. K'ang-hsi-ti, who was a man of considerable culture, had taken a personal interest in the question. He had taken the trouble to lay it down that there was no suspicion of idolatry in the homage paid to the tablets of Confucius or of one's ancestors. "We neither hope for nor expect anything from Confucius or the Ancestors," he wrote. "No one believes in their presence in the tablets. What is read in the rituals that might suggest the contrary is no more than one of the many metaphors in the Chinese language." He was hurt to find that his explanation was disregarded, and retaliated by the edict of May 17, 1717, which forbade the preaching of Christianity.[1]

The campaign of the Jansenists against the Jesuits had borne its fruits. China, after opening her doors to Christianity, sealed them once more.

The emperor K'ang-hsi-ti, who had caught cold while hunting in the park of Hai-tzu, died on December 20, 1722, at the age of sixty-nine. He left the throne to his fourth son, whose reign-title was Yung-cheng (1723–1735).

Yung-cheng-ti, who was forty-six years of age when he came to the throne, imprisoned most of his brothers or arranged for their disappearance. In spite of this unfortunate beginning, he was a diligent and hard-working ruler, careful of the public good; but he was a pale figure in comparison with his father. Whereas the latter had shown an independence of spirit which he owed, no doubt, to his Manchu upbringing, Yung-cheng-ti who was already much more under the influence of the mandarinate, often showed himself extremely narrow-minded, especially with regard to Christianity. In 1724 he ordered the expulsion of all missionaries except those who were tolerated at the court itself on account of their scientific knowledge. In foreign affairs, he resumed the struggle against the Sungars. In 1731 he sent an expeditionary force to their country; it occupied Kobdo, but two months later was taken by surprise and annihilated. In 1734 another Chinese force advanced to the region of Kobdo, but in the following year Yung-cheng-ti broke off hostilities.

Yung-cheng-ti died on October 7, 1735, leaving the throne to

[1] It was considered improper (and dangerous) for Chinese subjects to accept the dictates of a foreign ruler (the Pope).

his fourth son, a young man of twenty-four. The new reign-title was Ch'ien-lung (1736–1796).

Ch'ien-lung-ti, like his grandfather K'ang-hsi-ti, reigned for sixty years. His was the last great reign of the dynasty, and we shall see how he completed the work of K'ang-hsi-ti in Mongolia and in Tibet. These conquests were not carried out by the sovereign in person; for, unlike K'ang-hsi-ti, Ch'ien-lung-ti was not a soldier but a diplomat and administrator.

We have seen that Yung-cheng-ti failed in his attempt to annex Sungaria. Ch'ien-lung-ti was better served by circumstances. The Sungars were in the throes of a civil war; and in 1754 one of the Sungar pretenders, Amursana, took refuge in China. Ch'ien-lung-ti received him in Jehol, and sent him and his men as the vanguard of an imperial army to occupy Sungaria. But Amursana quarrelled with his protectors, and calling the Sungars to arms he fell upon the army of occupation, which sustained terrible losses. An energetic Manchu marshal, Chao-hui, retrieved the situation, crushed the rebels on the River Imil and in Tarbagataï, and occupied Kuldja, which was another centre of enemy resistance (1757). Amursana fled into Siberia, where he disappeared.

This defeat was the end of the Sungars as a nation. Sungaria, which roughly comprised the region of Kobdo, Tarbagataï, and the province of Kuldja along the River Ili, was directly annexed to the Ch'ing Empire. The Sungars were exterminated *en masse* (six hundred thousand were slaughtered); and Ch'ien-lung-ti repopulated the country with immigrants from all over the empire, among them Moslems from Kashgar and from Kansu. In 1771 he established the Turguts, who were Western Mongols and kinsmen of the Sungars, to the south and east of Kuldja; they had returned to their native land after a long period of existence in the region of Astrakhan, in Russia.

We have seen that in 1680 the Sungars had imposed their suzerainty on Kashgar, installing as their vassals the Moslem theocracy of the Hodjas. As soon as Sungaria had been conquered, the Manchu marshal, Chao Hui, invaded Kashgaria (1758) and, after two stubborn sieges, captured the cities of Kashgar and Yarkand (1759). The whole region of eastern Turkestan was annexed by Ch'ing and came to be known as the "New Marches", or Hsin-chiang (Sinkiang).

The conquest of Kashgar by the generals of Ch'ien-lung-ti marked the realization of a programme that was eighteen centuries old, the programme followed by the great dynasties of Han and T'ang.

In Tibet, too, Ch'ien-lung-ti completed the work of his grandfather. Despite the appointment of two imperial high commissioners at Lhasa to supervise the Dalai Lama, there had continued to be a pro-Sungar and anti-Chinese party in the Holy City. In 1750 this party incited a riot which resulted in the massacre of the two Chinese high commissioners and all the other Chinese residents. Ch'ien-lung-ti sent an army to Lhasa, and order was restored without any difficulty (1751); he then took the opportunity to attach Tibet more closely to the empire. The two Chinese high commissioners (*amban*) received full political power and henceforth had the deciding vote in the naming of a new Dalai Lama. The Lamaist church thus came within the framework of the Ch'ing administration. In order to compensate the Dalai Lama for his loss of independence, Ch'ien-lung-ti increased the honour and dignity of his position by formally investing him with the temporal title of King of Tibet. But as an extra precaution he took care to increase correspondingly the privileges accorded to the other Tibetan Pontiff, the head of the monastery of Tashilhunpo, whom he made King of Shigatse. In 1779 this prelate paid a visit to Ch'ien-lung-ti, who received him with great pomp at Jehol and in Peking. Tibet remained closely attached to the Ch'ing Empire until 1912.

The role of Ch'ien-lung-ti as protector of the Tibetan church led him to intervene in the affairs of Nepal. In 1791 the Gurkhas of Nepal made a plundering raid into Tibet; Ch'ien-lung-ti immediately sent an expeditionary force, which traversed the high plateaux, crossed the Himalayas, and came down into Nepal. This army inflicted a crushing defeat on the Gurkhas and forced them to become tributaries of Ch'ing (September, 1792).

In the south of China, the still forest-covered mountains and limestone plateaux of Kweichow had served as a refuge for the Miao-tzu, "aborigines" who up to this time had preserved their autonomy, the Chinese settlers having been content to clear the valleys only. In 1775 Ch'ien-lung-ti undertook to subdue these vigorous mountaineers. One after another their fortified retreats among the rocks and precipices were stormed; the population was decimated. The chieftains were carried off to Peking, where they perished as the victims of torture, and their severed heads were exposed in cages.

The subjugation of the Miao-tzu marked the end of an epoch. It completed the conquest of China by the Chinese, an immense undertaking begun by the legendary dynasties at the time of Babylon and Ur of the Chaldees, and terminated on the eve of the French Revolution. At the same time, the subjugation of Mongolia, Sungaria, Kashgaria, and Tibet, by K'ang-hsi-ti and Ch'ien-lung-ti, carried into effect the programme of Chinese expansion in Upper Asia that has been followed since the beginning of the Christian era. At the end of the period Ch'ien-lung, in 1796, the Chinese Empire again included, as it had at the zenith of Han and T'ang, the "closed continent" which is bounded by Siberia, the Altai, the T'ien Shan, the Pamirs, and the Himalayas.

From the economic and social point of view, the Ch'ing dynasty did much to help the Chinese people by its treatment of the agrarian problem. During the Ming dynasty there had developed, on a dangerously large scale, a type of privileged property or benefice exempt from forced labour and taxes. These latifundia created for the benefit of princes, courtiers, or officials, were cultivated by tenants and labourers who, under the *Statutes of Ming*, had no protection against the landowner. "The *Statutes of Ming*", points out Henri Maspero, "gave a master the right to punish his slaves or hired servants who were guilty of disobedience, and asked no redress from the master even if this punishment resulted in the death of the offender." At the same time, the imperial house itself had acquired enormous holdings of land, which of course were likewise exempt from taxation and which, despite the protests of the more honest members of the mandarinate, had steadily been extended. The agricultural population employed in the cultivation of these estates was at the mercy of every exaction of the officials in charge. The Ch'ing dynasty, to its credit, turned over to the state a part of the lands belonging to the imperial family. The privileged properties of rich families were confiscated, and were partially distributed among the peasants as their own property.

The Ch'ing dynasty did not stop at that. According to Henri Maspero, it constantly encouraged the development of small properties and maintained a strict supervision in order to prevent a return to the system of latifundia. Owners lost the right of coercion which had facilitated the exploitation of large estates by means of serfs and hired labourers. Strictly enforced laws provided that a master who caused the death of his serf or labourer by ill treatment should be punished with a hundred strokes and deportation for three years. Still more important was a provision that those whose families cultivated the same land for several generations finally acquired a legal right to the surface land, the owner retaining a right to the subsoil. Thus farmers were able to buy or sell "surface" land.

These measures and the spirit in which they were applied resulted in a general redistribution of the land.

In comparison with the Ming period, there was a great improvement in the condition of the rural masses, an improvement which resulted in a rapid increase in the population. If we are to believe Chinese statisticians, the population rose from 60,692,000 in 1578 (late Ming) to 104,700,000 in 1661 and to 182,076,000 in 1766; in 1872 it had reached 329,560,000.

Turning to the religious policy of Ch'ien-lung-ti we find that he, like his father, gave employment to talented Catholic missionaries. Thus it came about that the friar Castiglione, known to the Chinese as Lang Shih-ning, who arrived in Peking in 1715 and stayed there until he died in 1764, became one of the emperor's painters. Castiglione was commissioned by Ch'ien-lung-ti to make portraits of the ladies of the court; he also painted the emperor receiving a number of Kirghiz horses in tribute, a picture which can be seen in the Musée Guimet in Paris. Some time about 1760–1765 the emperor commissioned Castiglione, together with two other Jesuits (Attiret and Sickelpart) and the Augustinian Jean Damascène, to make a set of drawings depicting scenes from the conquest of Sungaria; these drawings were afterwards sent to France to be engraved under the direction of Bertin, secretary of the Académie des Beaux Arts (1765–1774).

However, his personal friendship for certain Jesuit painters and mathematicians did not prevent Ch'ien-lung-ti from forbidding his subjects to embrace Christianity (edict of April 24, 1736). Meanwhile the Jesuits were not deceived about his true feelings; taking a thoroughly objective view, Father de Ventavon wrote in 1769: "He is a great prince who sees and does everything himself. The older he grows the more favourable becomes his attitude towards Europeans. He and his nobles agree that our religion is good. If they forbid us to preach it in public and do not allow missionaries in their territories, it is for purely political reasons and for fear that under the pretext of religion we are concealing some other plan. They have a general knowledge of the conquests which Europeans have made in the Indies and are afraid lest something similar might happen in China." Moreover Europe itself seemed determined to stop the progress of the Catholic missions. In 1764 the government of Louis XV turned the Jesuit fathers out of France. Then, under pressure from the courts of Versailles and Madrid, the Holy See reluctantly gave way for the time being, and in 1773 the Society of Jesus had to disappear both in Europe and in China. The intelligentsia in Paris who applauded this measure little realized that France, by disowning the finest of her spiritual pioneers, was suffering a setback in the Far

East which was almost as great as the loss of those "few acres of snow" in Canada.

The periods of K'ang-hsi, Yung-cheng, and Ch'ien-lung were marked by an artistic renaissance, especially in the fields of architecture and ceramics.

We have seen how, between 1409 and 1424, the Ming emperor Yung-le-ti created the general scheme of the "Violet-purple Forbidden City" which lies in the centre of modern Peking. This incomparable group of buildings, which had been burnt down at the time of the fall of the Ming dynasty in 1644, was restored and completed by the three great Ch'ing emperors. Indeed, they understood the aspirations of the Ming architects so well that they may well be said to be the second founders of the Forbidden City. Moreover it is only through their restorations that we can judge the work of Yung-le-ti.

As is well known, the buildings of the Forbidden City conform not only to aesthetic rules, but also to a series of geometrical and astronomical considerations which played a fundamental part in ancient Chinese religion. The whole arrangement of porticoes, staircases, terraces, palaces, and throne rooms, oriented towards the south but progressing in importance from south to north, was "in harmony with the cosmic order". It was at the same time in harmony with the human order, since everything led up to the imperial throne, which was the centre of the world. Entering the Forbidden City by the Meridian Gate (*Wu-men*), where the emperor used to receive his victorious armies, one crosses the River of Gold, an ornamental stream which winds between its marble bridges. One then passes through the Gate of Supreme Harmony (*T'ai-he-men*) and arrives in the great ceremonial courtyard, which is surrounded by marble terraces each surmounted by a palace. In the centre is the Throne Room of Supreme Harmony (*T'ai-he-tien*) with its gilded roof; this hall was intended for certain solemn ceremonies, such as those of the New Year, and was in fact "the centre of the ceremonial life of the empire"—the centre of the imperial religion.

Behind this building and in the same group are two other throne rooms of equal importance, the *Chung-he-tien* and the *Pao-he-tien*. The former was the place where the emperor examined the agricultural implements before the spring ploughing ceremony, and the second was where he received his vassal princes. A little farther north, and still on the central axis, lies the Palace of Celestial Purity (*Ch'ien-ch'ing-kung*), the hall for imperial audiences, where the emperor attended to affairs of state. On the same axis, but outside the northern wall of the Forbidden City, rises Coal Hill (*Mei-shan*; more correctly called *Ching-shan*, or Prospect Hill), with its five hillocks surmounted by as many pavilions.

Almost bordering the Forbidden City to the west are the Three Seas, being one stretch of water twice divided by a bridge and a neck of land; on an islet just north of the Marble Bridge, which divides the North Sea from the Middle Sea, is the *Pai-t'a*, an artificial hill surmounted by a white dagoba (Tibetan pagoda), which was built by Shun-chih-ti.

On the way from the White Dagoba to Coal Hill one passes the *Ta-kao-tien*, a temple with yellow glazed tiles, which was built during the Ming period of Chia-tsing (1522–1566) and embellished during the Ch'ing periods of Yung-cheng and Ch'ien-lung. Here the emperors went to pray for rain in times of drought.

In the southern quarter of Peking, and not far from the outer wall, in a great park planted with acacias, pines, and cypresses, is the Altar of Heaven (*T'ien-t'an*); in reality it comprises no less than five altars and temples, which were built by the Ming emperor Yung-le-ti in 1420, and were restored by Ch'ien-lung-ti. Every year the emperor, in his role of grand pontiff of the three-thousand-year-old religion, would proceed there on three solemn occasions: at the winter solstice, when he came to the "Round Hill" (*Yüan-ch'iu*), a great circular marble altar consisting of three superimposed, concentric platforms, to render to Heaven an account of his Mandate; at the first moon, when he returned to be invested by Heaven with his Mandate to govern during the year; and towards the end of spring, when he came to offer prayers to Heaven for fertilizing rains and a good harvest. Beyond two white marble porticoes stood the Temple of Heaven (*Huang-chiung-yü*), a round building with a circular roof supported by eight columns. To the west of the Temple of Heaven lies the Temple of Agriculture (*Hsien-nung-t'an*), constructed during the Ming dynasty and restored by the emperor Ch'ien-lung-ti.

K'ang-hsi-ti, Yung-cheng-ti, and Ch'ien-lung-ti were not content with restoring and perfecting buildings started by the Ming dynasty. In the northwestern suburbs of Peking they built a "sort of Chinese Versailles" known as the Summer Palace. This consisted of two groups of buildings: the "Garden of Prolonged Spring" (*Ch'ang-ch'un-yüan*), used by K'ang-hsi-ti, and the "Garden of Round Brightness" (*Yüan-ming-yüan*), a resort of Yung-cheng-ti. Ch'ien-lung-ti joined the two palaces together, and in this work he employed the missionaries Castiglione and Attiret, who were chosen for their skill as painters. Father Attiret has left us a pleasing description of the site:

> Little hillocks of a height of twenty to sixty feet have been constructed, creating an infinity of little valleys. Canals of clear water, which has its source in the high mountains of the region, irrigate these valleys and, after separating, come together again in several places to form basins, pools and "seas". The slopes of the mountains and hills are covered with those flowering trees which are so common in China. The canals are not constructed in straight lines, and the rustic stones which edge them are placed with such artistry that one would say it was the work of nature; for the watercourses widen out, narrow down, and twist about in the most natural fashion. The banks are sown with flowers which grow up among the rocks, and each season has its own flowers.

The description written by the celebrated Jesuit forms one of the best possible studies on the art of gardening as practised in China during the middle of the eighteenth century—an art which was obviously based on the canons of Ming and Ch'ing painting. Attiret continues:

> On reaching a valley one observes buildings. The entire façade is made up of columns and windows; the woodwork is gilded, painted

or varnished; the walls are of grey brick, well cut and well polished; and the roofs are covered with glazed tiles of red, yellow, blue, and violet, which by their mingling and arrangement produce a pleasant variety of patterns. Each valley has its pavilion, small in comparison with the surroundings but large enough to house the greatest of our nobles and his attendants. Several of these houses are built of cedarwood, which has been brought over distances of five hundred leagues; and it is possible to count over two hundred palaces in this vast enclosure, to say nothing of the pavilions inhabited by the eunuchs.

The canals are spanned by bridges of the most varied forms. The balustrades of some of these bridges are of white marble skilfully fashioned and sculptured with bas-reliefs. On a rock in the middle of the large lake is a little palace, which the architect has constructed in a central position so that from it one may survey all the beauty spots of the park. One sails up and down the largest stretches of water in magnificent boats.

From this we can see the trend of artistic expression during the periods of K'ang-hsi, Yung-cheng, and Ch'ien-lung. If painting and sculpture had fallen into decadence, architecture, and above all the arts of the urban architect and the landscape gardener, had attained to heights hitherto unknown. And it was during these periods that the last masterpieces of Chinese ceramics were made.

During the period of K'ang-hsi (1662–1722) the imperial manufactory at Ching-te-chen, in Kiangsi, was reconstructed (1680), and the art of porcelain reached its peak in dazzling monochromes such as *sang de boeuf*, peach-bloom and sapphire blue, and above all in pieces with painted decoration, such as the *famille verte* (where the green forms a background for a pleasing arrangement of polychromes), the soft powder blues, or the very rare *famille noire*. During the period Yung-cheng (1723–1735) there appeared the extremely delicate pieces with painted decoration which we call the *famille rose*. The period Ch'ien-lung (1736–1796) produced in addition a beautiful decoration known as *mille fleurs*. But almost immediately after this, decadence set in as Chinese potters began to work for export to European markets; Europe demanded *chinoiserie*, and was served accordingly.

This artistic decline was symptomatic of the decay of Ch'ing, a decay that can be traced back to the eighteenth century—to the period when the philosophers of the Age of Reason were praising Chinese enlightenment. It is the pattern of Chinese history that imperial dynasties fall into decay after producing two or three generations of capable rulers; the ancient empire, which has been reconstructed by the founder of the dynasty, is once more broken up. The Manchu clan which obtained the throne in 1644, was no exception to this law. From the time of the fifth ruler, Chia-ch'ing-ti (1796–1820), the degeneracy became increasingly pronounced. Unfortunately this dynastic exhaustion coincided with the period when the rest of the world was flourishing under the influence of science and mechanization. In the latter half of the seventeenth century China was still on a level with Europe, as was indicated by the expulsion of the Dutch from Formosa and the Russian setback at Albazin. Between 1820 and 1850, China suddenly found herself several centuries behind. To expanding Europe, China was now a barbarous land, though a land with unlimited possibilities for evangelization and commercial exploitation.

The first European campaign against China was launched by Great Britain in 1840; since it was largely provoked by Chinese official reluctance to accept a commodity that most conveniently maintained a trade balance it is called the Opium War. Ten years later there broke out the great T'ai-p'ing revolution, which today is regarded as a precursor of the recent Communist revolution. For some fifteen years the civil war devastated Central China and nearly marked the end of the Ch'ing empire. The failure of this revolution seems to have been due to three main causes: firstly, the corruption of the leaders, which brought internal dissension and failure to implement reforms. Secondly, there was the opposition of the literati to a military regime with an anti-Confucian ideology (the T'ai-p'ing "Heavenly King" had been inspired by Christian teaching, and claimed to be the brother of Jesus Christ). Lastly, the British and French, after occupying Peking in 1860 and securing terms which virtually abrogated Chinese sovereignty, lent assistance to the Ch'ing government in its suppression of the rebels.

From 1860 until its final abdication in 1912 the dynasty persisted as nominal rulers of a bankrupt and slowly disintegrating empire, threatened alternately by invasion and rebellion. The danger of invasion increased with the growing industrialization of the Western powers, but it was also lessened by the rivalry between them. The danger of rebellion lay mainly in the traditional growth of provincial autonomy during a period of decline; but towards the turn of the century there also developed a considerable wave of reformist sentiment. The dynasty refused to accept the programme of the "Westernizers", and instead encouraged the abortive rising of the so-called Boxers (*I-he-ch'üan*, the Harmonious Fist society). Its suppression by an army of foreign powers was followed by measures of reform too long delayed, and in 1912 the Ch'ing dynasty abdicated in favour of a nominal republic, which was under the control of provincial warlords. Meanwhile the whole of the North-east (Manchuria) lay in dispute between Russia and Japan, while other powers held their "spheres of influence" in various parts of the country.

Had China remained in isolation, a talented general might have established a new dynasty to succeed Ch'ing; but Western power and Western ideas had undermined the traditional political conceptions. Unprecedented material and ideological factors entered into the struggle for power, and the imperial structure finally became obsolete.

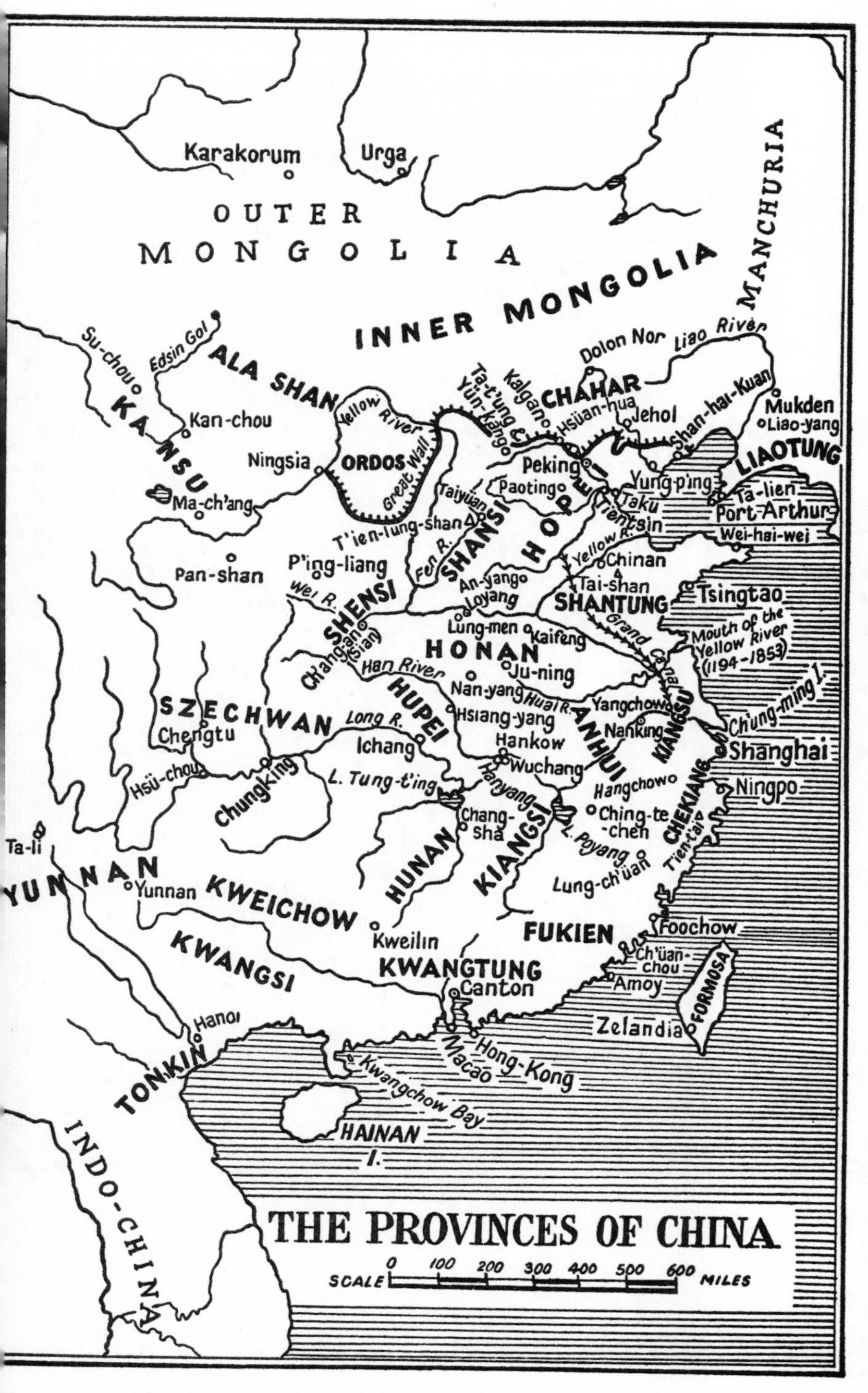
THE PROVINCES OF CHINA
SCALE
0
100
200
300
400
500
600
MILES
OUTER MONGOLIA
INNER MONGOLIA
MANCHURIA
Karakorum
Urga
Su-chou
Edsin Gol
ALA SHAN
KANSU
Kan-chou
Ningsia
ORDOS
Yellow River
Great Wall
Ma-ch'ang
Pan-shan
P'ing-liang
Wei R.
Dolon Nor
Liao River
CHAHAR
Kalgan
Ta-t'ung & Yün-kang
Hsüan-hua
Jehol
Shan-hai-Kuan
Mukden
Liao-yang
LIAOTUNG
Peking
Paoting
HOPEI
Yung-p'ing
Taku
Tientsin
Ta-lien
Port Arthur
Wei-hai-wei
Taiyüan
T'ien-lung-shan
SHANSI
Fen R.
Yellow R.
Chinan
Tai-shan
SHANTUNG
Tsingtao
Grand Canal
Mouth of the Yellow River (1194-1853)
An-yang
Loyang
SHENSI
Ch'ang-an (Sian)
Lung-men
Kaifeng
HONAN
Ju-ning
Han River
HUPEI
Nan-yang
Huai R.
Yangchow
KIANGSU
Ch'ung-ming I.
SZECHWAN
Chengtu
Long R.
Hsiang-yang
ANHUI
Nanking
Shanghai
Ichang
Hankow
Wuchang
Hanyang
Hsü-chou
Chungking
L. Tung-t'ing
Hangchow
Ningpo
CHEKIANG
Chang-sha
HUNAN
KIANGSI
Ching-te-chen
L. Poyang
Tien-t'ai
Lung-ch'üan
Ta-li
YUNNAN
Yunnan
KWEICHOW
Kweilin
FUKIEN
Foochow
Ch'üan-chou
Amoy
FORMOSA
Zelandia
KWANGSI
KWANGTUNG
Canton
Hanoi
TONKIN
Macao
Hong-Kong
Kwangchow Bay
HAINAN I.
INDO-CHINA

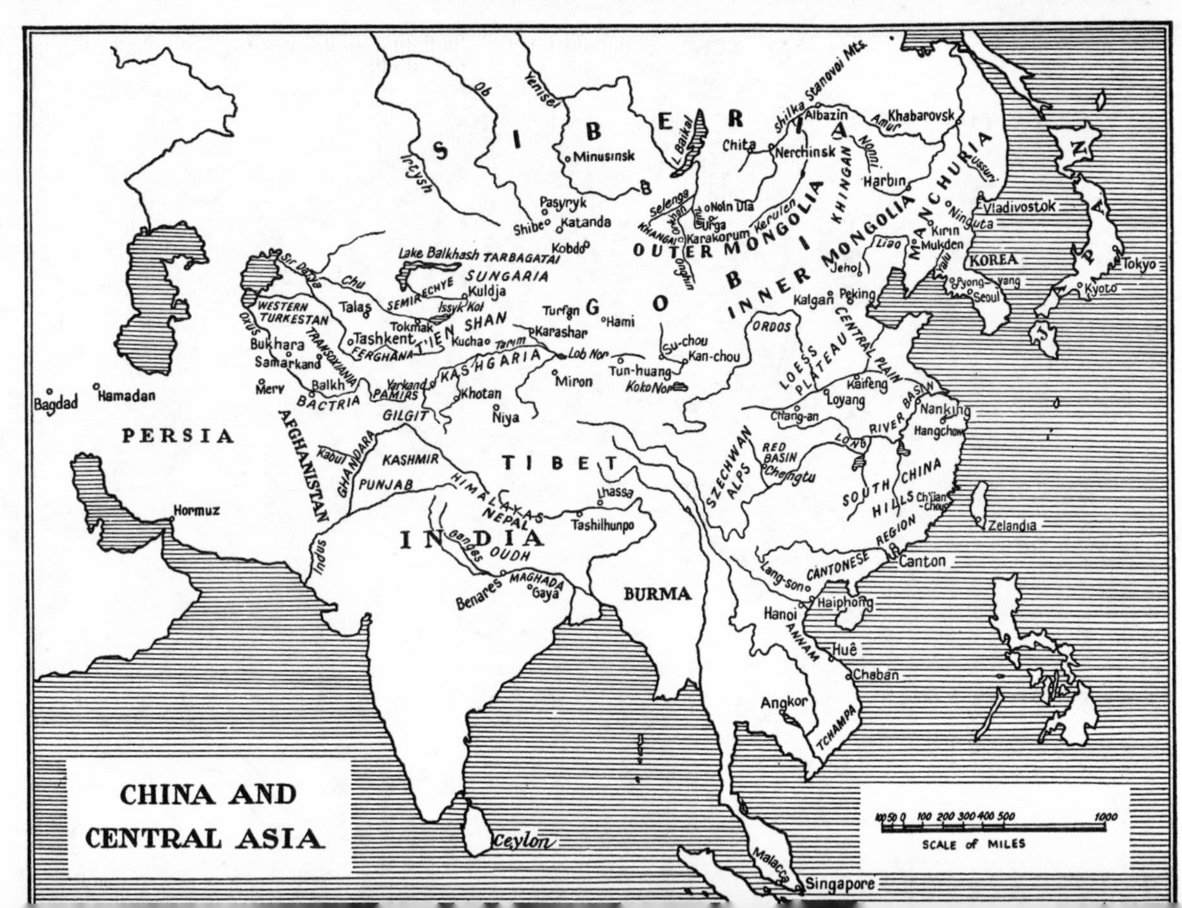
CHINA AND CENTRAL ASIA
SIBERIA
Ob
Yenisei
Irtysh
Minusinsk
L. Baikal
Chita
Shilka
Stanovoi Mts.
Albazin
Amur
Khabarovsk
Nerchinsk
Nonni
KHINGAN
Harbin
MANCHURIA
Ussuri
Vladivostok
Ninguta
Kirin
Mukden
Liao
Jehol
KOREA
Yalu
Pyong-yang
Seoul
JAPAN
Tokyo
Kyoto
Pasyryk
Shibe
Katanda
Kobdo
Selenga
Orkhon
Tula
Urga
Noin Ula
KHANGAI
Karakorum
Kerulen
Onghin
OUTER MONGOLIA
INNER MONGOLIA
GOBI
Kalgan
Peking
Lake Balkhash
TARBAGATAI
SUNGARIA
Kuldja
SEMIRECHYE
Issyk Kol
Chu
Talas
Sir Darya
WESTERN TURKESTAN
Oxus
Tokmak
Tashkent
T'IEN SHAN
Kuchao
Tarim
Karashar
Turfan
Hami
Su-chou
Kan-chou
Lob Nor
Tun-huang
Koko Nor
Miron
KASHGARIA
FERGHANA
TRANSOXIANIA
Bukhara
Samarkand
Merv
Balkh
BACTRIA
Yarkand
PAMIRS
Khotan
Niya
GILGIT
Bagdad
Hamadan
PERSIA
AFGHANISTAN
Kabul
GHANDARA
KASHMIR
PUNJAB
TIBET
Lhassa
HIMALAYAS
NEPAL
Tashilhunpo
INDIA
Ganges
OUDH
Indus
Hormuz
Benares
MAGHADA
Gaya
BURMA
Ceylon
ORDOS
LOESS PLATEAU
CENTRAL PLAIN
Kaifeng
Loyang
Ch'ang-an
BASIN
Nanking
Hangchow
RIVER
LONG
RED BASIN
Chengtu
SZECHWAN ALPS
SOUTH CHINA HILLS
Ch'üan-chou
Zelandia
REGION
CANTONESE
Canton
Lang-son
Haiphong
Hanoi
ANNAM
Huê
Chaban
Angkor
TCHAMPA
Malacca
Singapore
100 50 0 100 200 300 400 500 1000
SCALE of MILES

INDEX